Teen Titans

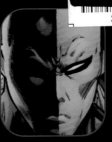

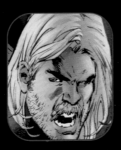

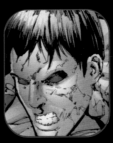

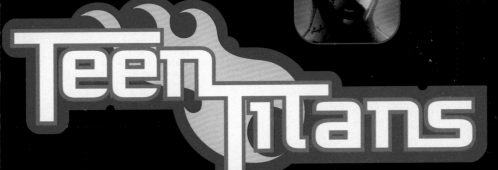

TITANS EAST

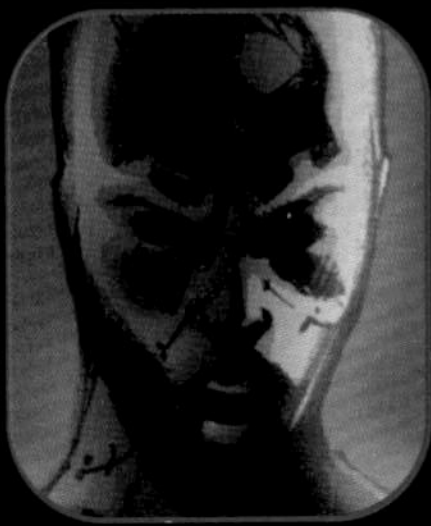

Cover art by Tony S. Daniel and the Hories

TEEN TITANS: TITANS EAST

Published by DC Comics. Cover and
compilation copyright © 2007 DC Comics.
All Rights Reserved.

Originally published in single magazine form as: TEEN TITANS
42-47 Copyright © 2007 DC Comics. All Rights Reserved. All
characters, their distinctive likenesses and related elements
featured in this publication are trademarks of DC Comics.
The stories, characters and incidents featured in this
publication are entirely fictional. DC Comics does not read or
accept unsolicited submissions of ideas, stories or artwork.

DC Comics, 1700 Broadway, New York, NY 10019
A Warner Bros. Entertainment Company
Printed in Canada. First Printing.
ISBN: 1-4012-1447-9
ISBN 13: 978-1-4012-1447-0

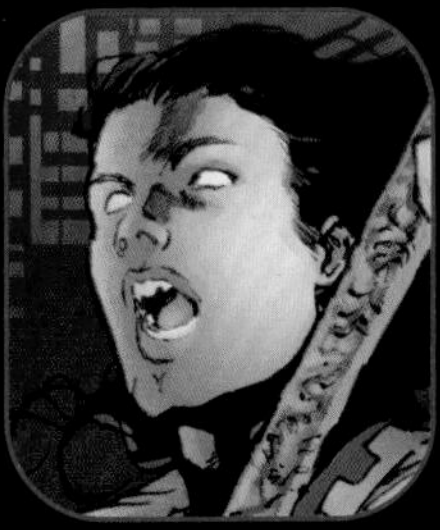

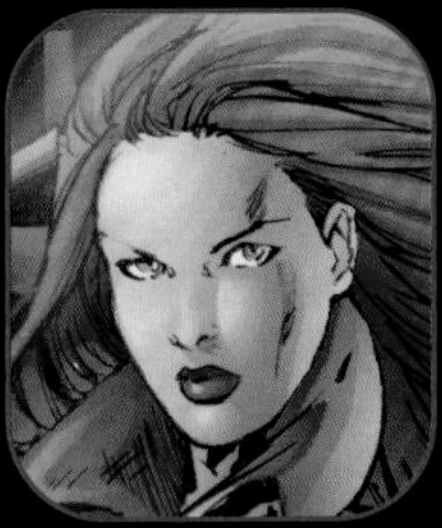

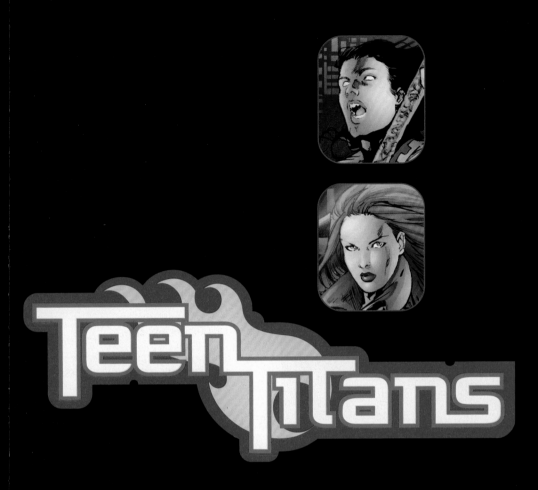

Teen Titans

TITANS EAST

Since the days Robin first appeared, teenaged heroes have gathered together to take on evil, and learn from each other, as the

Teen Titans

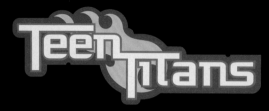

ROBIN:
TIM DRAKE. BATMAN'S CURRENT PROTÉGÉ.

WONDER GIRL:
CASSIE SANDSMARK. BLESSED WITH THE POWERS OF THE GODS.

RAVEN:
EMPATHIC DAUGHTER OF THE DEMON TRIGON.

KID DEVIL:
EDDIE BLOOMBERG. INNOCENT DEMON SIDEKICK TO BLUE DEVIL.

MISS MARTIAN:
M'GANN M'OORZ. MYSTERIOUS ALIEN SWEETHEART.

CYBORG:
VICTOR STONE. HALF-MAN. HALF-MACHINE.

JERICHO:
JOSEPH WILSON. BODY SNATCHER SON OF DEATH-STROKE, THE WORLD'S DEADLIEST ASSASSIN.

RAVAGER:
ROSE WILSON. MARTIAL ARTIST DAUGHTER OF DEATHSTROKE, THE WORLD'S DEADLIEST ASSASSIN.

NIGHTWING:
DICK GRAYSON. THE FIRST ROBIN AND BATMAN'S FORMER PROTÉGÉ.

TROIA:
DONNA TROY. BEING OF INFINITE POSSIBILITIES.

FLASH:
BART ALLEN. THE LATEST SUPER SPEEDSTER FOLLOWING THE LEGACY OF THE FLASH.

BEAST BOY:
GARFIELD LOGAN. ANIMAL SHAPE SHIFTER.

Since the day Deathstroke first appeared, new villains have gathered together to figh the Teen Titans. Now they seek to corrupt their name and do Slade's bidding as the

Teen Titans EAS

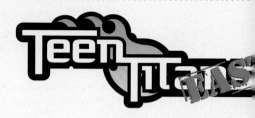

BATGIRL:
CASSANDRA CAIN. BATMAN'S FORMER PROTÉGÉ.

MATCH:
A BIZARRE IMPERFECT CLONE OF CONNER KENT.

INERTIA:
CLONE OF BART ALLEN, THE FORMER KID FLASH.

KID CRUSADER:
VIGILANTE DEMON-SLAYER.

SUNGIRL:
HERO FROM THE FUTURE WHO HARNESSES THE POWER OF THE SUN.

RISK:
CODY DRISCOLL. FORMER TEEN TITAN. ONE-ARME DAREDEVIL WITH FIVE TIMES THE SPEED, STRENGT AND STAMINA AS A NORMAL HUMAN.

JOKER'S DAUGHTER:
JDUELA DENT. FORMER TEEN TITAN. PRANKSTER DAUGHTER OF AN UNKNOWN SUPER-VILLAIN.

RIDDLER'S DAUGHTER:
FORMER TEEN TITAN. THE GIRL IS AN ENIGMA.

RED HOOD:
JASON TODD. THE SECOND ROBIN AND BATMAN'S FORMER PROTÉGÉ.

DEATHSTROKE:
SLADE WILSON. LEADER OF TITANS EAST. THE WORLD'S DEADLIEST ASSASSIN.

BOMBSHELL:
FORMER TEEN TITAN. HOST TO A METAL ALIEN SKIN, WHICH GIVES HER ENERGY POWERS.

NERON:
EVIL COLLECTOR OF SOULS – ONE OF THE DEVILS OF HELL.

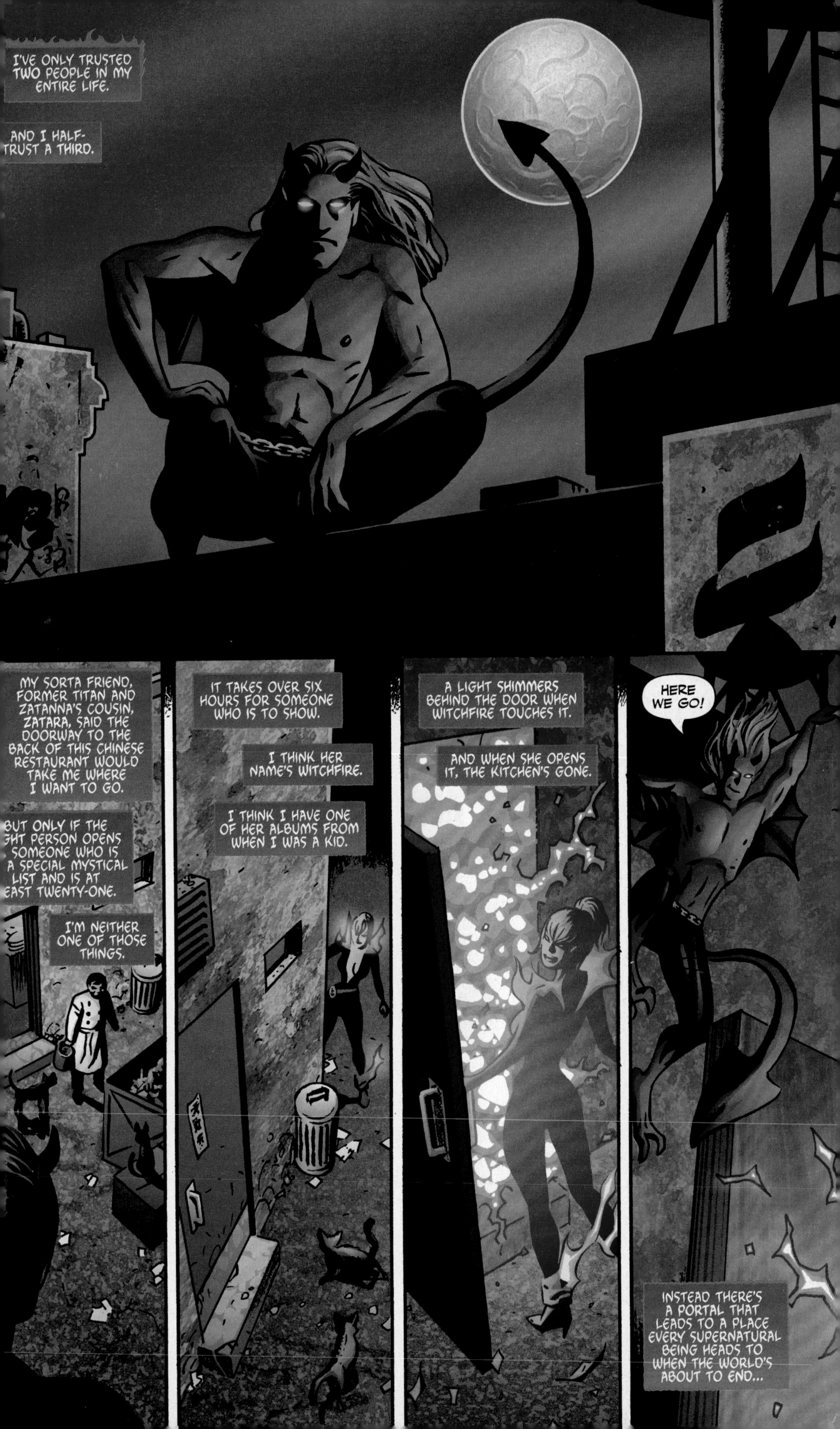

I'VE ONLY TRUSTED TWO PEOPLE IN MY ENTIRE LIFE.
AND I HALF-TRUST A THIRD.
MY SORTA FRIEND, FORMER TITAN AND ZATANNA'S COUSIN, ZATARA, SAID THE DOORWAY TO THE BACK OF THIS CHINESE RESTAURANT WOULD TAKE ME WHERE I WANT TO GO.
BUT ONLY IF THE GHT PERSON OPENS SOMEONE WHO IS A SPECIAL MYSTICAL LIST AND IS AT EAST TWENTY-ONE.
I'M NEITHER ONE OF THOSE THINGS.
IT TAKES OVER SIX HOURS FOR SOMEONE WHO IS TO SHOW.
I THINK HER NAME'S WITCHFIRE.
I THINK I HAVE ONE OF HER ALBUMS FROM WHEN I WAS A KID.
A LIGHT SHIMMERS BEHIND THE DOOR WHEN WITCHFIRE TOUCHES IT.
AND WHEN SHE OPENS IT, THE KITCHEN'S GONE.
HERE WE GO!
INSTEAD THERE'S A PORTAL THAT LEADS TO A PLACE EVERY SUPERNATURAL BEING HEADS TO WHEN THE WORLD'S ABOUT TO END...

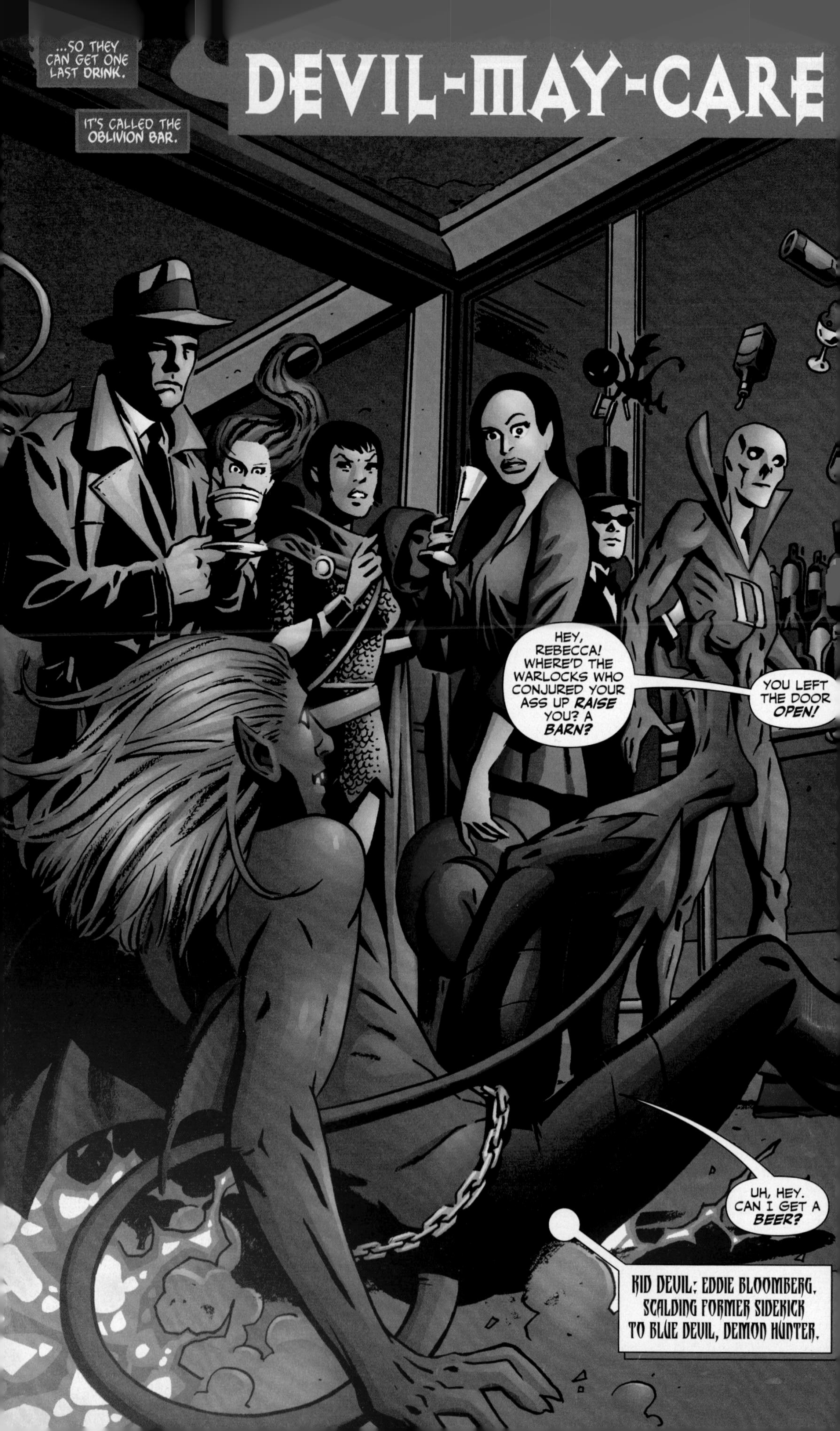
...SO THEY CAN GET ONE LAST DRINK.
DEVIL-MAY-CARE
IT'S CALLED THE OBLIVION BAR.
HEY, REBECCA! WHERE'D THE WARLOCKS WHO CONJURED YOUR ASS UP RAISE YOU? A BARN?
YOU LEFT THE DOOR OPEN!
UH, HEY. CAN I GET A BEER?
KID DEVIL: EDDIE BLOOMBERG. SCALDING FORMER SIDEKICK TO BLUE DEVIL, DEMON HUNTER.

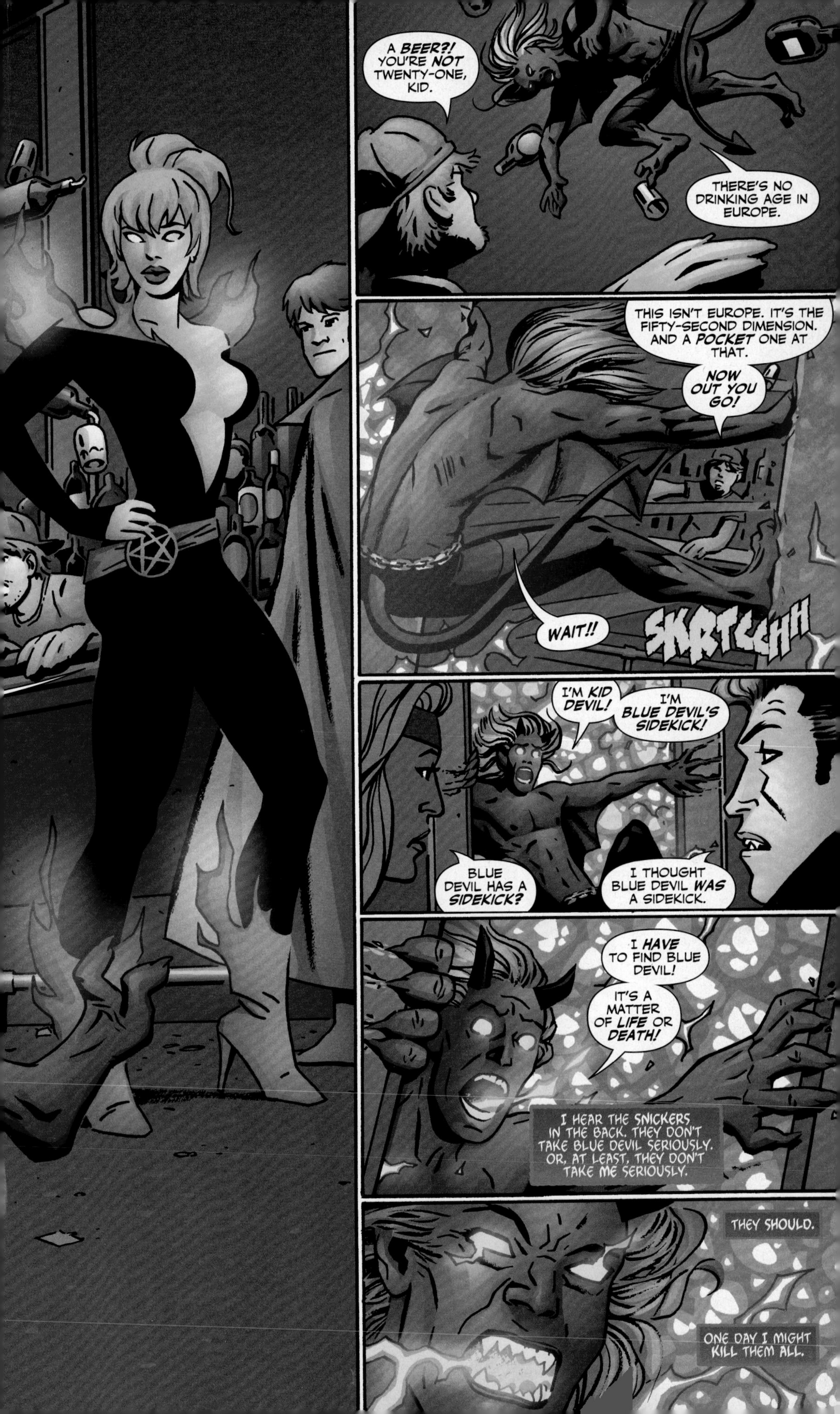

A BEER?! YOU'RE NOT TWENTY-ONE, KID.
THERE'S NO DRINKING AGE IN EUROPE.
THIS ISN'T EUROPE. IT'S THE FIFTY-SECOND DIMENSION. AND A POCKET ONE AT THAT.
NOW OUT YOU GO!
WAIT!!
SKRTCCHH
I'M KID DEVIL!
I'M BLUE DEVIL'S SIDEKICK!
BLUE DEVIL HAS A SIDEKICK?
I THOUGHT BLUE DEVIL WAS A SIDEKICK.
I HAVE TO FIND BLUE DEVIL!
IT'S A MATTER OF LIFE OR DEATH!
I HEAR THE SNICKERS IN THE BACK. THEY DON'T TAKE BLUE DEVIL SERIOUSLY. OR, AT LEAST, THEY DON'T TAKE ME SERIOUSLY.
THEY SHOULD.
ONE DAY I MIGHT KILL THEM ALL.

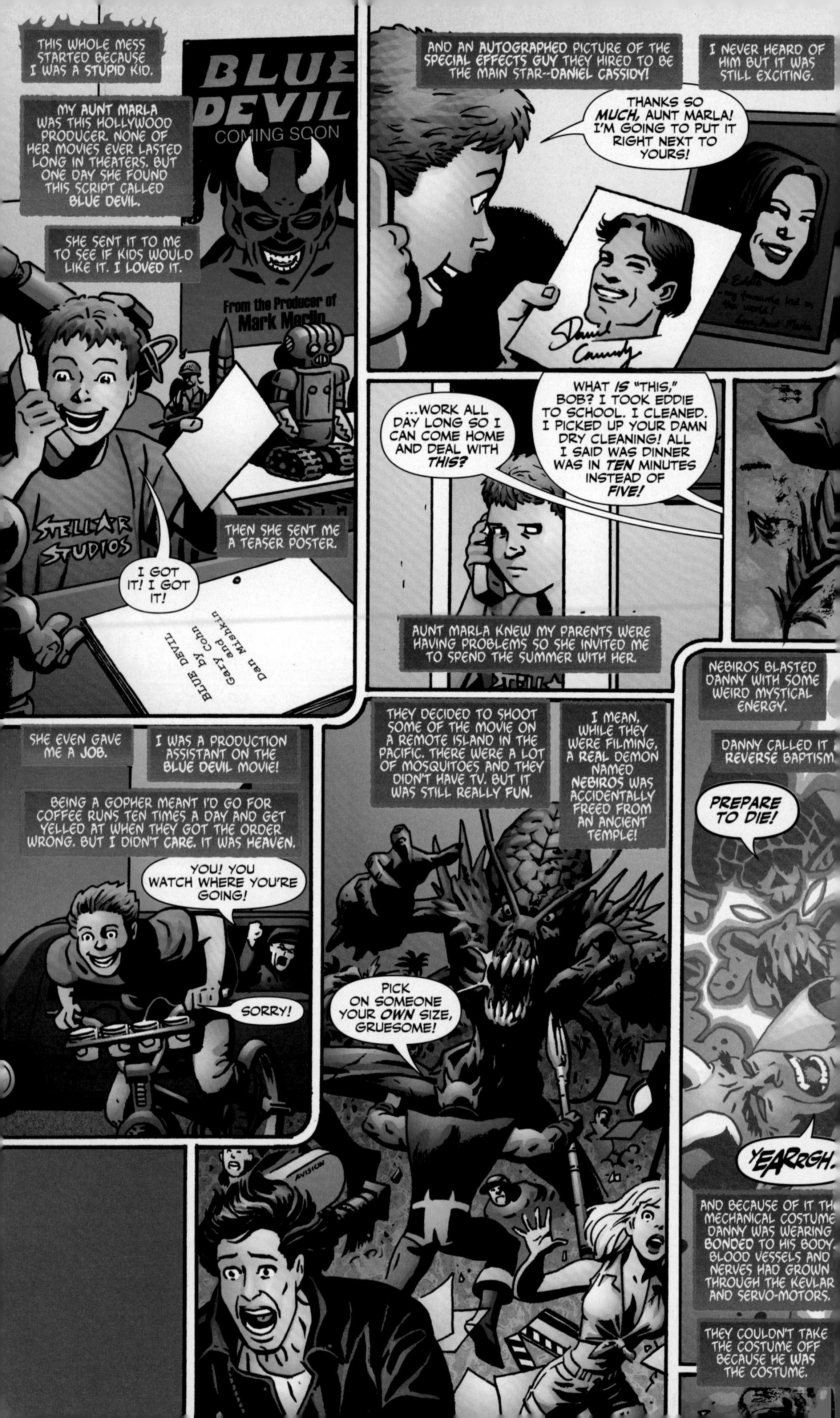
THIS WHOLE MESS STARTED BECAUSE I WAS A STUPID KID.
MY AUNT MARLA WAS THIS HOLLYWOOD PRODUCER. NONE OF HER MOVIES EVER LASTED LONG IN THEATERS. BUT ONE DAY SHE FOUND THIS SCRIPT CALLED BLUE DEVIL.
BLUE DEVIL COMING SOON
From the Producer of Mark Merlin
SHE SENT IT TO ME TO SEE IF KIDS WOULD LIKE IT. I LOVED IT.
STELLAR STUDIOS
THEN SHE SENT ME A TEASER POSTER.
I GOT IT! I GOT IT!
BLUE DEVIL by Gary Cohn and Dan Mishkin
AND AN AUTOGRAPHED PICTURE OF THE SPECIAL EFFECTS GUY THEY HIRED TO BE THE MAIN STAR--DANIEL CASSIDY!
I NEVER HEARD OF HIM BUT IT WAS STILL EXCITING.
THANKS SO MUCH, AUNT MARLA! I'M GOING TO PUT IT RIGHT NEXT TO YOURS!
...WORK ALL DAY LONG SO I CAN COME HOME AND DEAL WITH THIS?
WHAT IS "THIS," BOB? I TOOK EDDIE TO SCHOOL. I CLEANED. I PICKED UP YOUR DAMN DRY CLEANING! ALL I SAID WAS DINNER WAS IN TEN MINUTES INSTEAD OF FIVE!
AUNT MARLA KNEW MY PARENTS WERE HAVING PROBLEMS SO SHE INVITED ME TO SPEND THE SUMMER WITH HER.
SHE EVEN GAVE ME A JOB.
I WAS A PRODUCTION ASSISTANT ON THE BLUE DEVIL MOVIE!
BEING A GOPHER MEANT I'D GO FOR COFFEE RUNS TEN TIMES A DAY AND GET YELLED AT WHEN THEY GOT THE ORDER WRONG. BUT I DIDN'T CARE. IT WAS HEAVEN.
YOU! YOU WATCH WHERE YOU'RE GOING!
SORRY!
THEY DECIDED TO SHOOT SOME OF THE MOVIE ON A REMOTE ISLAND IN THE PACIFIC. THERE WERE A LOT OF MOSQUITOES AND THEY DIDN'T HAVE TV. BUT IT WAS STILL REALLY FUN.
I MEAN, WHILE THEY WERE FILMING, A REAL DEMON NAMED NEBIROS WAS ACCIDENTALLY FREED FROM AN ANCIENT TEMPLE!
PICK ON SOMEONE YOUR OWN SIZE, GRUESOME!
NEBIROS BLASTED DANNY WITH SOME WEIRD MYSTICAL ENERGY.
DANNY CALLED IT REVERSE BAPTISM.
PREPARE TO DIE!
YEARRGH!
AND BECAUSE OF IT THE MECHANICAL COSTUME DANNY WAS WEARING BONDED TO HIS BODY. BLOOD VESSELS AND NERVES HAD GROWN THROUGH THE KEVLAR AND SERVO-MOTORS.
THEY COULDN'T TAKE THE COSTUME OFF BECAUSE HE WAS THE COSTUME.

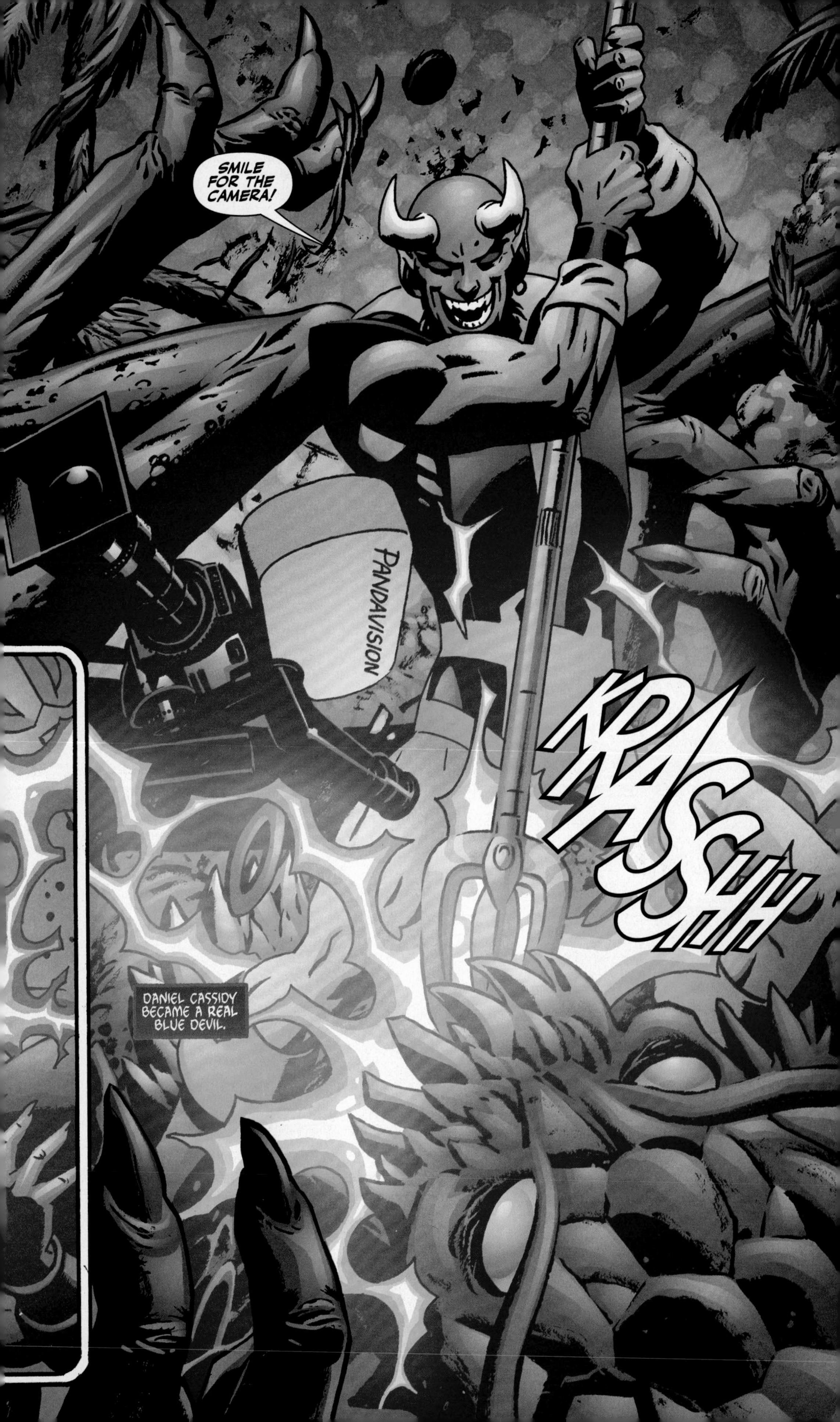
SMILE FOR THE CAMERA!
PANDAVISION
KRASSHH
DANIEL CASSIDY BECAME A REAL BLUE DEVIL.

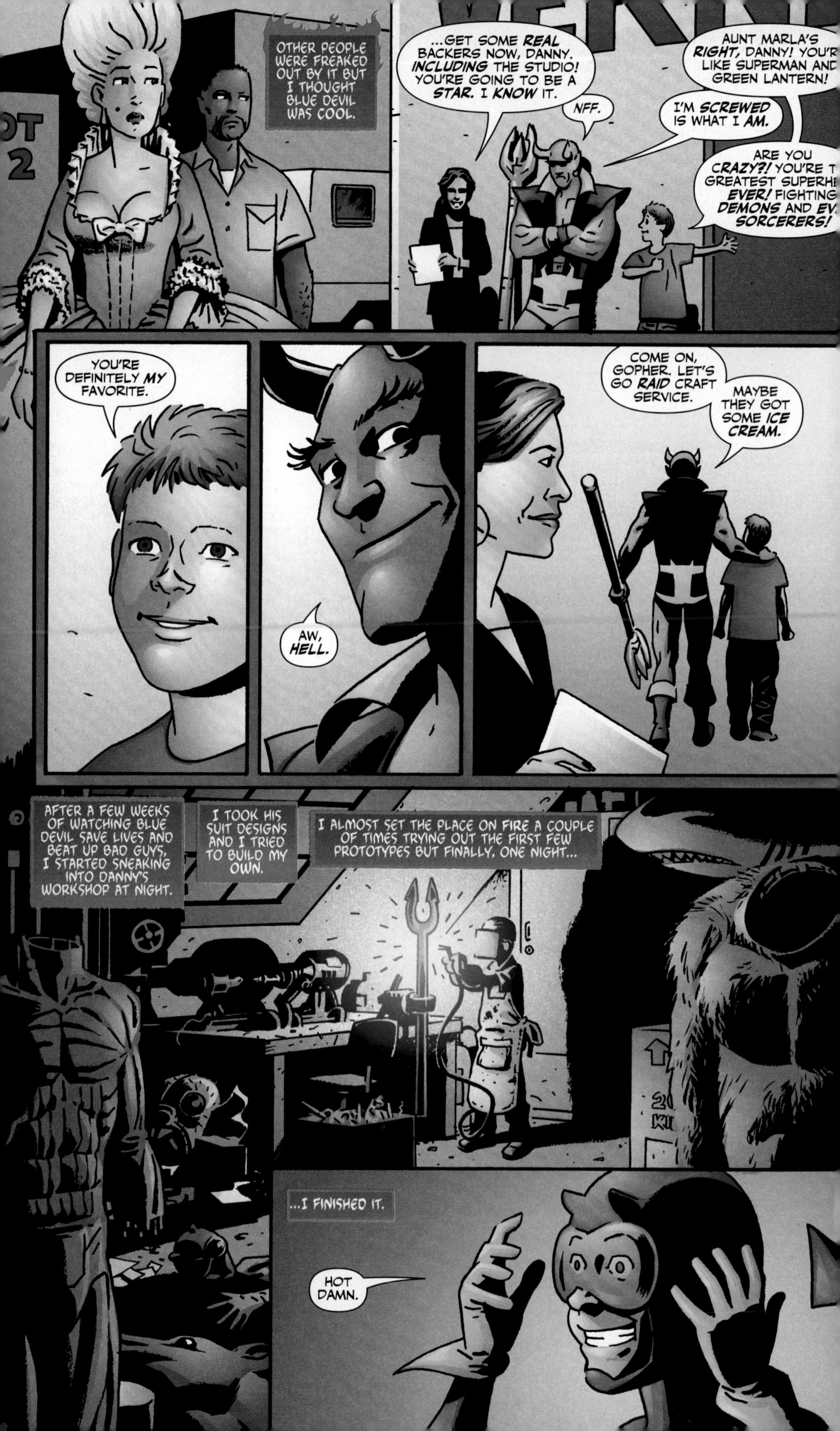
OTHER PEOPLE WERE FREAKED OUT BY IT BUT I THOUGHT BLUE DEVIL WAS COOL.
...GET SOME REAL BACKERS NOW, DANNY. INCLUDING THE STUDIO! YOU'RE GOING TO BE A STAR. I KNOW IT.
NFF.
AUNT MARLA'S RIGHT, DANNY! YOU'R LIKE SUPERMAN AND GREEN LANTERN!
I'M SCREWED IS WHAT I AM.
ARE YOU CRAZY?! YOU'RE T GREATEST SUPERHE EVER! FIGHTING DEMONS AND EV SORCERERS!
YOU'RE DEFINITELY MY FAVORITE.
AW, HELL.
COME ON, GOPHER. LET'S GO RAID CRAFT SERVICE.
MAYBE THEY GOT SOME ICE CREAM.
AFTER A FEW WEEKS OF WATCHING BLUE DEVIL SAVE LIVES AND BEAT UP BAD GUYS, I STARTED SNEAKING INTO DANNY'S WORKSHOP AT NIGHT.
I TOOK HIS SUIT DESIGNS AND I TRIED TO BUILD MY OWN.
I ALMOST SET THE PLACE ON FIRE A COUPLE OF TIMES TRYING OUT THE FIRST FEW PROTOTYPES BUT FINALLY, ONE NIGHT...
...I FINISHED IT.
HOT DAMN.

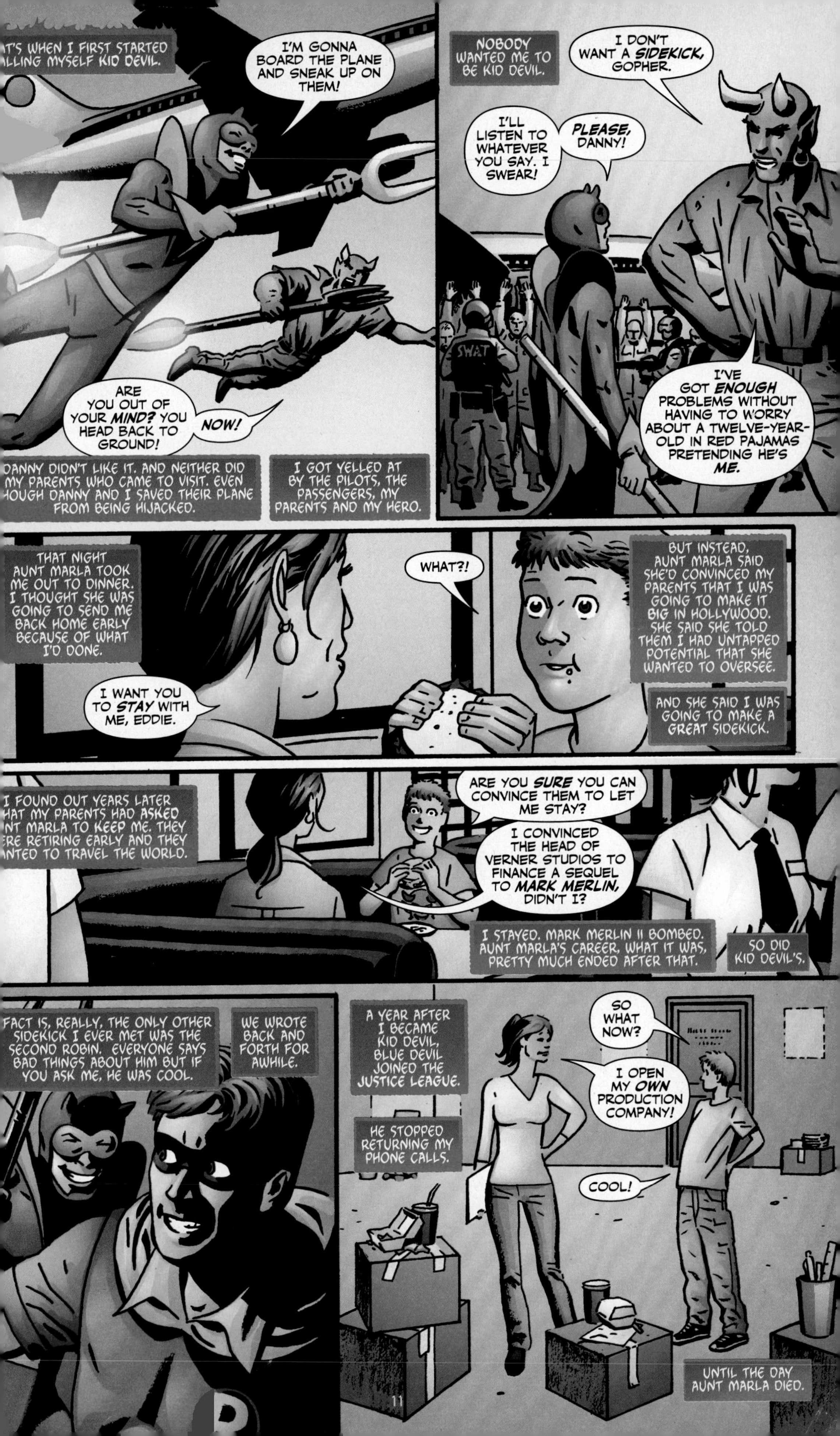

T'S WHEN I FIRST STARTED
LLING MYSELF KID DEVIL.
I'M GONNA BOARD THE PLANE AND SNEAK UP ON THEM!
ARE YOU OUT OF YOUR MIND? YOU HEAD BACK TO GROUND!
NOW!
DANNY DIDN'T LIKE IT. AND NEITHER DID MY PARENTS WHO CAME TO VISIT. EVEN
HOUGH DANNY AND I SAVED THEIR PLANE FROM BEING HIJACKED.
I GOT YELLED AT BY THE PILOTS, THE PASSENGERS, MY PARENTS AND MY HERO.
NOBODY WANTED ME TO BE KID DEVIL.
I DON'T WANT A SIDEKICK, GOPHER.
PLEASE, DANNY!
I'LL LISTEN TO WHATEVER YOU SAY. I SWEAR!
SWAT
I'VE GOT ENOUGH PROBLEMS WITHOUT HAVING TO WORRY ABOUT A TWELVE-YEAR-OLD IN RED PAJAMAS PRETENDING HE'S ME.
THAT NIGHT AUNT MARLA TOOK ME OUT TO DINNER. I THOUGHT SHE WAS GOING TO SEND ME BACK HOME EARLY BECAUSE OF WHAT I'D DONE.
I WANT YOU TO STAY WITH ME, EDDIE.
WHAT?!
BUT INSTEAD, AUNT MARLA SAID SHE'D CONVINCED MY PARENTS THAT I WAS GOING TO MAKE IT BIG IN HOLLYWOOD. SHE SAID SHE TOLD THEM I HAD UNTAPPED POTENTIAL THAT SHE WANTED TO OVERSEE.
AND SHE SAID I WAS GOING TO MAKE A GREAT SIDEKICK.
I FOUND OUT YEARS LATER
HAT MY PARENTS HAD ASKED
NT MARLA TO KEEP ME. THEY
RE RETIRING EARLY AND THEY
NTED TO TRAVEL THE WORLD.
ARE YOU SURE YOU CAN CONVINCE THEM TO LET ME STAY?
I CONVINCED THE HEAD OF VERNER STUDIOS TO FINANCE A SEQUEL TO MARK MERLIN, DIDN'T I?
I STAYED. MARK MERLIN II BOMBED. AUNT MARLA'S CAREER, WHAT IT WAS, PRETTY MUCH ENDED AFTER THAT.
SO DID KID DEVIL'S.
FACT IS, REALLY, THE ONLY OTHER SIDEKICK I EVER MET WAS THE SECOND ROBIN. EVERYONE SAYS BAD THINGS ABOUT HIM BUT IF YOU ASK ME, HE WAS COOL.
WE WROTE BACK AND FORTH FOR AWHILE.
A YEAR AFTER I BECAME KID DEVIL, BLUE DEVIL JOINED THE JUSTICE LEAGUE.
HE STOPPED RETURNING MY PHONE CALLS.
SO WHAT NOW?
I OPEN MY OWN PRODUCTION COMPANY!
COOL!
UNTIL THE DAY AUNT MARLA DIED.

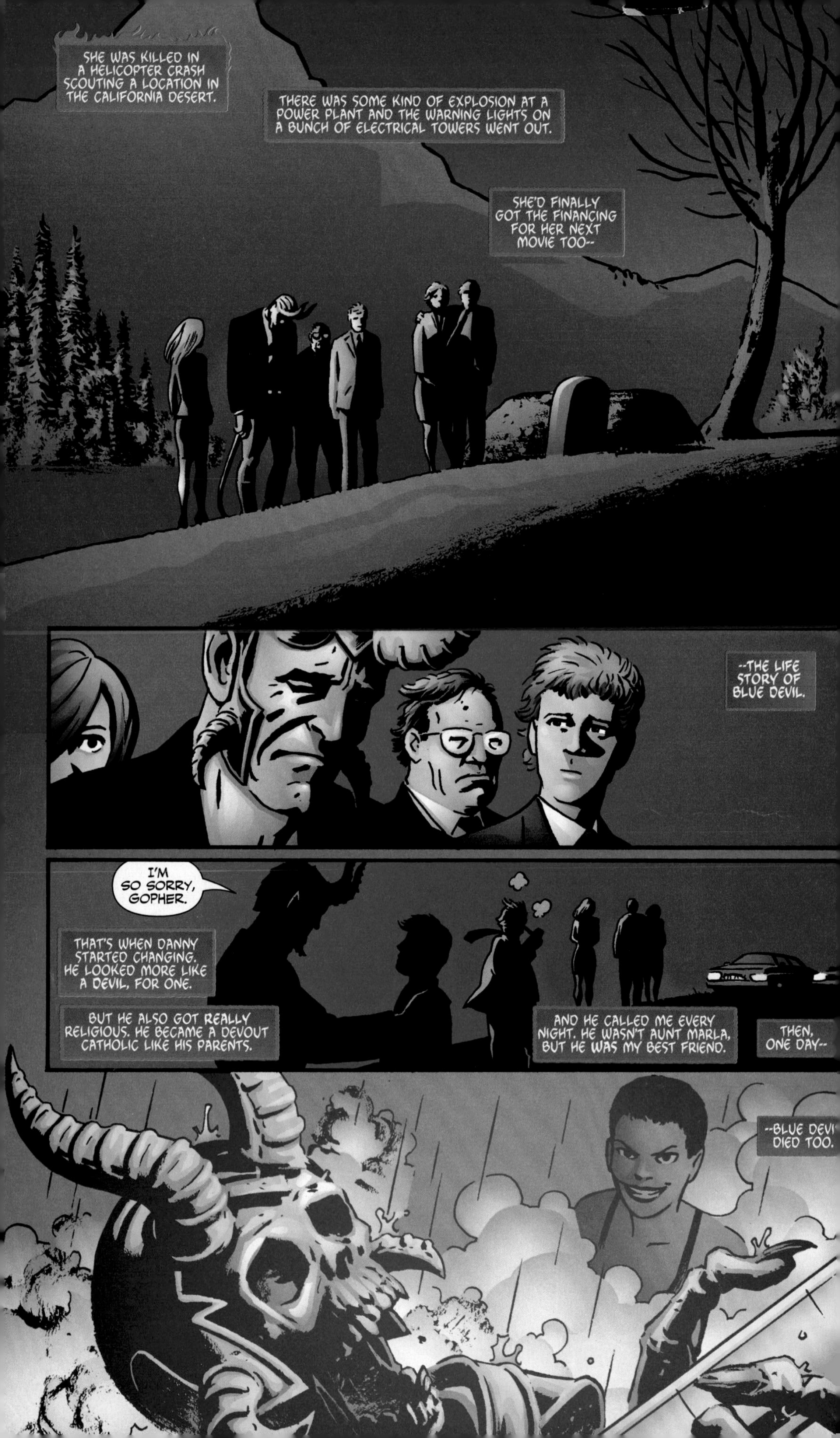
SHE WAS KILLED IN A HELICOPTER CRASH SCOUTING A LOCATION IN THE CALIFORNIA DESERT.
THERE WAS SOME KIND OF EXPLOSION AT A POWER PLANT AND THE WARNING LIGHTS ON A BUNCH OF ELECTRICAL TOWERS WENT OUT.
SHE'D FINALLY GOT THE FINANCING FOR HER NEXT MOVIE TOO--
--THE LIFE STORY OF BLUE DEVIL.
I'M SO SORRY, GOPHER.
THAT'S WHEN DANNY STARTED CHANGING. HE LOOKED MORE LIKE A DEVIL, FOR ONE.
BUT HE ALSO GOT REALLY RELIGIOUS. HE BECAME A DEVOUT CATHOLIC LIKE HIS PARENTS.
AND HE CALLED ME EVERY NIGHT. HE WASN'T AUNT MARLA, BUT HE WAS MY BEST FRIEND.
THEN, ONE DAY--
--BLUE DEVI
DIED TOO.

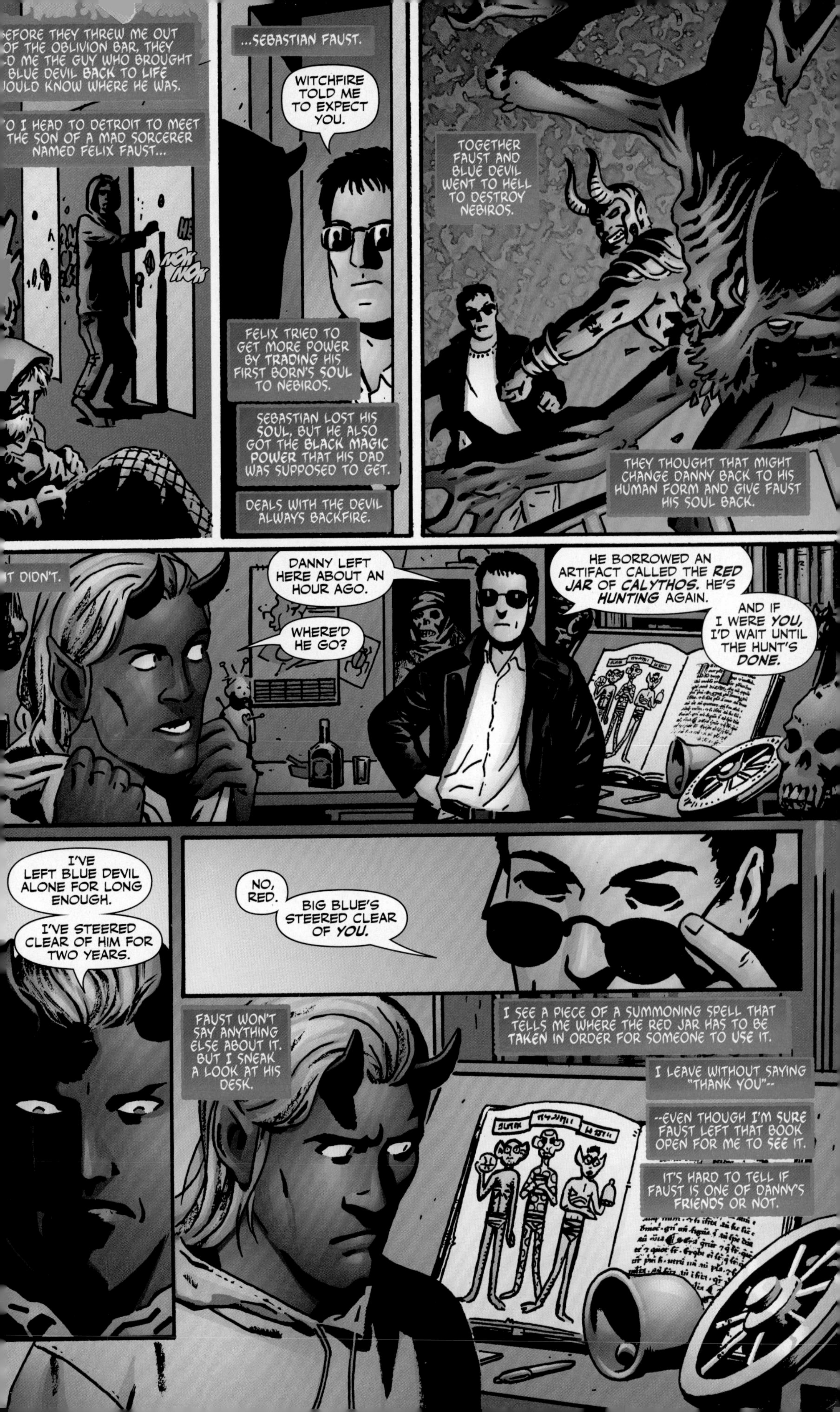
EFORE THEY THREW ME OUT OF THE OBLIVION BAR, THEY D ME THE GUY WHO BROUGHT BLUE DEVIL BACK TO LIFE OULD KNOW WHERE HE WAS.
O I HEAD TO DETROIT TO MEET THE SON OF A MAD SORCERER NAMED FELIX FAUST...
KNOK KNOK
...SEBASTIAN FAUST.
WITCHFIRE TOLD ME TO EXPECT YOU.
FELIX TRIED TO GET MORE POWER BY TRADING HIS FIRST BORN'S SOUL TO NEBIROS.
SEBASTIAN LOST HIS SOUL, BUT HE ALSO GOT THE BLACK MAGIC POWER THAT HIS DAD WAS SUPPOSED TO GET.
DEALS WITH THE DEVIL ALWAYS BACKFIRE.
TOGETHER FAUST AND BLUE DEVIL WENT TO HELL TO DESTROY NEBIROS.
THEY THOUGHT THAT MIGHT CHANGE DANNY BACK TO HIS HUMAN FORM AND GIVE FAUST HIS SOUL BACK.
T DIDN'T.
DANNY LEFT HERE ABOUT AN HOUR AGO.
WHERE'D HE GO?
HE BORROWED AN ARTIFACT CALLED THE *RED JAR* OF *CALYTHOS.* HE'S *HUNTING* AGAIN.
AND IF I WERE *YOU,* I'D WAIT UNTIL THE HUNT'S *DONE.*
I'VE LEFT BLUE DEVIL ALONE FOR LONG ENOUGH.
I'VE STEERED CLEAR OF HIM FOR TWO YEARS.
NO, RED.
BIG BLUE'S STEERED CLEAR OF *YOU.*
FAUST WON'T SAY ANYTHING ELSE ABOUT IT. BUT I SNEAK A LOOK AT HIS DESK.
I SEE A PIECE OF A SUMMONING SPELL THAT TELLS ME WHERE THE RED JAR HAS TO BE TAKEN IN ORDER FOR SOMEONE TO USE IT.
I LEAVE WITHOUT SAYING "THANK YOU"--
--EVEN THOUGH I'M SURE FAUST LEFT THAT BOOK OPEN FOR ME TO SEE IT.
IT'S HARD TO TELL IF FAUST IS ONE OF DANNY'S FRIENDS OR NOT.

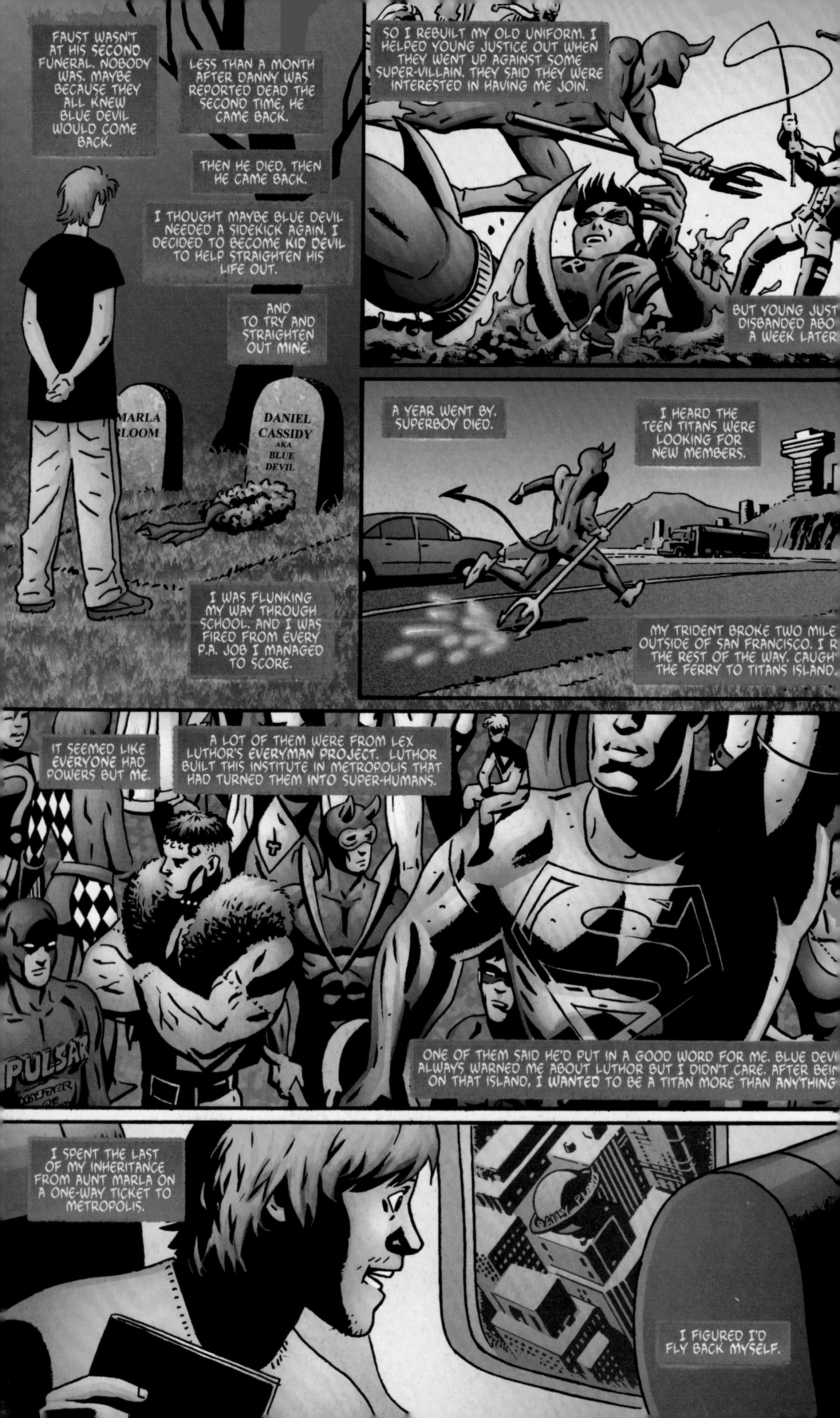
FAUST WASN'T AT HIS SECOND FUNERAL. NOBODY WAS. MAYBE BECAUSE THEY ALL KNEW BLUE DEVIL WOULD COME BACK.
LESS THAN A MONTH AFTER DANNY WAS REPORTED DEAD THE SECOND TIME, HE CAME BACK.
THEN HE DIED. THEN HE CAME BACK.
I THOUGHT MAYBE BLUE DEVIL NEEDED A SIDEKICK AGAIN. I DECIDED TO BECOME KID DEVIL TO HELP STRAIGHTEN HIS LIFE OUT.
AND TO TRY AND STRAIGHTEN OUT MINE.
MARLA BLOOM
DANIEL CASSIDY AKA BLUE DEVIL
I WAS FLUNKING MY WAY THROUGH SCHOOL. AND I WAS FIRED FROM EVERY P.A. JOB I MANAGED TO SCORE.
SO I REBUILT MY OLD UNIFORM. I HELPED YOUNG JUSTICE OUT WHEN THEY WENT UP AGAINST SOME SUPER-VILLAIN. THEY SAID THEY WERE INTERESTED IN HAVING ME JOIN.
BUT YOUNG JUST DISBANDED ABO A WEEK LATER
A YEAR WENT BY. SUPERBOY DIED.
I HEARD THE TEEN TITANS WERE LOOKING FOR NEW MEMBERS.
MY TRIDENT BROKE TWO MILE OUTSIDE OF SAN FRANCISCO. I R THE REST OF THE WAY. CAUGH THE FERRY TO TITANS ISLAND.
IT SEEMED LIKE EVERYONE HAD POWERS BUT ME.
A LOT OF THEM WERE FROM LEX LUTHOR'S EVERYMAN PROJECT. LUTHOR BUILT THIS INSTITUTE IN METROPOLIS THAT HAD TURNED THEM INTO SUPER-HUMANS.
PULSAR
ONE OF THEM SAID HE'D PUT IN A GOOD WORD FOR ME. BLUE DEVI ALWAYS WARNED ME ABOUT LUTHOR BUT I DIDN'T CARE. AFTER BEIN ON THAT ISLAND, I WANTED TO BE A TITAN MORE THAN ANYTHING
I SPENT THE LAST OF MY INHERITANCE FROM AUNT MARLA ON A ONE-WAY TICKET TO METROPOLIS.
I FIGURED I'D FLY BACK MYSELF.

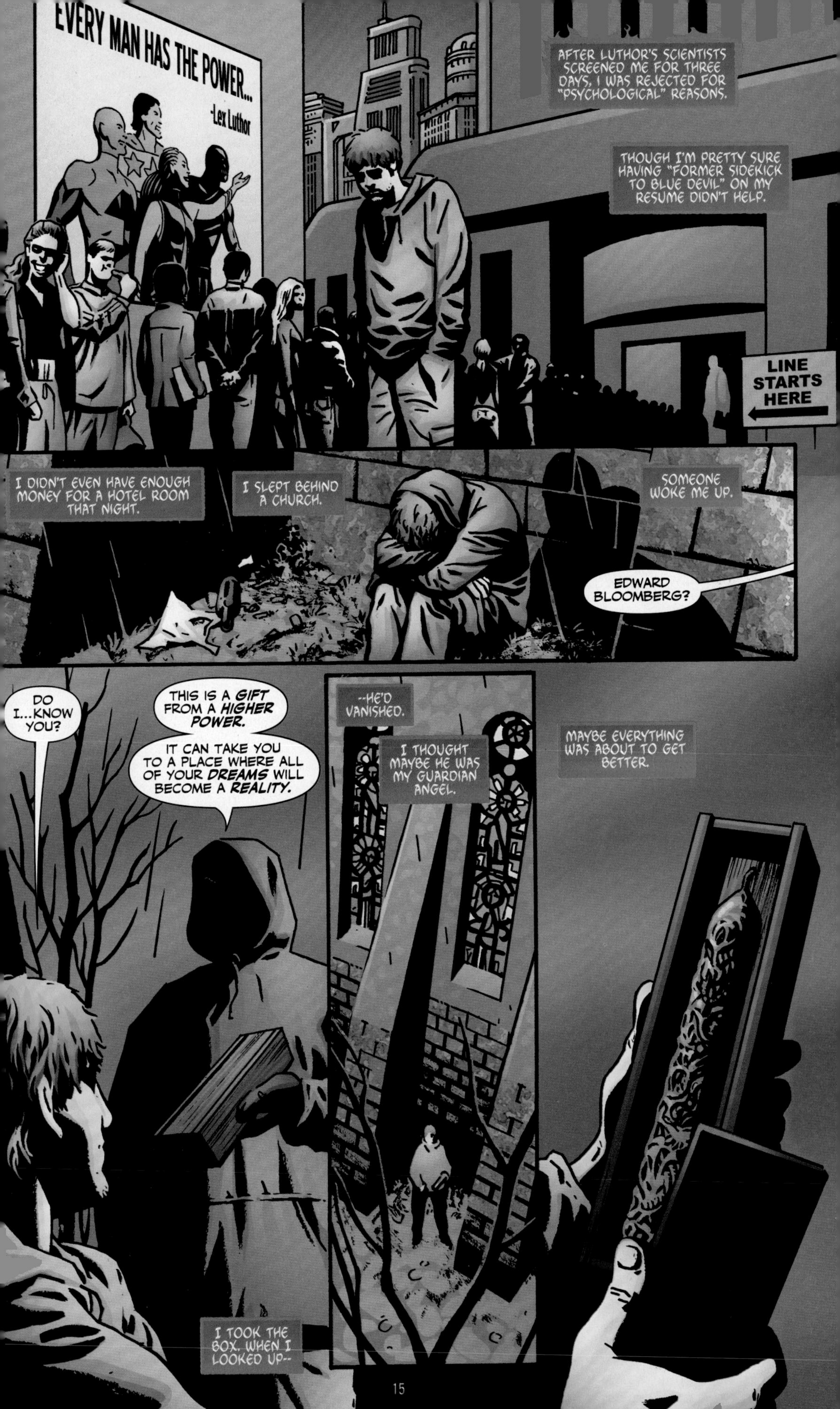

EVERY MAN HAS THE POWER...
-Lex Luthor
AFTER LUTHOR'S SCIENTISTS SCREENED ME FOR THREE DAYS, I WAS REJECTED FOR "PSYCHOLOGICAL" REASONS.
THOUGH I'M PRETTY SURE HAVING "FORMER SIDEKICK TO BLUE DEVIL" ON MY RESUME DIDN'T HELP.
LINE STARTS HERE
I DIDN'T EVEN HAVE ENOUGH MONEY FOR A HOTEL ROOM THAT NIGHT.
I SLEPT BEHIND A CHURCH.
SOMEONE WOKE ME UP.
EDWARD BLOOMBERG?
DO I...KNOW YOU?
THIS IS A GIFT FROM A HIGHER POWER.
IT CAN TAKE YOU TO A PLACE WHERE ALL OF YOUR DREAMS WILL BECOME A REALITY.
I TOOK THE BOX. WHEN I LOOKED UP--
--HE'D VANISHED.
I THOUGHT MAYBE HE WAS MY GUARDIAN ANGEL.
MAYBE EVERYTHING WAS ABOUT TO GET BETTER.

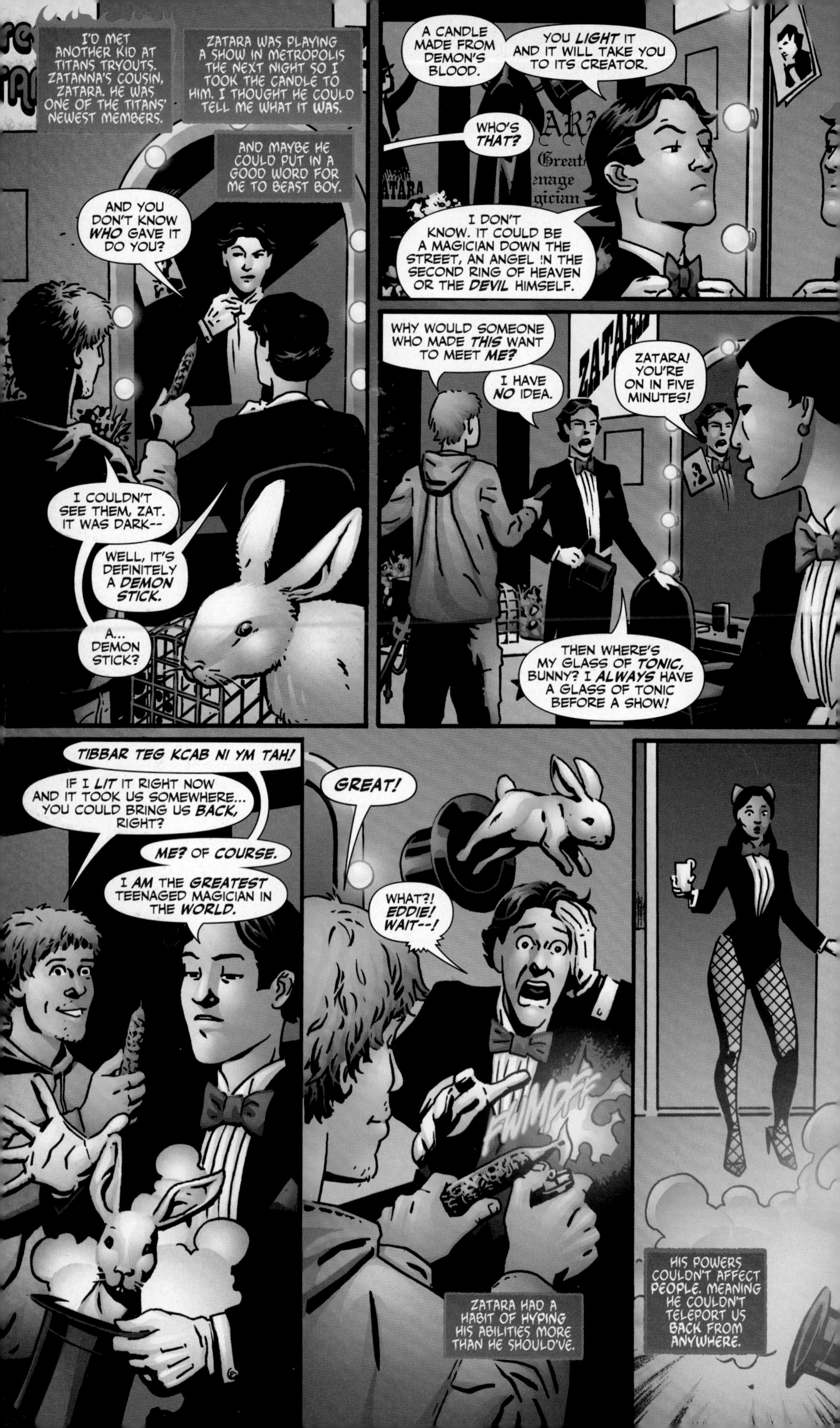
I'D MET ANOTHER KID AT TITANS TRYOUTS. ZATANNA'S COUSIN, ZATARA. HE WAS ONE OF THE TITANS' NEWEST MEMBERS.
ZATARA WAS PLAYING A SHOW IN METROPOLIS THE NEXT NIGHT SO I TOOK THE CANDLE TO HIM. I THOUGHT HE COULD TELL ME WHAT IT WAS.
AND MAYBE HE COULD PUT IN A GOOD WORD FOR ME TO BEAST BOY.
AND YOU DON'T KNOW WHO GAVE IT DO YOU?
I COULDN'T SEE THEM, ZAT. IT WAS DARK--
WELL, IT'S DEFINITELY A DEMON STICK.
A... DEMON STICK?
A CANDLE MADE FROM DEMON'S BLOOD.
YOU LIGHT IT AND IT WILL TAKE YOU TO ITS CREATOR.
WHO'S THAT?
I DON'T KNOW. IT COULD BE A MAGICIAN DOWN THE STREET, AN ANGEL IN THE SECOND RING OF HEAVEN OR THE DEVIL HIMSELF.
WHY WOULD SOMEONE WHO MADE THIS WANT TO MEET ME?
I HAVE NO IDEA.
ZATARA! YOU'RE ON IN FIVE MINUTES!
THEN WHERE'S MY GLASS OF TONIC, BUNNY? I ALWAYS HAVE A GLASS OF TONIC BEFORE A SHOW!
TIBBAR TEG KCAB NI YM TAH!
IF I LIT IT RIGHT NOW AND IT TOOK US SOMEWHERE... YOU COULD BRING US BACK, RIGHT?
ME? OF COURSE.
I AM THE GREATEST TEENAGED MAGICIAN IN THE WORLD.
GREAT!
WHAT?! EDDIE! WAIT--!
FWIMPF
ZATARA HAD A HABIT OF HYPING HIS ABILITIES MORE THAN HE SHOULD'VE.
HIS POWERS COULDN'T AFFECT PEOPLE. MEANING HE COULDN'T TELEPORT US BACK FROM ANYWHERE.

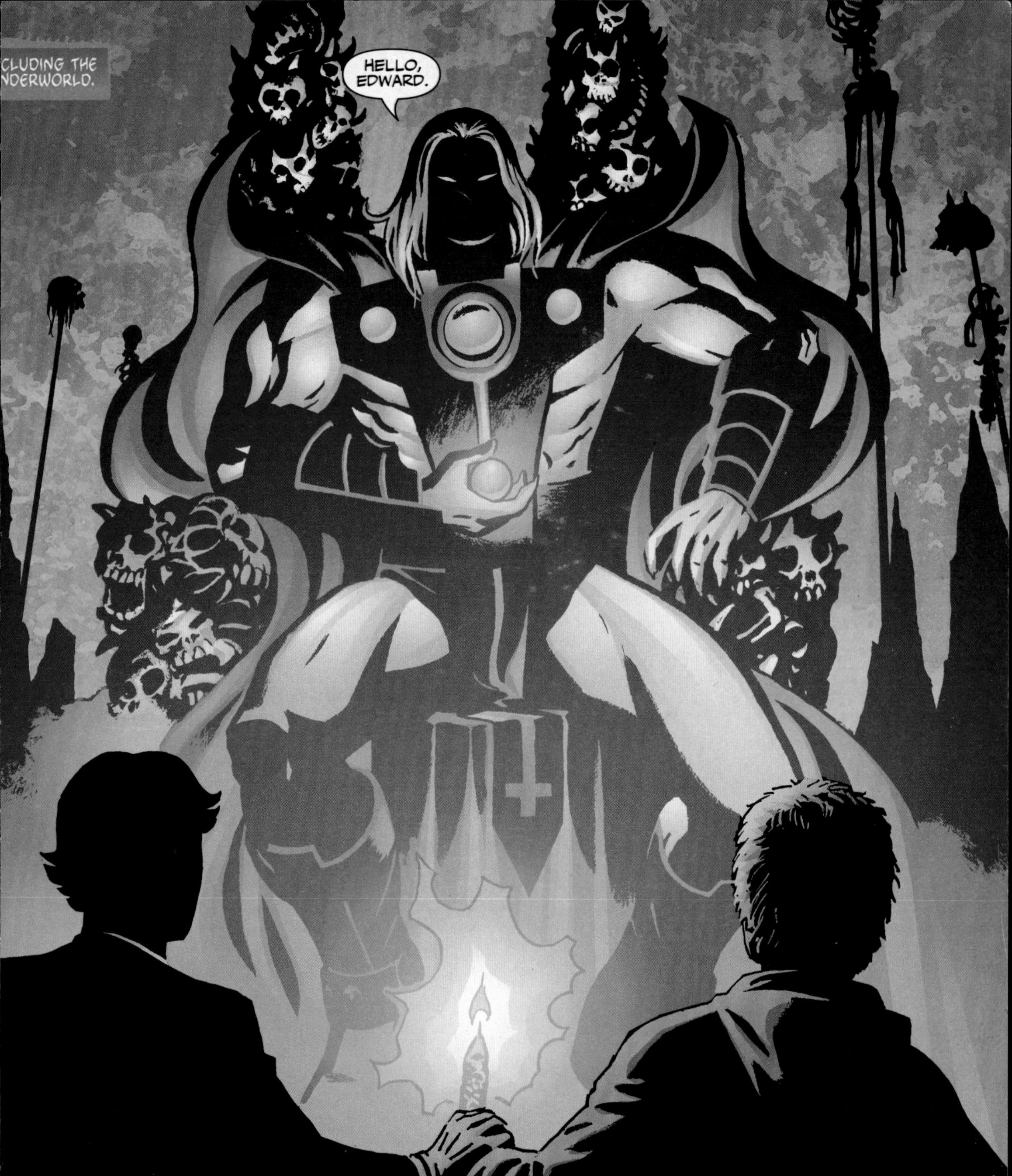
CLUDING THE
NDERWORLD.
HELLO, EDWARD.

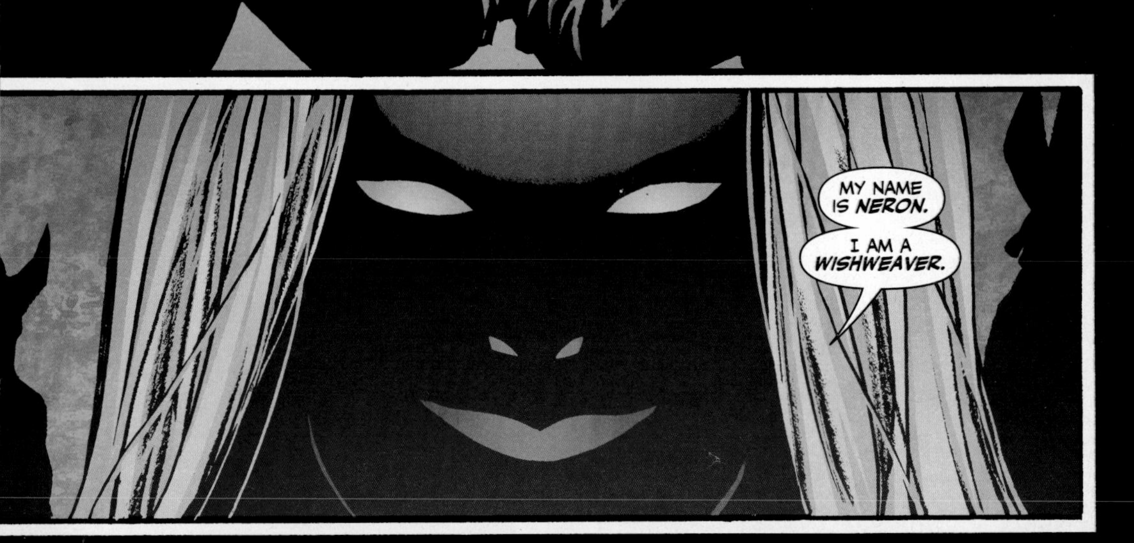
MY NAME IS *NERON*.
I AM A *WISHWEAVER*.

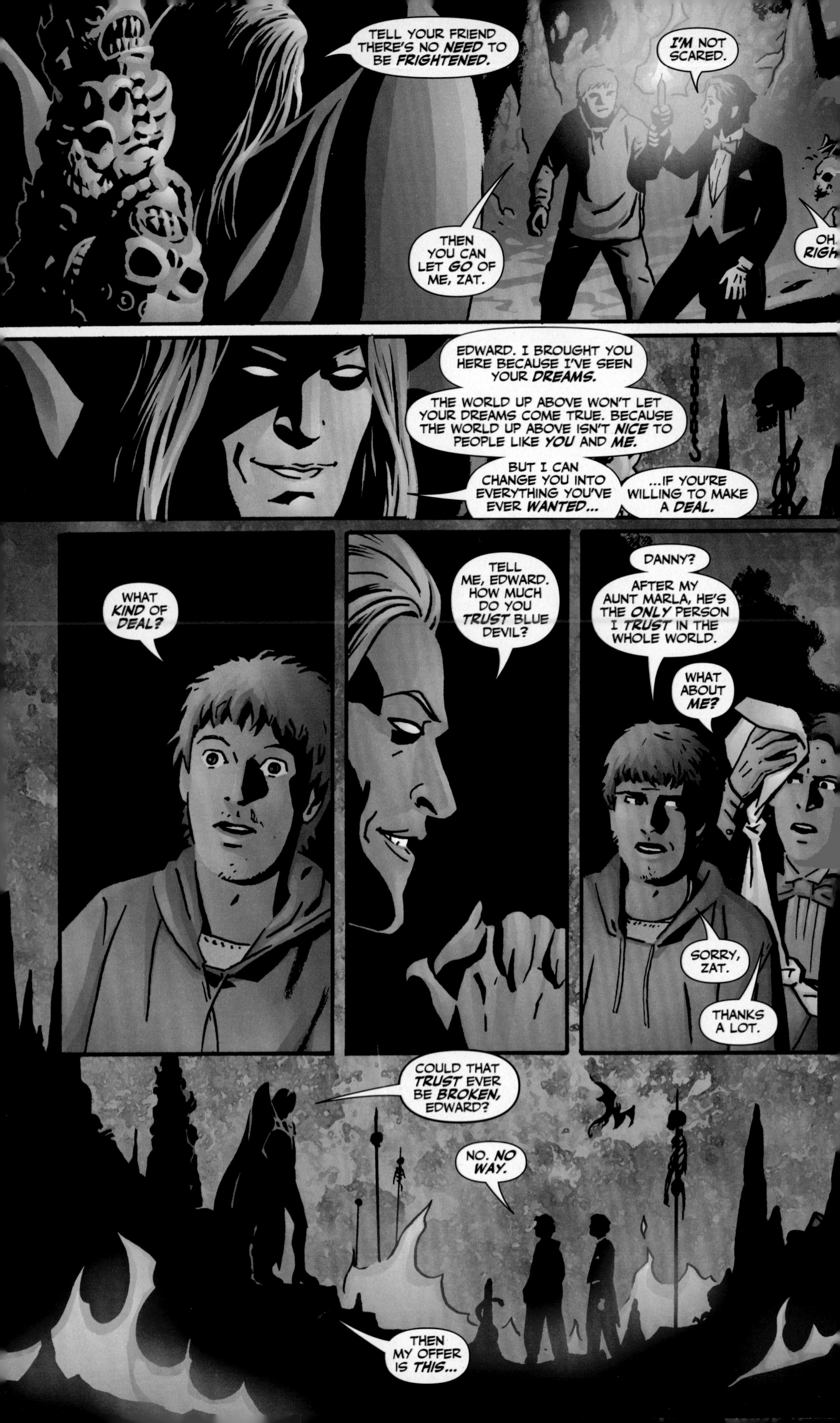
TELL YOUR FRIEND THERE'S NO *NEED* TO BE *FRIGHTENED.*
I'M NOT SCARED.
THEN YOU CAN LET *GO* OF ME, ZAT.
OH. *RIGH*
EDWARD. I BROUGHT YOU HERE BECAUSE I'VE SEEN YOUR *DREAMS.*
THE WORLD UP ABOVE WON'T LET YOUR DREAMS COME TRUE. BECAUSE THE WORLD UP ABOVE ISN'T *NICE* TO PEOPLE LIKE *YOU* AND *ME.*
BUT I CAN CHANGE YOU INTO EVERYTHING YOU'VE EVER *WANTED...*
...IF YOU'RE WILLING TO MAKE A *DEAL.*
WHAT *KIND* OF *DEAL?*
TELL ME, EDWARD. HOW MUCH DO YOU *TRUST* BLUE DEVIL?
DANNY?
AFTER MY AUNT MARLA, HE'S THE *ONLY* PERSON I *TRUST* IN THE WHOLE WORLD.
WHAT ABOUT *ME?*
SORRY, ZAT.
THANKS A LOT.
COULD THAT *TRUST* EVER BE *BROKEN,* EDWARD?
NO. *NO WAY.*
THEN MY OFFER IS *THIS...*

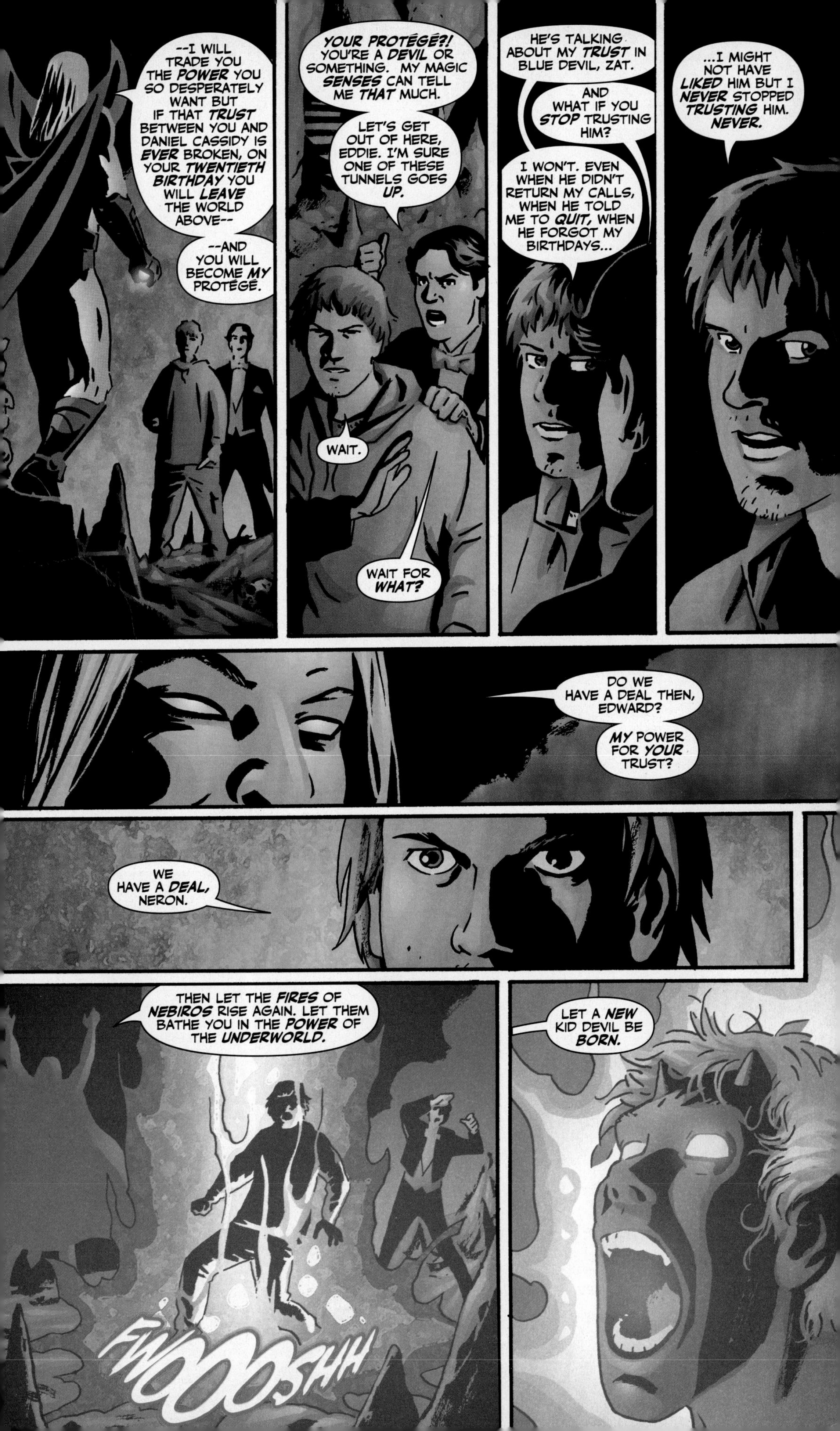
--I WILL TRADE YOU THE POWER YOU SO DESPERATELY WANT BUT IF THAT TRUST BETWEEN YOU AND DANIEL CASSIDY IS EVER BROKEN, ON YOUR TWENTIETH BIRTHDAY YOU WILL LEAVE THE WORLD ABOVE--
--AND YOU WILL BECOME MY PROTÉGÉ.
YOUR PROTÉGÉ?! YOU'RE A DEVIL OR SOMETHING. MY MAGIC SENSES CAN TELL ME THAT MUCH.
LET'S GET OUT OF HERE, EDDIE. I'M SURE ONE OF THESE TUNNELS GOES UP.
WAIT.
WAIT FOR WHAT?
HE'S TALKING ABOUT MY TRUST IN BLUE DEVIL, ZAT.
AND WHAT IF YOU STOP TRUSTING HIM?
I WON'T. EVEN WHEN HE DIDN'T RETURN MY CALLS, WHEN HE TOLD ME TO QUIT, WHEN HE FORGOT MY BIRTHDAYS...
...I MIGHT NOT HAVE LIKED HIM BUT I NEVER STOPPED TRUSTING HIM. NEVER.
DO WE HAVE A DEAL THEN, EDWARD?
MY POWER FOR YOUR TRUST?
WE HAVE A DEAL, NERON.
THEN LET THE FIRES OF NEBIROS RISE AGAIN. LET THEM BATHE YOU IN THE POWER OF THE UNDERWORLD.
FWOOOSHH
LET A NEW KID DEVIL BE BORN.

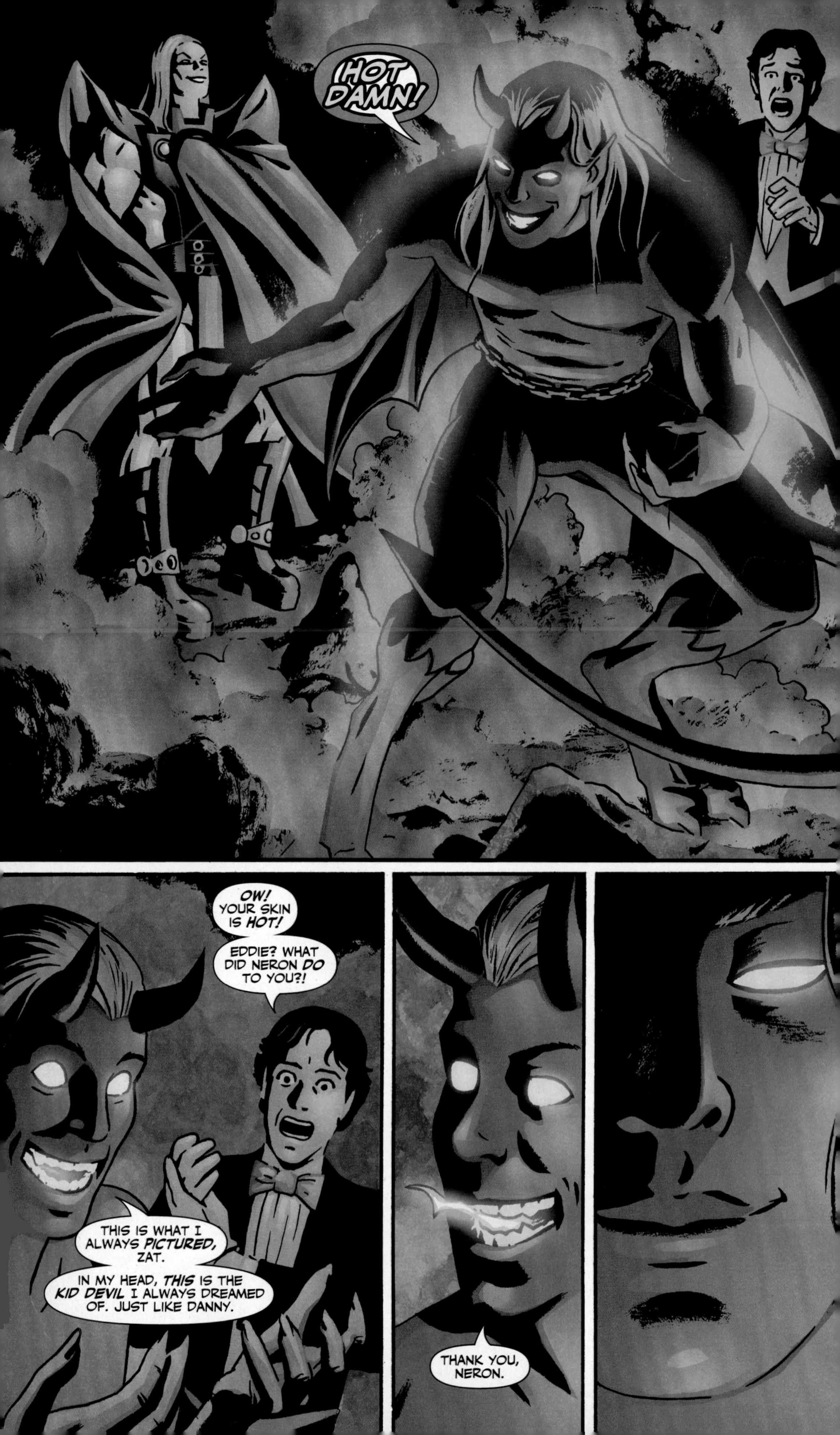
HOT DAMN!
OW! YOUR SKIN IS HOT!
EDDIE? WHAT DID NERON DO TO YOU?!
THIS IS WHAT I ALWAYS PICTURED, ZAT.
IN MY HEAD, THIS IS THE KID DEVIL I ALWAYS DREAMED OF. JUST LIKE DANNY.
THANK YOU, NERON.

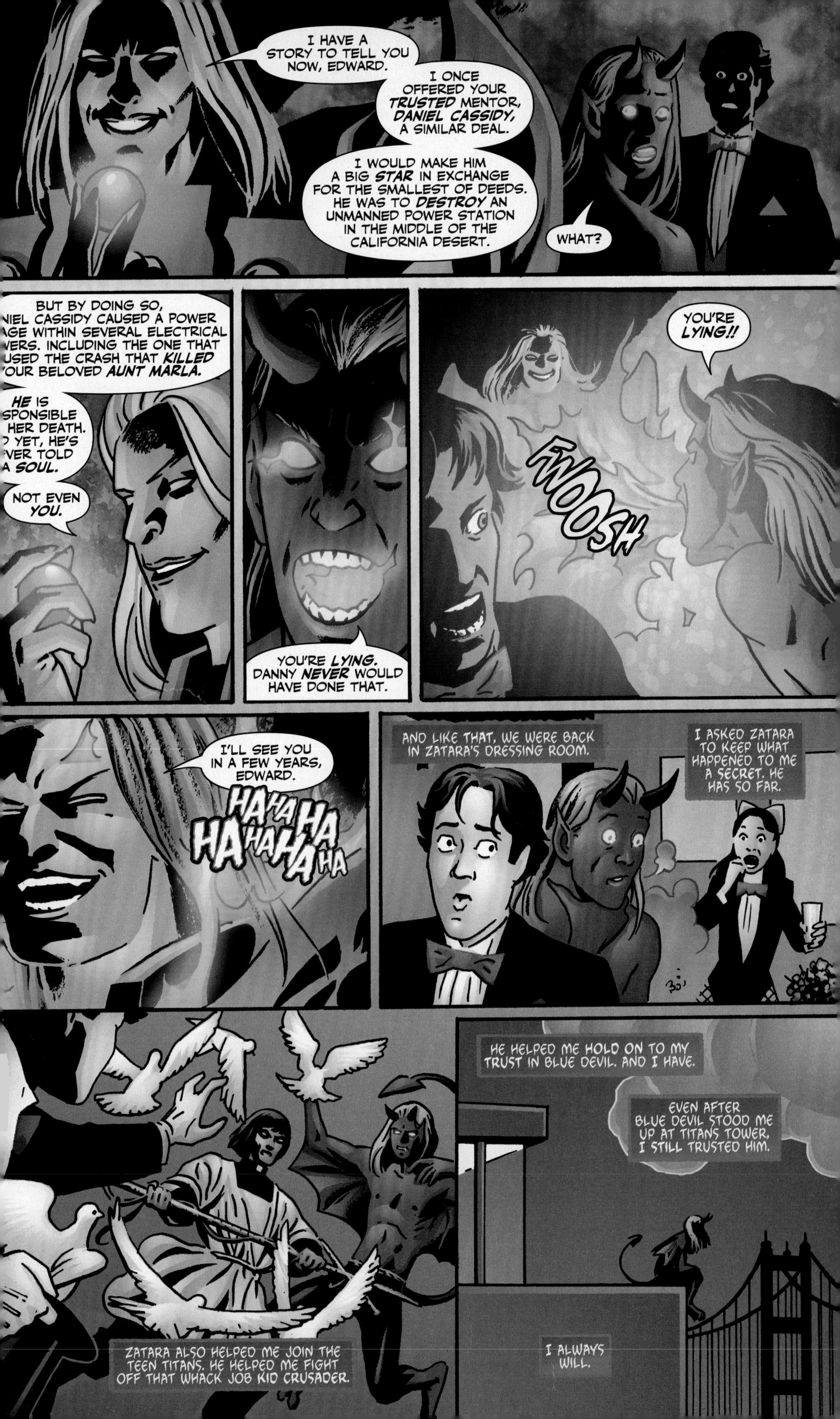

I HAVE A STORY TO TELL YOU NOW, EDWARD.
I ONCE OFFERED YOUR TRUSTED MENTOR, DANIEL CASSIDY, A SIMILAR DEAL.
I WOULD MAKE HIM A BIG STAR IN EXCHANGE FOR THE SMALLEST OF DEEDS. HE WAS TO DESTROY AN UNMANNED POWER STATION IN THE MIDDLE OF THE CALIFORNIA DESERT.
WHAT?
BUT BY DOING SO, NIEL CASSIDY CAUSED A POWER AGE WITHIN SEVERAL ELECTRICAL WERS. INCLUDING THE ONE THAT USED THE CRASH THAT KILLED YOUR BELOVED AUNT MARLA.
HE IS SPONSIBLE HER DEATH. D YET, HE'S VER TOLD A SOUL.
NOT EVEN YOU.
YOU'RE LYING. DANNY NEVER WOULD HAVE DONE THAT.
YOU'RE LYING!!
FWOOSH
I'LL SEE YOU IN A FEW YEARS, EDWARD.
HAHAHA HAHAHAHA
AND LIKE THAT, WE WERE BACK IN ZATARA'S DRESSING ROOM.
I ASKED ZATARA TO KEEP WHAT HAPPENED TO ME A SECRET. HE HAS SO FAR.
ZATARA ALSO HELPED ME JOIN THE TEEN TITANS. HE HELPED ME FIGHT OFF THAT WHACK JOB KID CRUSADER.
HE HELPED ME HOLD ON TO MY TRUST IN BLUE DEVIL. AND I HAVE.
EVEN AFTER BLUE DEVIL STOOD ME UP AT TITANS TOWER, I STILL TRUSTED HIM.
I ALWAYS WILL.

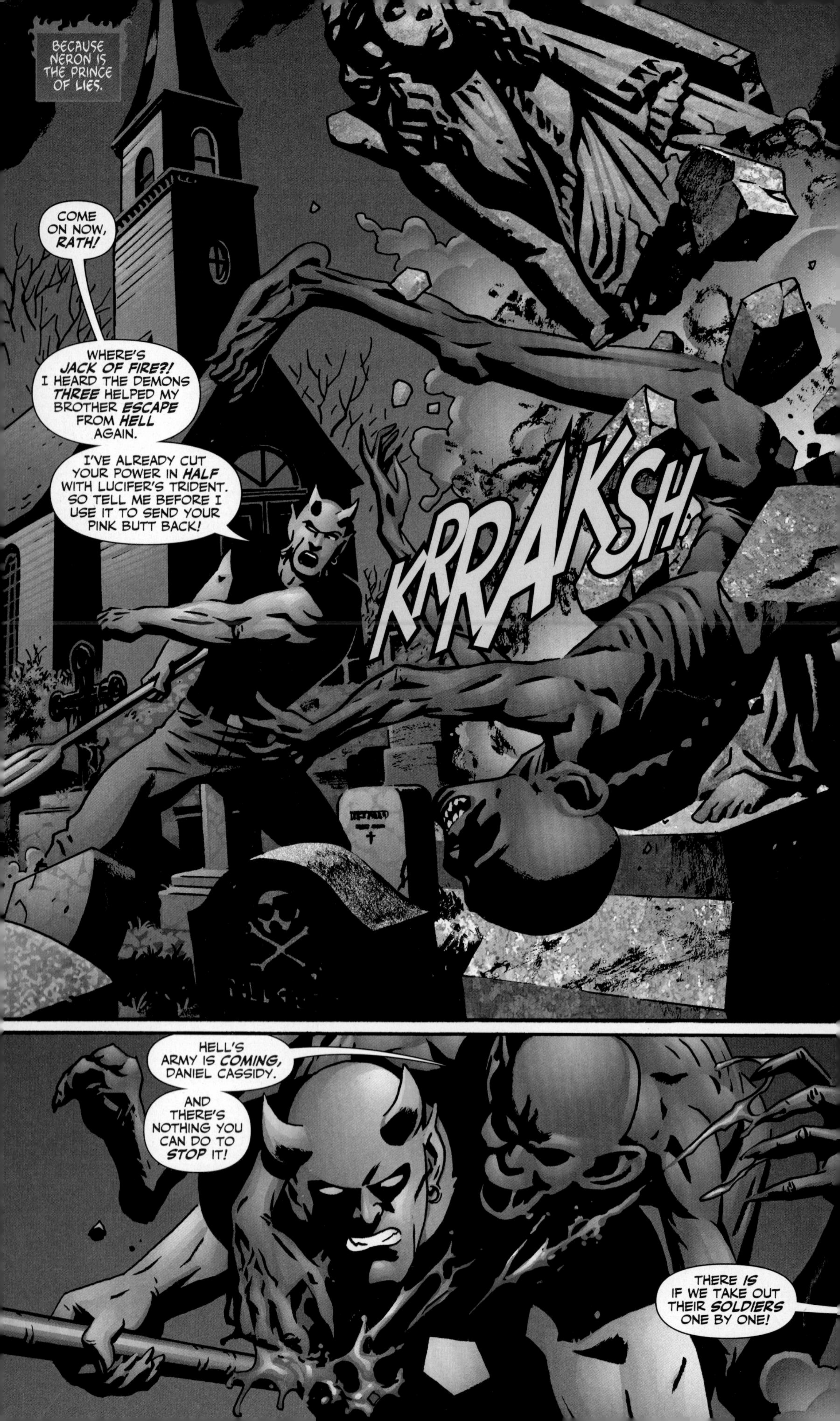
BECAUSE NERON IS THE PRINCE OF LIES.
COME ON NOW, RATH!
WHERE'S JACK OF FIRE?! I HEARD THE DEMONS THREE HELPED MY BROTHER ESCAPE FROM HELL AGAIN.
I'VE ALREADY CUT YOUR POWER IN HALF WITH LUCIFER'S TRIDENT. SO TELL ME BEFORE I USE IT TO SEND YOUR PINK BUTT BACK!
KRRAKSH
HELL'S ARMY IS COMING, DANIEL CASSIDY.
AND THERE'S NOTHING YOU CAN DO TO STOP IT!
THERE IS IF WE TAKE OUT THEIR SOLDIERS ONE BY ONE!

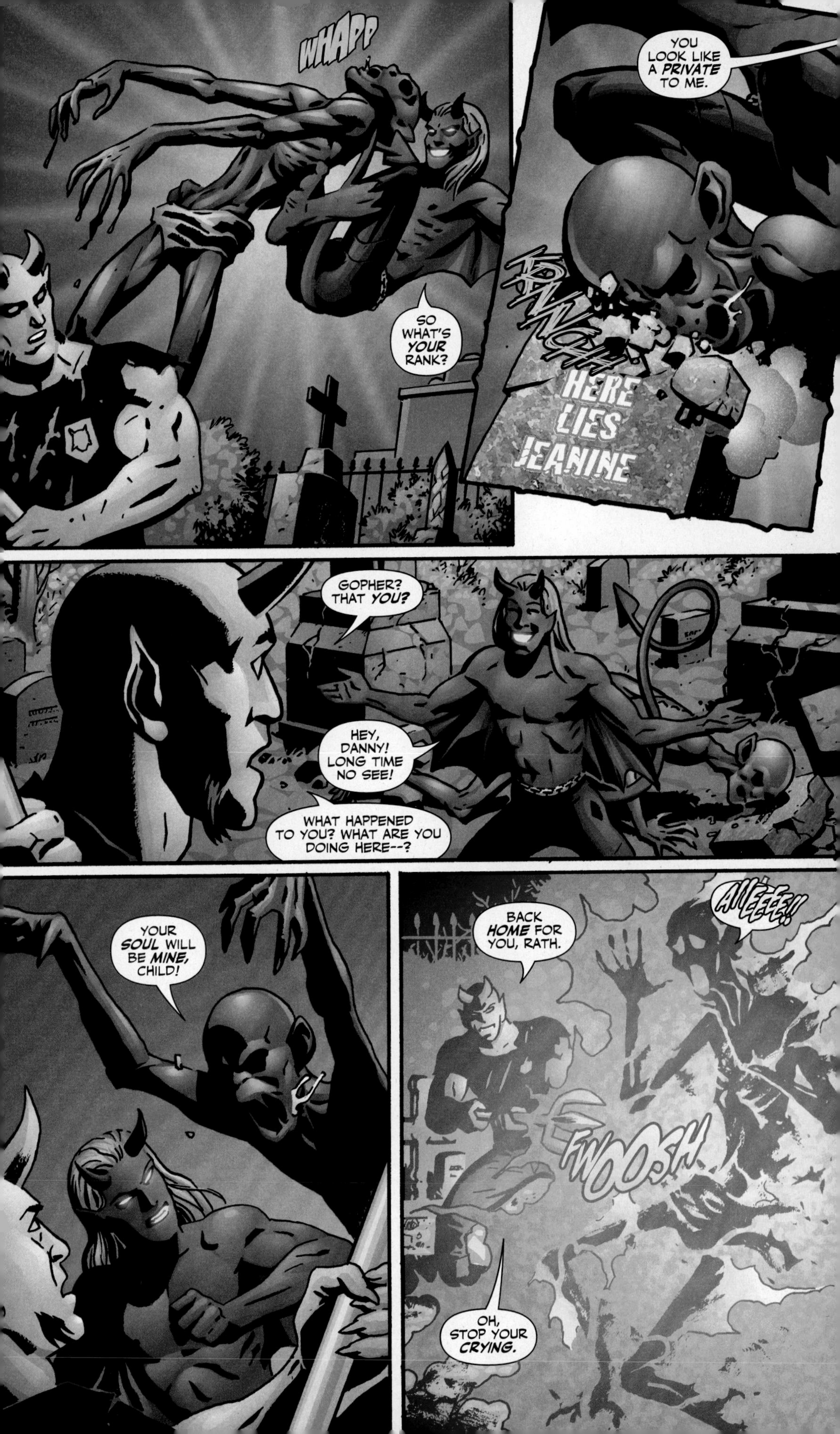
WHAPP
SO WHAT'S YOUR RANK?
YOU LOOK LIKE A PRIVATE TO ME.
KRUNCH
HERE LIES JEANINE
GOPHER? THAT YOU?
HEY, DANNY! LONG TIME NO SEE!
WHAT HAPPENED TO YOU? WHAT ARE YOU DOING HERE--?
YOUR SOUL WILL BE MINE, CHILD!
BACK HOME FOR YOU, RATH.
AIEEEE!!
FWOOSH
OH, STOP YOUR CRYING.

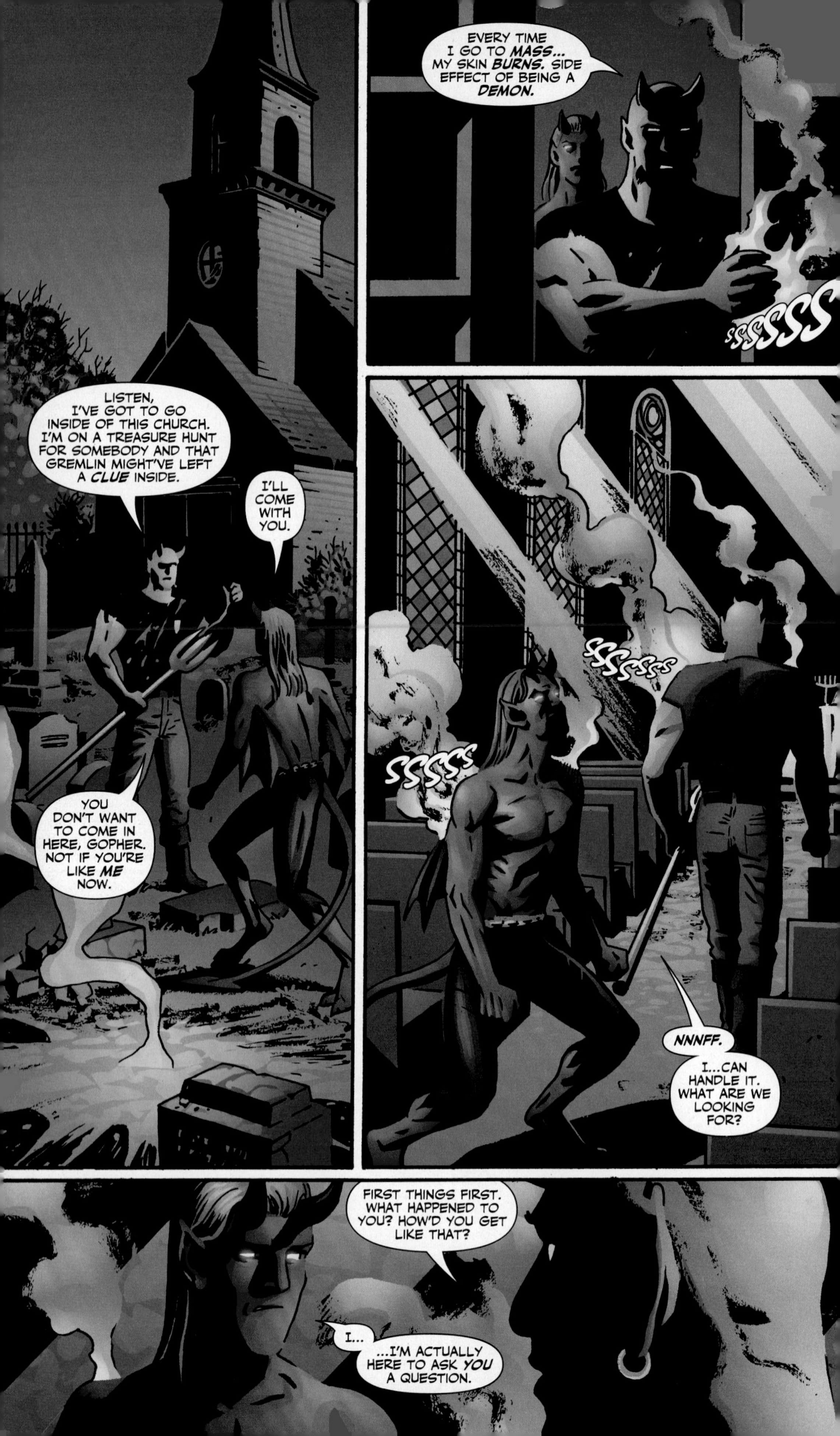

LISTEN, I'VE GOT TO GO INSIDE OF THIS CHURCH. I'M ON A TREASURE HUNT FOR SOMEBODY AND THAT GREMLIN MIGHT'VE LEFT A CLUE INSIDE.
I'LL COME WITH YOU.
YOU DON'T WANT TO COME IN HERE, GOPHER. NOT IF YOU'RE LIKE ME NOW.
EVERY TIME I GO TO MASS... MY SKIN BURNS. SIDE EFFECT OF BEING A DEMON.
SSSSSS
SSSSSS
SSSSS
NNNFF.
I...CAN HANDLE IT. WHAT ARE WE LOOKING FOR?
FIRST THINGS FIRST. WHAT HAPPENED TO YOU? HOW'D YOU GET LIKE THAT?
I...
...I'M ACTUALLY HERE TO ASK YOU A QUESTION.

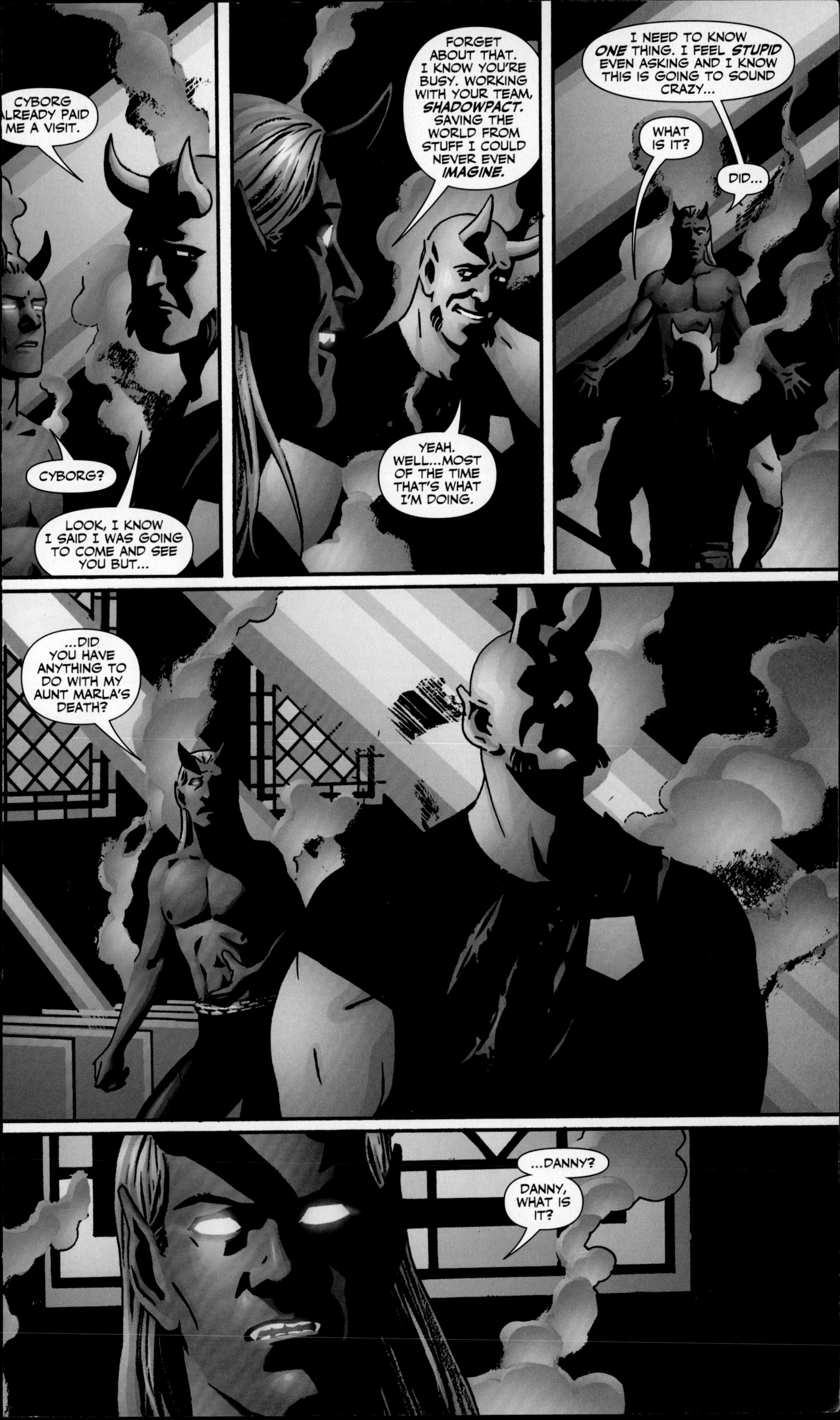

CYBORG ALREADY PAID ME A VISIT.
CYBORG?
LOOK, I KNOW I SAID I WAS GOING TO COME AND SEE YOU BUT...
FORGET ABOUT THAT. I KNOW YOU'RE BUSY. WORKING WITH YOUR TEAM, SHADOWPACT. SAVING THE WORLD FROM STUFF I COULD NEVER EVEN IMAGINE.
YEAH. WELL...MOST OF THE TIME THAT'S WHAT I'M DOING.
I NEED TO KNOW ONE THING. I FEEL STUPID EVEN ASKING AND I KNOW THIS IS GOING TO SOUND CRAZY...
WHAT IS IT?
DID...
...DID YOU HAVE ANYTHING TO DO WITH MY AUNT MARLA'S DEATH?
...DANNY?
DANNY, WHAT IS IT?

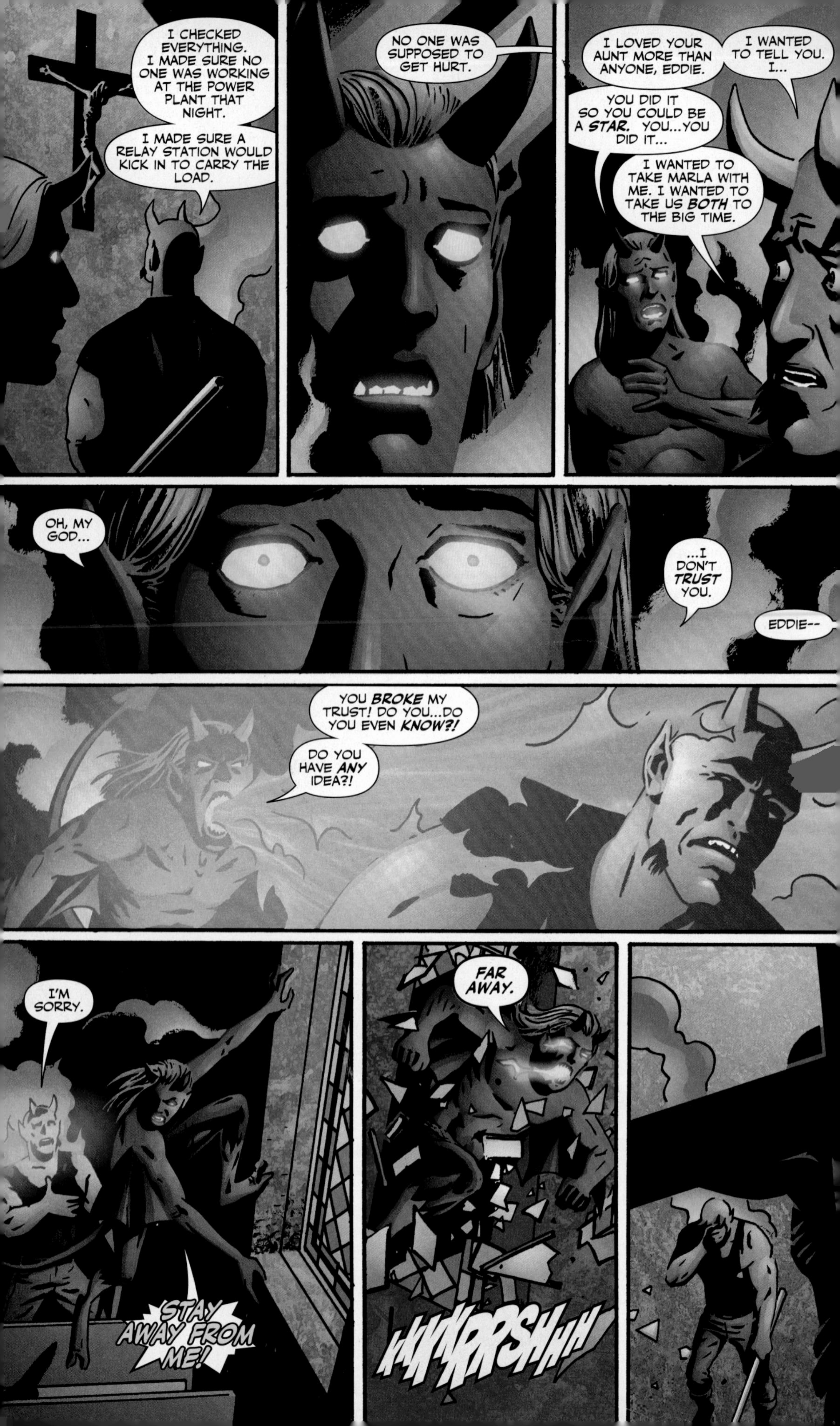
I CHECKED EVERYTHING. I MADE SURE NO ONE WAS WORKING AT THE POWER PLANT THAT NIGHT.
I MADE SURE A RELAY STATION WOULD KICK IN TO CARRY THE LOAD.
NO ONE WAS SUPPOSED TO GET HURT.
I LOVED YOUR AUNT MORE THAN ANYONE, EDDIE.
I WANTED TO TELL YOU. I...
YOU DID IT SO YOU COULD BE A STAR. YOU...YOU DID IT...
I WANTED TO TAKE MARLA WITH ME. I WANTED TO TAKE US BOTH TO THE BIG TIME.
OH, MY GOD...
...I DON'T TRUST YOU.
EDDIE--
YOU BROKE MY TRUST! DO YOU...DO YOU EVEN KNOW?!
DO YOU HAVE ANY IDEA?!
I'M SORRY.
STAY AWAY FROM ME!
FAR AWAY.
KKKKRRSHHH

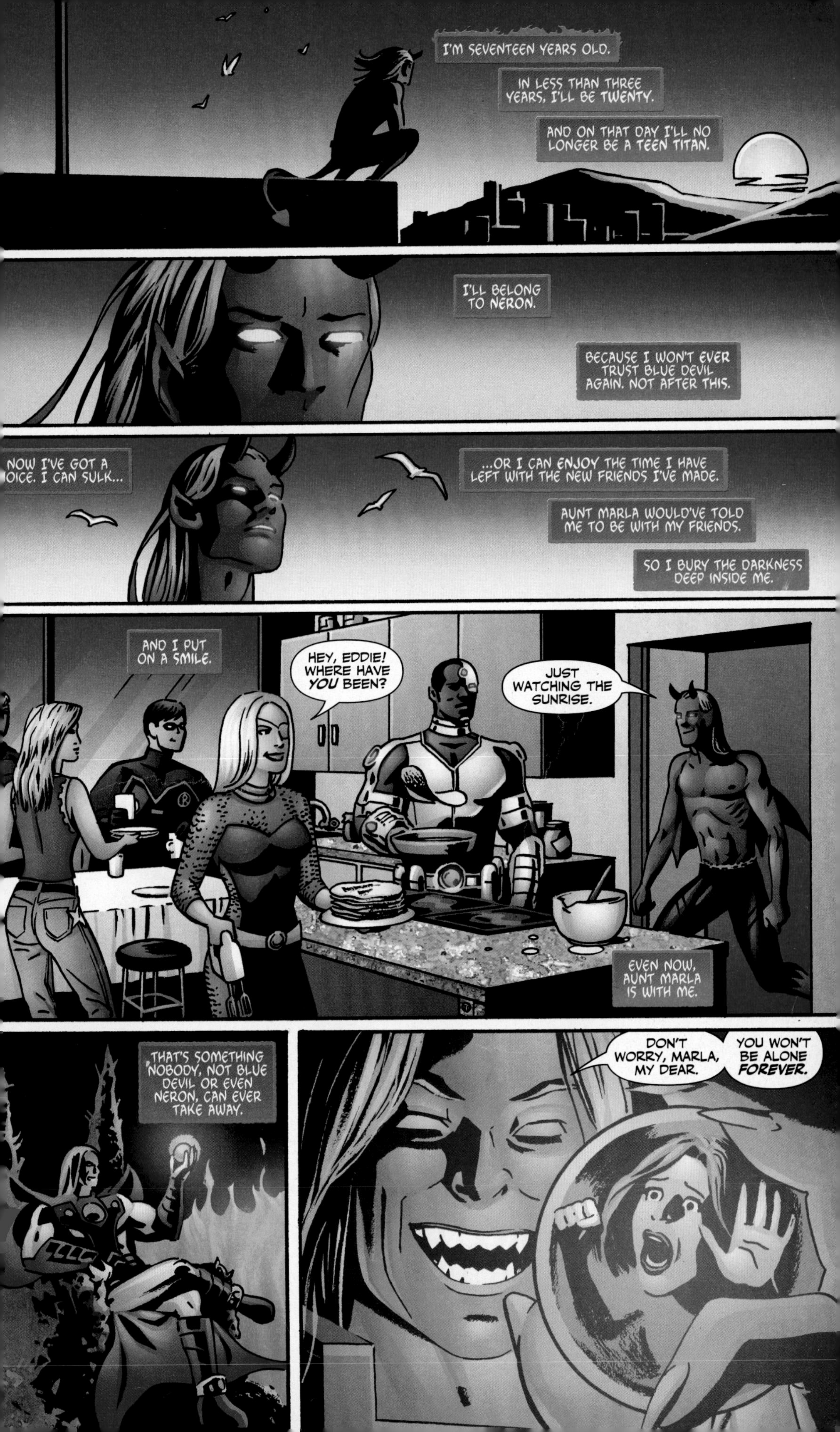
I'M SEVENTEEN YEARS OLD.
IN LESS THAN THREE YEARS, I'LL BE TWENTY.
AND ON THAT DAY I'LL NO LONGER BE A TEEN TITAN.
I'LL BELONG TO NERON.
BECAUSE I WON'T EVER TRUST BLUE DEVIL AGAIN. NOT AFTER THIS.
NOW I'VE GOT A OICE. I CAN SULK...
...OR I CAN ENJOY THE TIME I HAVE LEFT WITH THE NEW FRIENDS I'VE MADE.
AUNT MARLA WOULD'VE TOLD ME TO BE WITH MY FRIENDS.
SO I BURY THE DARKNESS DEEP INSIDE ME.
AND I PUT ON A SMILE.
HEY, EDDIE! WHERE HAVE YOU BEEN?
JUST WATCHING THE SUNRISE.
EVEN NOW, AUNT MARLA IS WITH ME.
THAT'S SOMETHING NOBODY, NOT BLUE DEVIL OR EVEN NERON, CAN EVER TAKE AWAY.
DON'T WORRY, MARLA, MY DEAR.
YOU WON'T BE ALONE FOREVER.

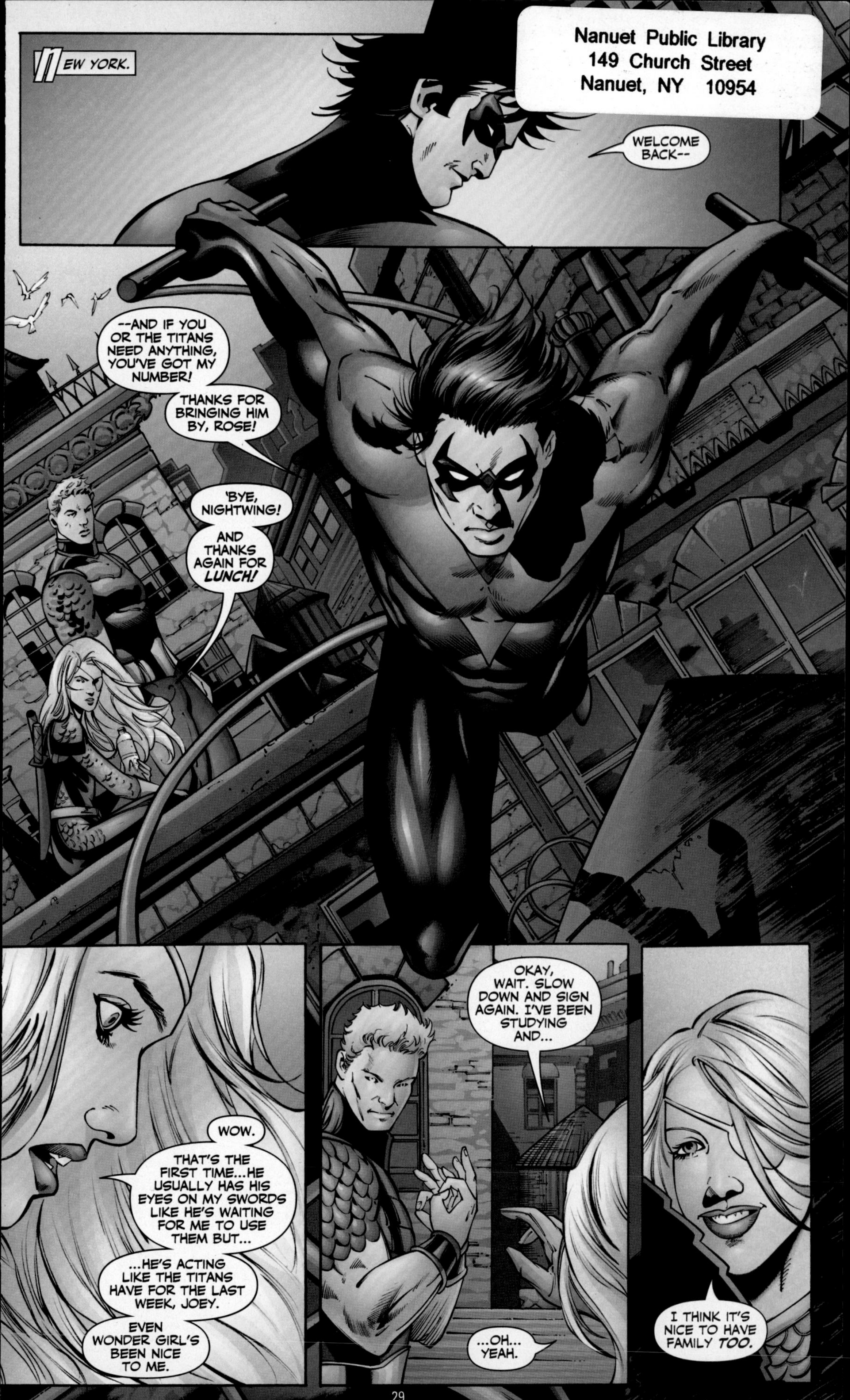
NEW YORK.
WELCOME BACK--
--AND IF YOU OR THE TITANS NEED ANYTHING, YOU'VE GOT MY NUMBER!
THANKS FOR BRINGING HIM BY, ROSE!
'BYE, NIGHTWING!
AND THANKS AGAIN FOR *LUNCH!*
WOW.
THAT'S THE FIRST TIME...HE USUALLY HAS HIS EYES ON MY SWORDS LIKE HE'S WAITING FOR ME TO USE THEM BUT...
...HE'S ACTING LIKE THE TITANS HAVE FOR THE LAST WEEK, JOEY.
EVEN WONDER GIRL'S BEEN NICE TO ME.
OKAY, WAIT. SLOW DOWN AND SIGN AGAIN. I'VE BEEN STUDYING AND...
...OH... YEAH.
I THINK IT'S NICE TO HAVE FAMILY *TOO.*

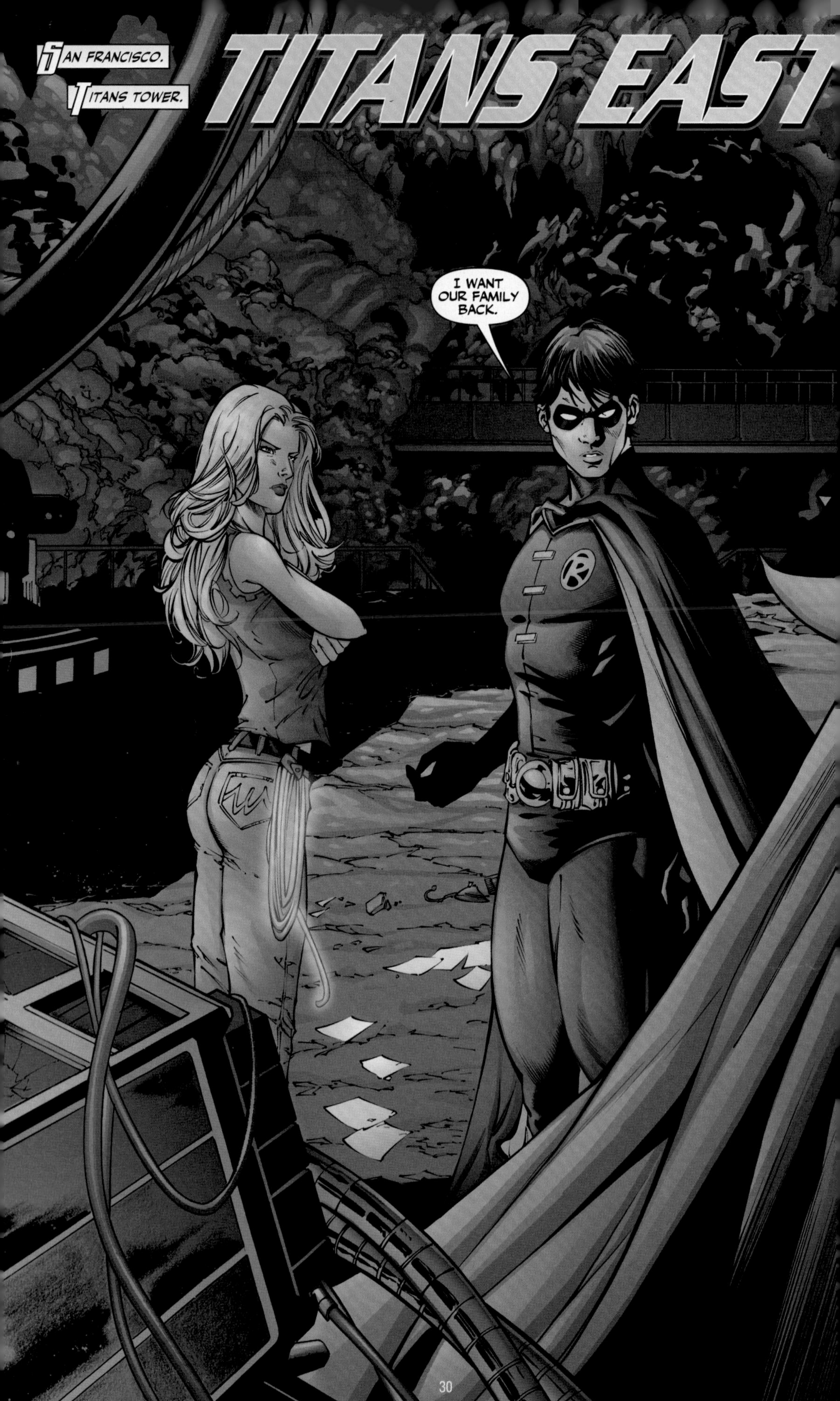
SAN FRANCISCO.
TITANS TOWER.
TITANS EAST
I WANT OUR FAMILY BACK.

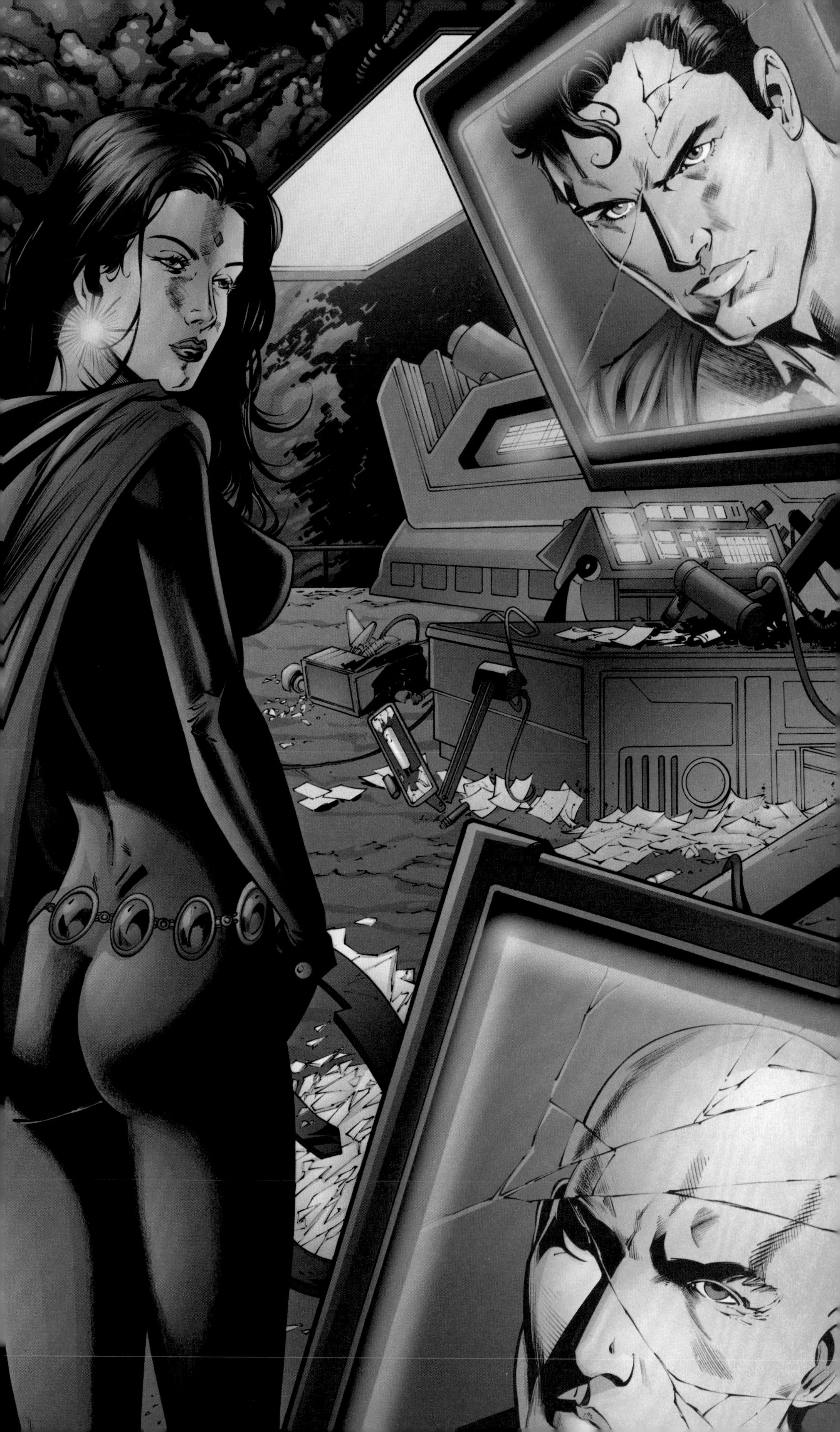

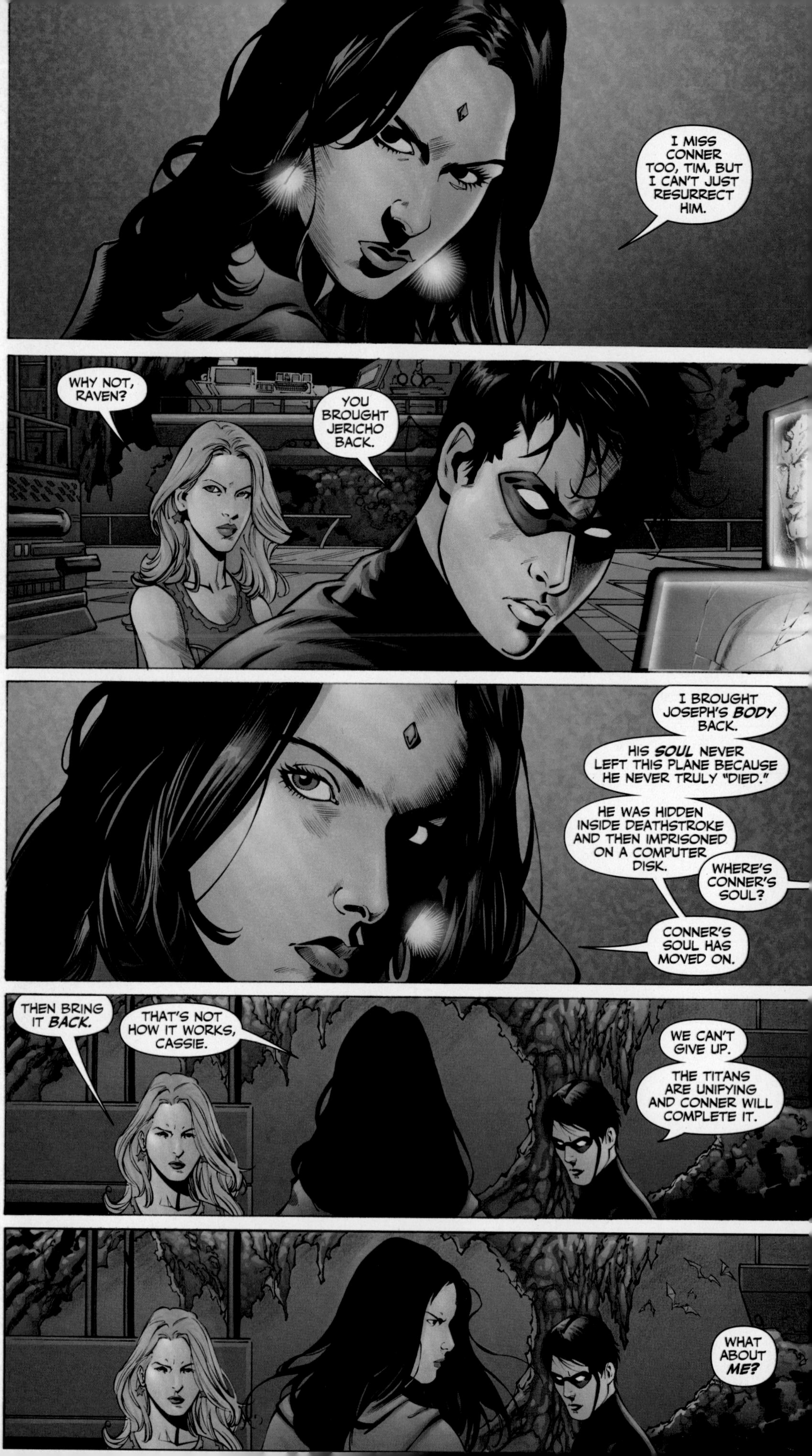

I MISS CONNER TOO, TIM, BUT I CAN'T JUST RESURRECT HIM.
WHY NOT, RAVEN?
YOU BROUGHT JERICHO BACK.
I BROUGHT JOSEPH'S *BODY* BACK.
HIS *SOUL* NEVER LEFT THIS PLANE BECAUSE HE NEVER TRULY "DIED."
HE WAS HIDDEN INSIDE DEATHSTROKE AND THEN IMPRISONED ON A COMPUTER DISK.
WHERE'S CONNER'S SOUL?
CONNER'S SOUL HAS MOVED ON.
THEN BRING IT *BACK.*
THAT'S NOT HOW IT WORKS, CASSIE.
WE CAN'T GIVE UP.
THE TITANS ARE UNIFYING AND CONNER WILL COMPLETE IT.
WHAT ABOUT *ME?*

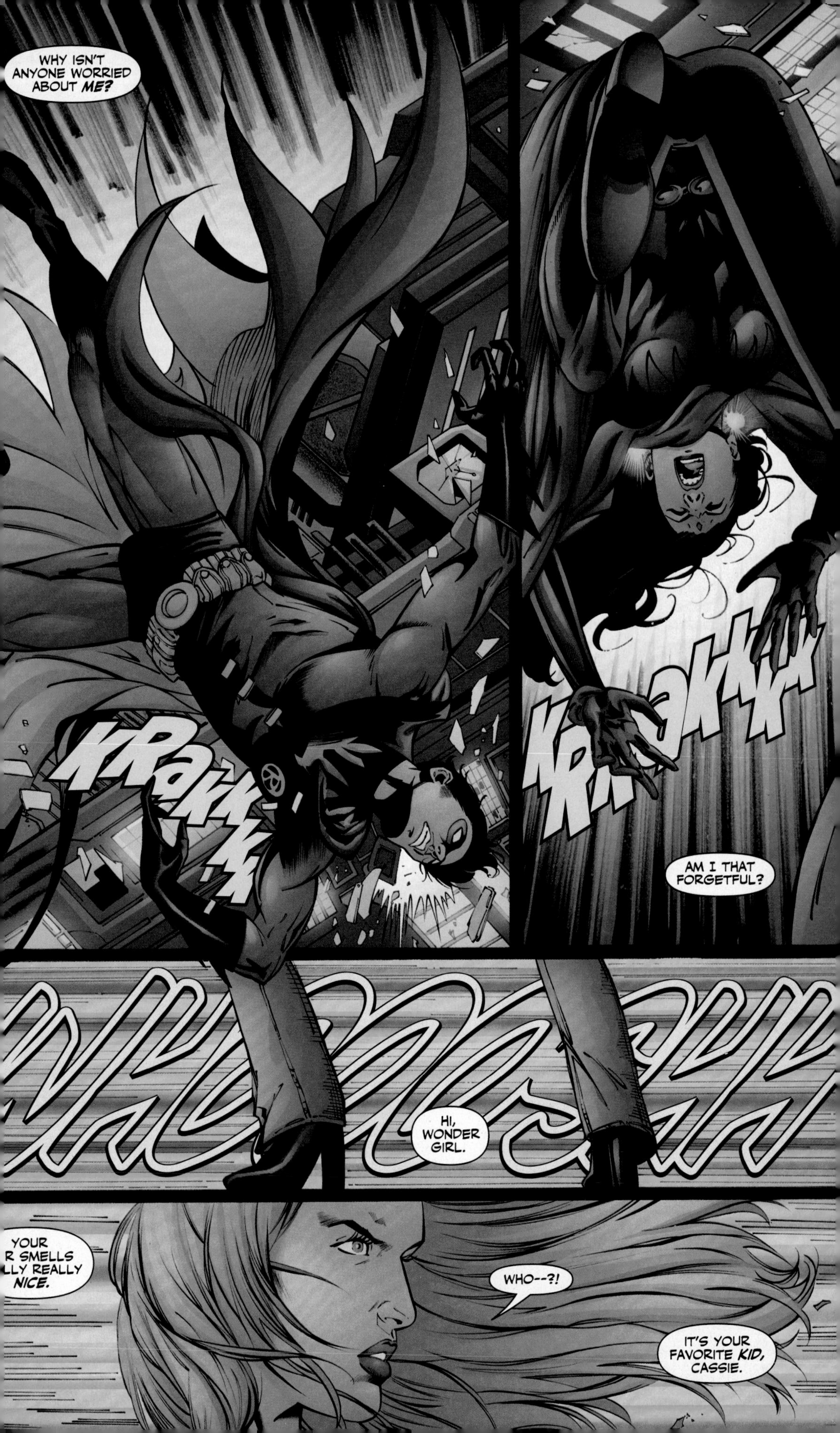
WHY ISN'T ANYONE WORRIED ABOUT *ME?*
KRAKKK
KRAKKK
AM I THAT FORGETFUL?
WHOOOSH
HI, WONDER GIRL.
YOUR R SMELLS LLY REALLY *NICE.*
WHO--?!
IT'S YOUR FAVORITE *KID,* CASSIE.

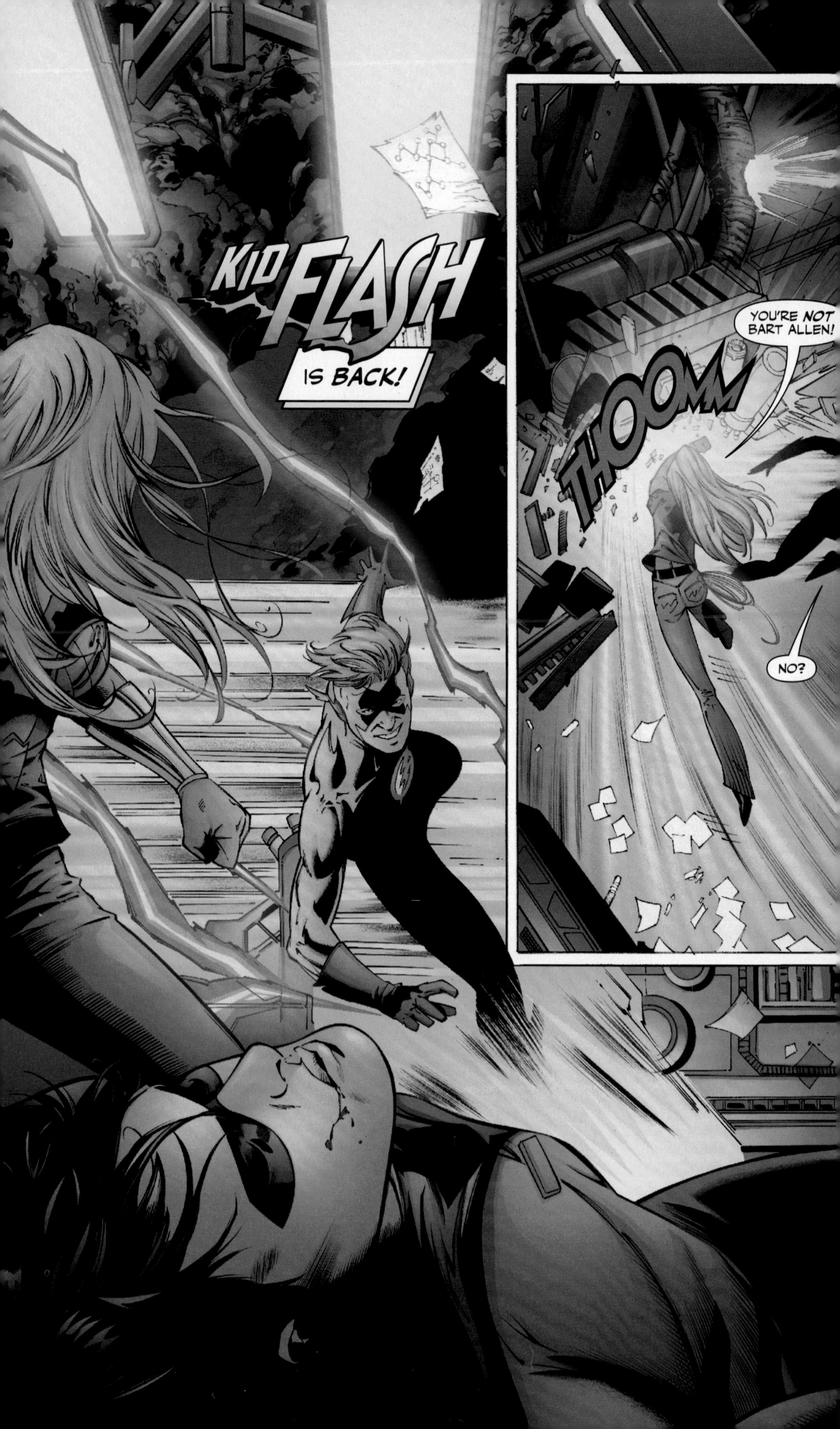
KID FLASH
IS BACK!
THOOM
YOU'RE NOT BART ALLEN!
NO?

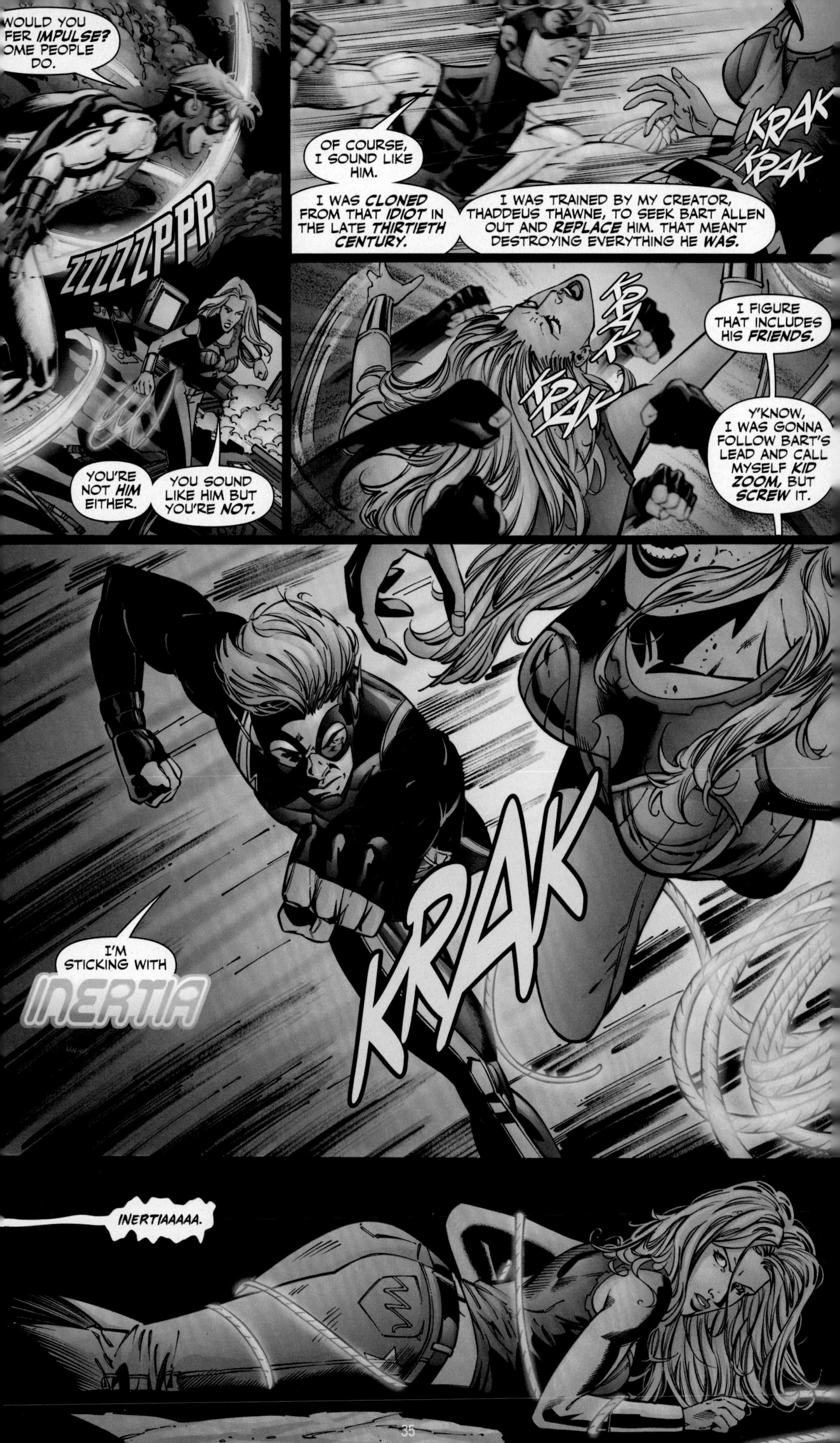
WOULD YOU
FER *IMPULSE?*
OME PEOPLE
DO.
OF COURSE, I SOUND LIKE HIM.
I WAS *CLONED* FROM THAT *IDIOT* IN THE LATE *THIRTIETH CENTURY.*
I WAS TRAINED BY MY CREATOR, THADDEUS THAWNE, TO SEEK BART ALLEN OUT AND *REPLACE* HIM. THAT MEANT DESTROYING EVERYTHING HE *WAS.*
KRAK KRAK
ZZZZZPPP
YOU'RE NOT *HIM* EITHER.
YOU SOUND LIKE HIM BUT YOU'RE *NOT.*
KRAK
KRAK
I FIGURE THAT INCLUDES HIS *FRIENDS.*
Y'KNOW, I WAS GONNA FOLLOW BART'S LEAD AND CALL MYSELF *KID ZOOM,* BUT *SCREW* IT.
I'M STICKING WITH
INERTIA
KRAK
INERTIAAAAA.

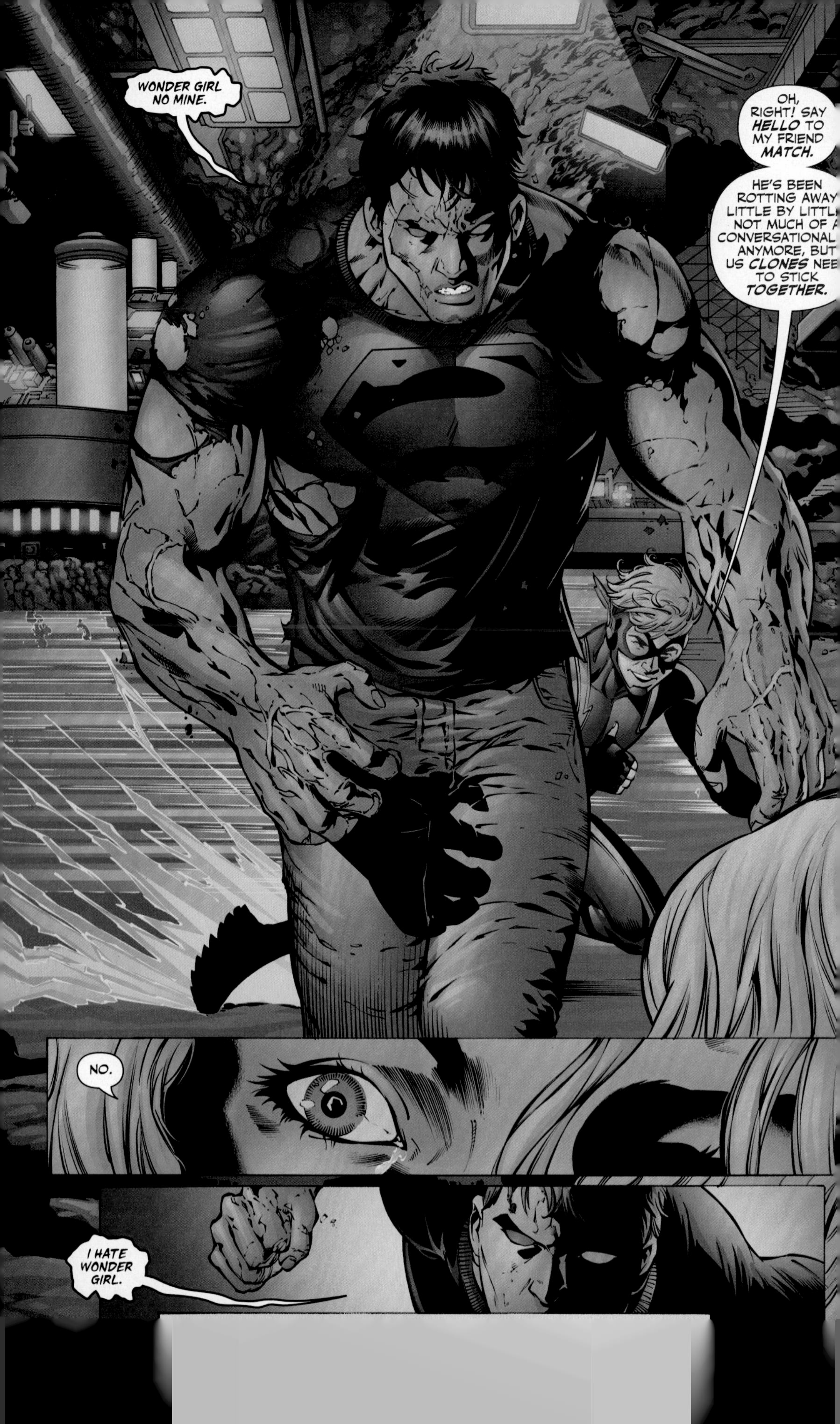
WONDER GIRL NO MINE.
OH, RIGHT! SAY HELLO TO MY FRIEND MATCH.
HE'S BEEN ROTTING AWAY LITTLE BY LITTL, NOT MUCH OF A CONVERSATIONAL ANYMORE, BUT US CLONES NEE TO STICK TOGETHER.
NO.
I HATE WONDER GIRL.

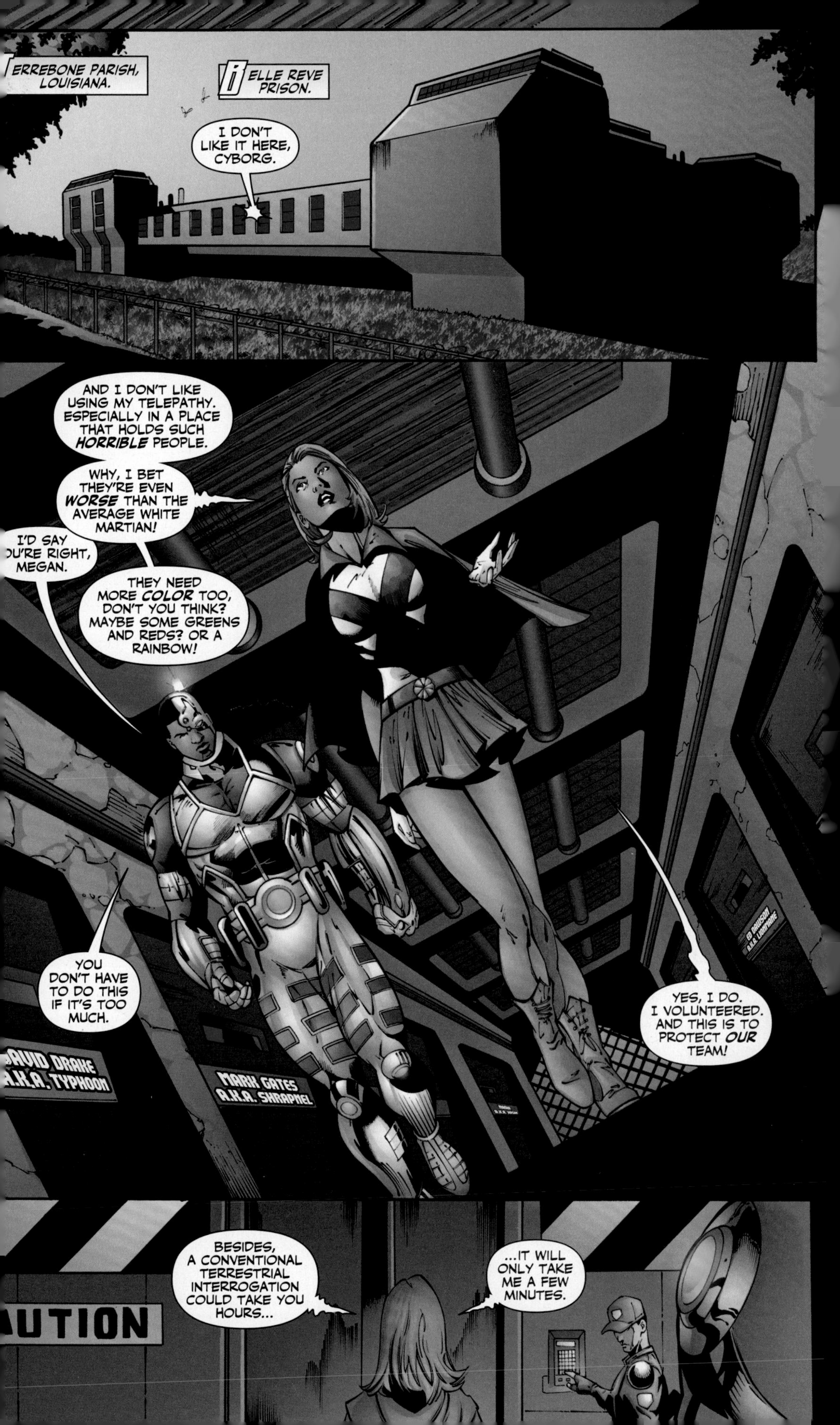

ERREBONE PARISH, LOUISIANA.
BELLE REVE PRISON.
I DON'T LIKE IT HERE, CYBORG.
AND I DON'T LIKE USING MY TELEPATHY. ESPECIALLY IN A PLACE THAT HOLDS SUCH HORRIBLE PEOPLE.
WHY, I BET THEY'RE EVEN WORSE THAN THE AVERAGE WHITE MARTIAN!
I'D SAY YOU'RE RIGHT, MEGAN.
THEY NEED MORE COLOR TOO, DON'T YOU THINK? MAYBE SOME GREENS AND REDS? OR A RAINBOW!
YOU DON'T HAVE TO DO THIS IF IT'S TOO MUCH.
YES, I DO. I VOLUNTEERED. AND THIS IS TO PROTECT OUR TEAM!
DAVID DRAKE A.K.A. TYPHOON
MARK GATES A.K.A. SHRAPNEL
BESIDES, A CONVENTIONAL TERRESTRIAL INTERROGATION COULD TAKE YOU HOURS...
...IT WILL ONLY TAKE ME A FEW MINUTES.
AUTION

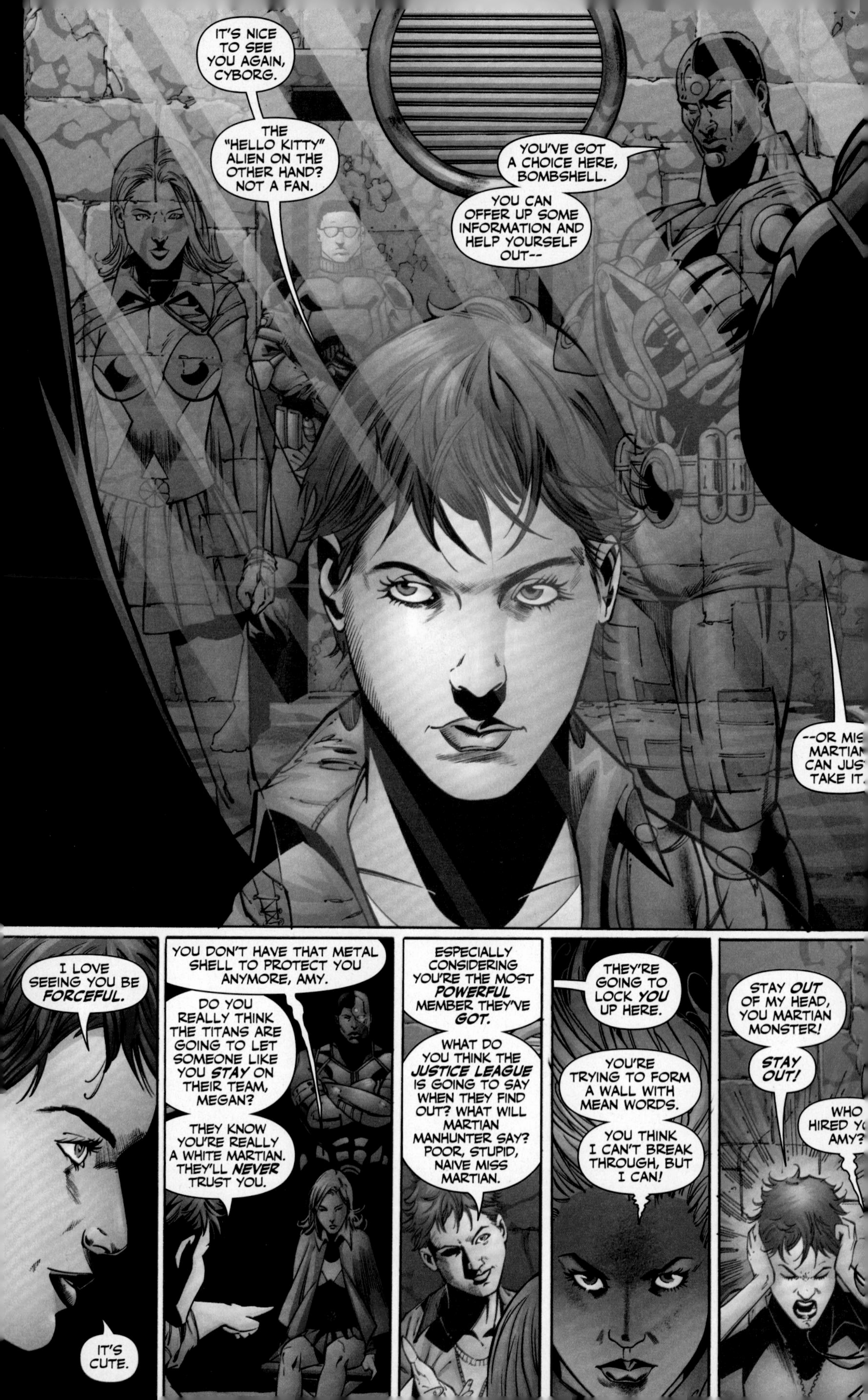
IT'S NICE TO SEE YOU AGAIN, CYBORG.
THE "HELLO KITTY" ALIEN ON THE OTHER HAND? NOT A FAN.
YOU'VE GOT A CHOICE HERE, BOMBSHELL.
YOU CAN OFFER UP SOME INFORMATION AND HELP YOURSELF OUT--
--OR MIS MARTIAN CAN JUST TAKE IT.
I LOVE SEEING YOU BE FORCEFUL.
IT'S CUTE.
YOU DON'T HAVE THAT METAL SHELL TO PROTECT YOU ANYMORE, AMY.
DO YOU REALLY THINK THE TITANS ARE GOING TO LET SOMEONE LIKE YOU STAY ON THEIR TEAM, MEGAN?
THEY KNOW YOU'RE REALLY A WHITE MARTIAN. THEY'LL NEVER TRUST YOU.
ESPECIALLY CONSIDERING YOU'RE THE MOST POWERFUL MEMBER THEY'VE GOT.
WHAT DO YOU THINK THE JUSTICE LEAGUE IS GOING TO SAY WHEN THEY FIND OUT? WHAT WILL MARTIAN MANHUNTER SAY? POOR, STUPID, NAIVE MISS MARTIAN.
THEY'RE GOING TO LOCK YOU UP HERE.
YOU'RE TRYING TO FORM A WALL WITH MEAN WORDS.
YOU THINK I CAN'T BREAK THROUGH, BUT I CAN!
STAY OUT OF MY HEAD, YOU MARTIAN MONSTER!
STAY OUT!
WHO HIRED Y AMY?

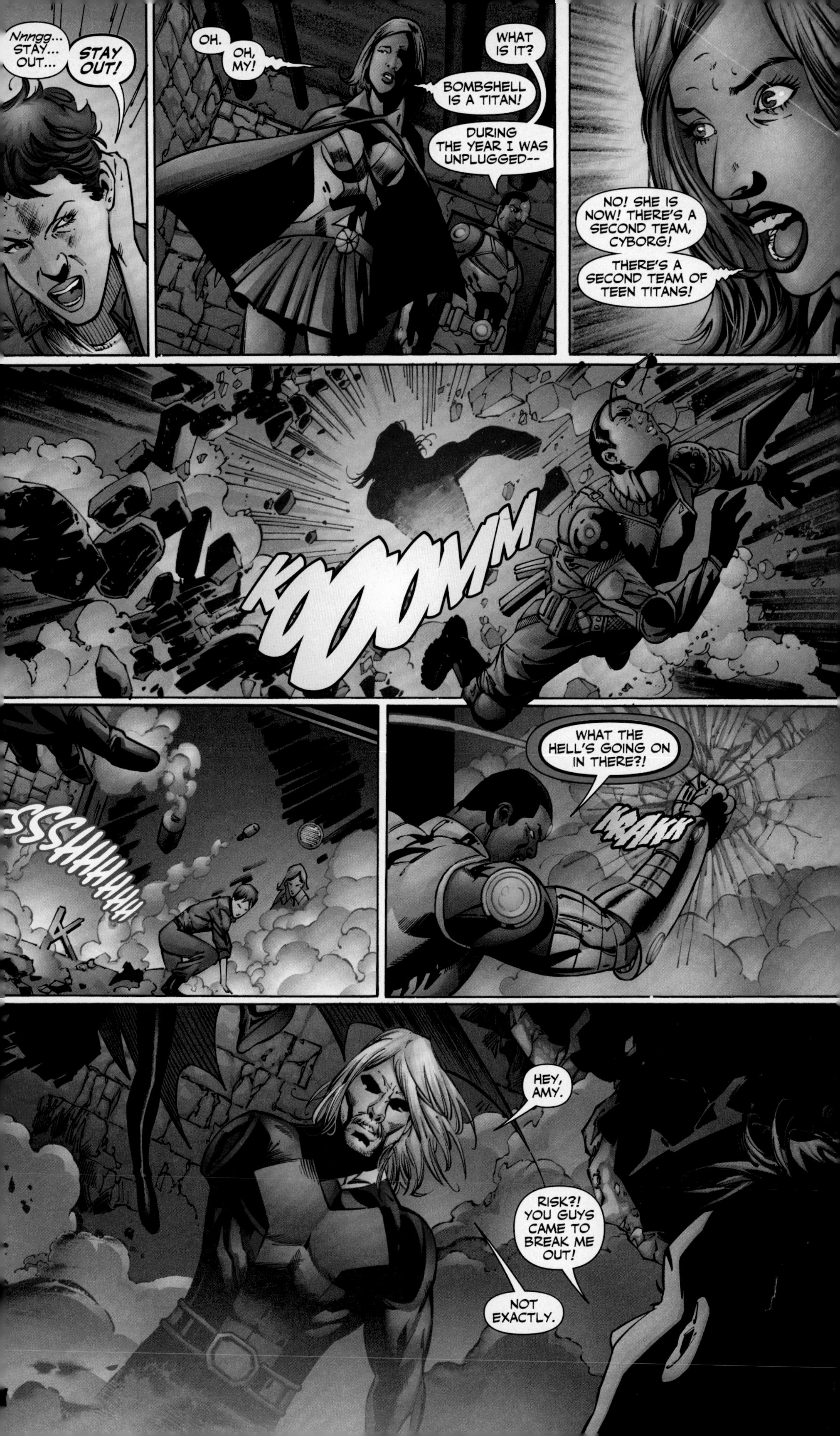
Nnngg... STAY... OUT...
STAY OUT!
OH.
OH, MY!
WHAT IS IT?
BOMBSHELL IS A TITAN!
DURING THE YEAR I WAS UNPLUGGED--
NO! SHE IS NOW! THERE'S A SECOND TEAM, CYBORG!
THERE'S A SECOND TEAM OF TEEN TITANS!
KOOOMM
SSSHHHHHH
WHAT THE HELL'S GOING ON IN THERE?!
KRAKK
HEY, AMY.
RISK?! YOU GUYS CAME TO BREAK ME OUT!
NOT EXACTLY.

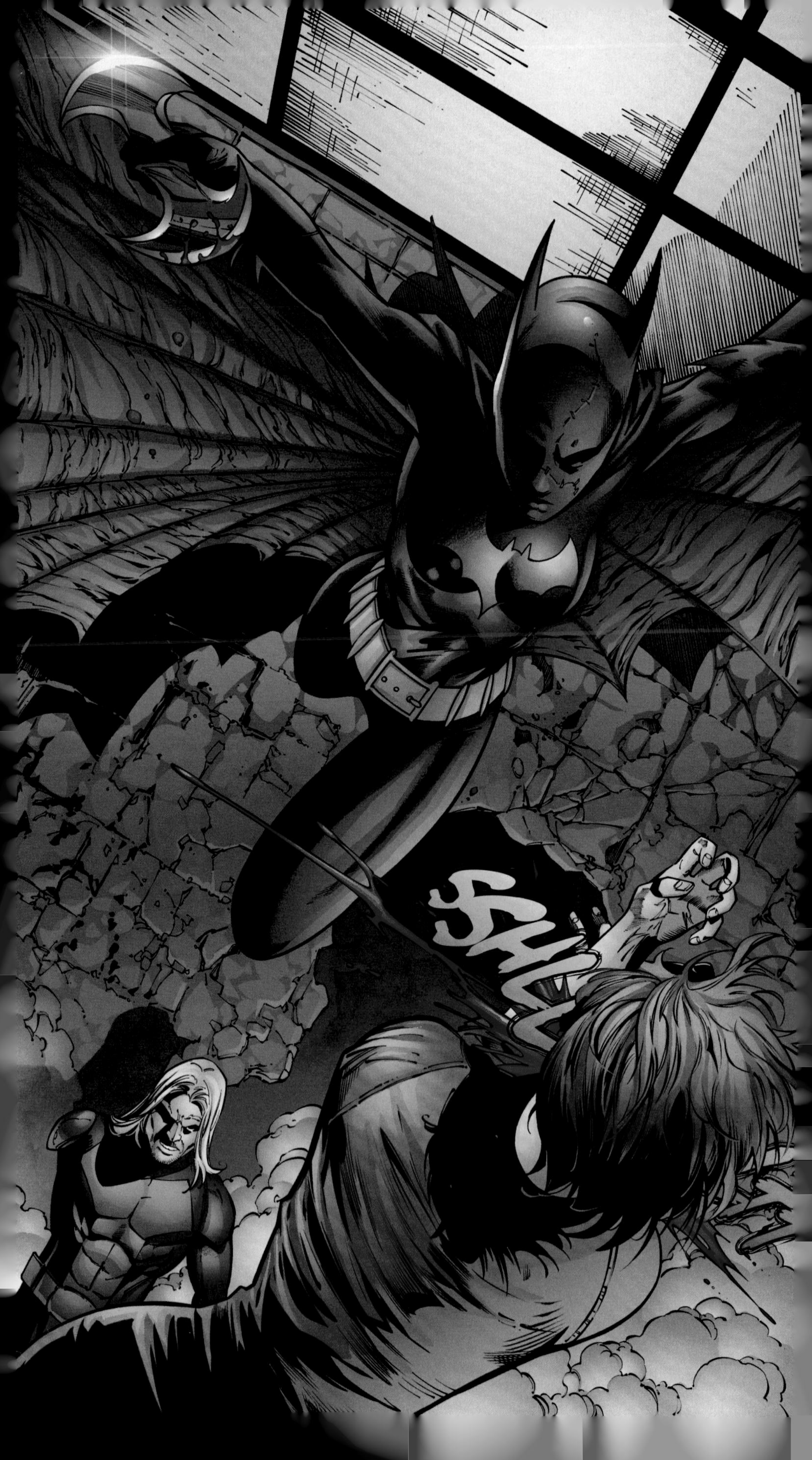

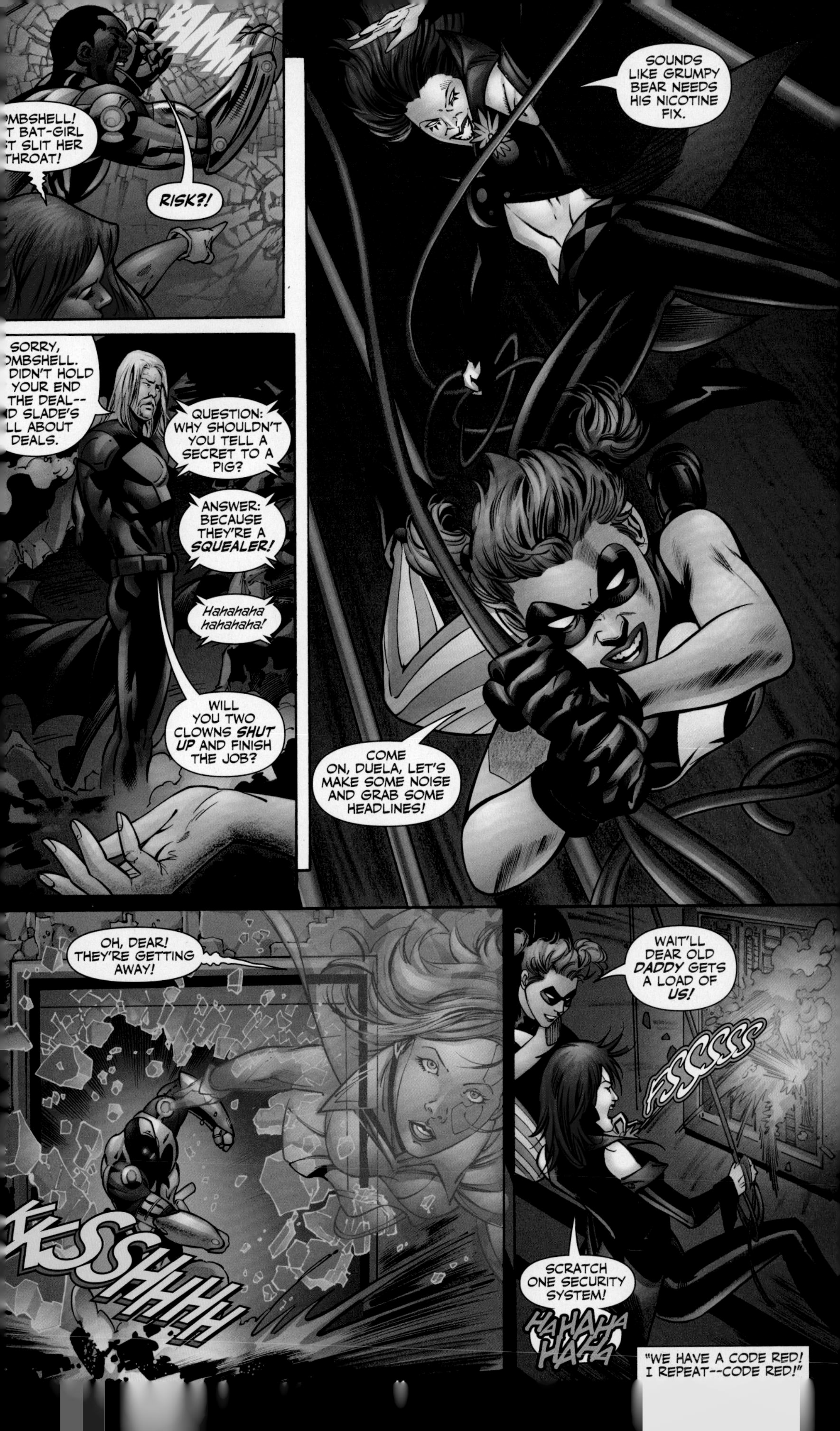
BAMM
OMBSHELL! T BAT-GIRL T SLIT HER THROAT!
RISK?!
SOUNDS LIKE GRUMPY BEAR NEEDS HIS NICOTINE FIX.
SORRY, OMBSHELL. DIDN'T HOLD YOUR END THE DEAL-- D SLADE'S LL ABOUT DEALS.
QUESTION: WHY SHOULDN'T YOU TELL A SECRET TO A PIG?
ANSWER: BECAUSE THEY'RE A SQUEALER!
Hahahaha hahahaha!
WILL YOU TWO CLOWNS SHUT UP AND FINISH THE JOB?
COME ON, DUELA, LET'S MAKE SOME NOISE AND GRAB SOME HEADLINES!
OH, DEAR! THEY'RE GETTING AWAY!
KSSHHHH
WAIT'LL DEAR OLD DADDY GETS A LOAD OF US!
FSSSSS
SCRATCH ONE SECURITY SYSTEM!
HAHAHA HAHA
"WE HAVE A CODE RED! I REPEAT--CODE RED!"

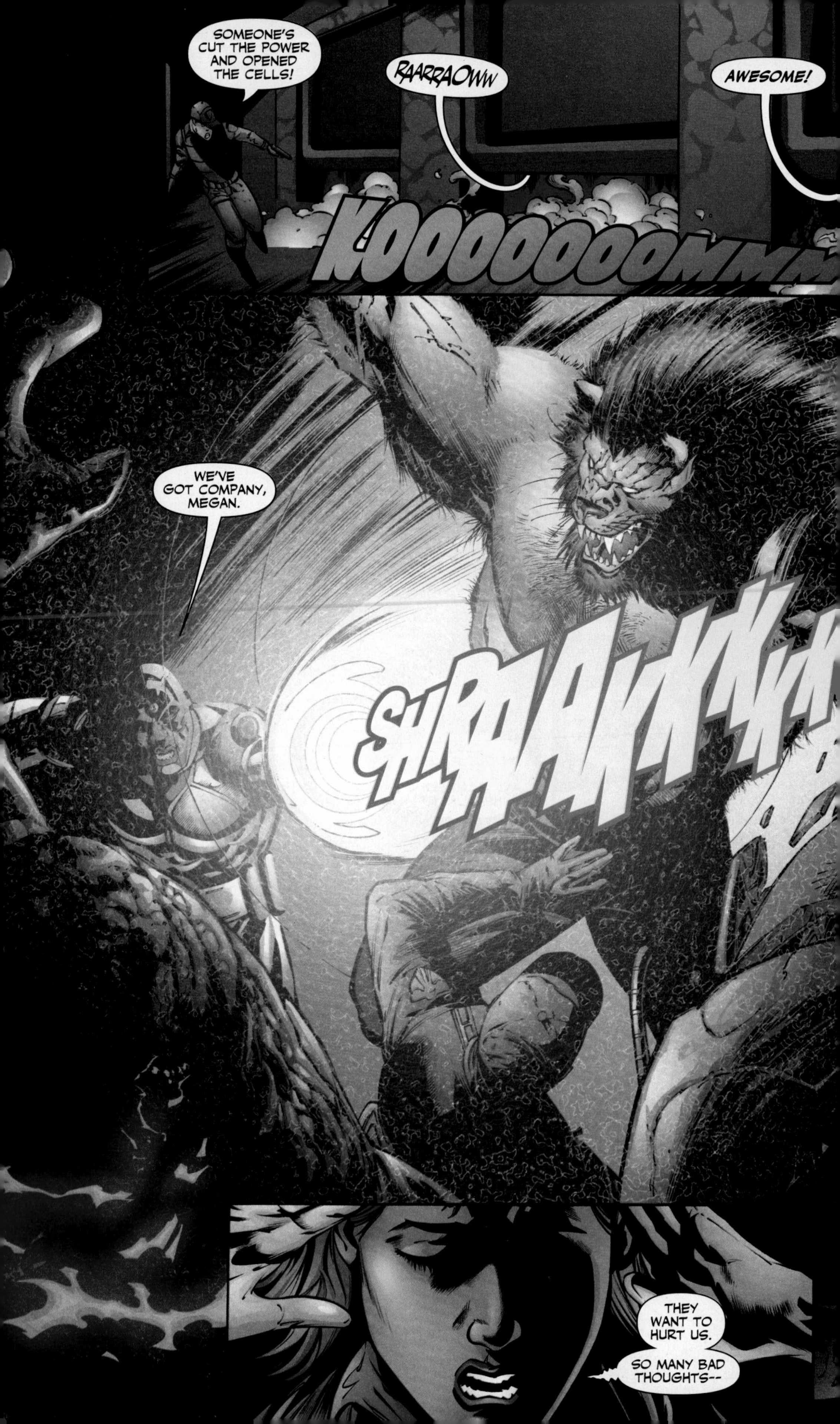
SOMEONE'S CUT THE POWER AND OPENED THE CELLS!
RAARRAOWW
AWESOME!
KOOOOOOOOMMM
WE'VE GOT COMPANY, MEGAN.
SHRAAKKKK
THEY WANT TO HURT US.
SO MANY BAD THOUGHTS--

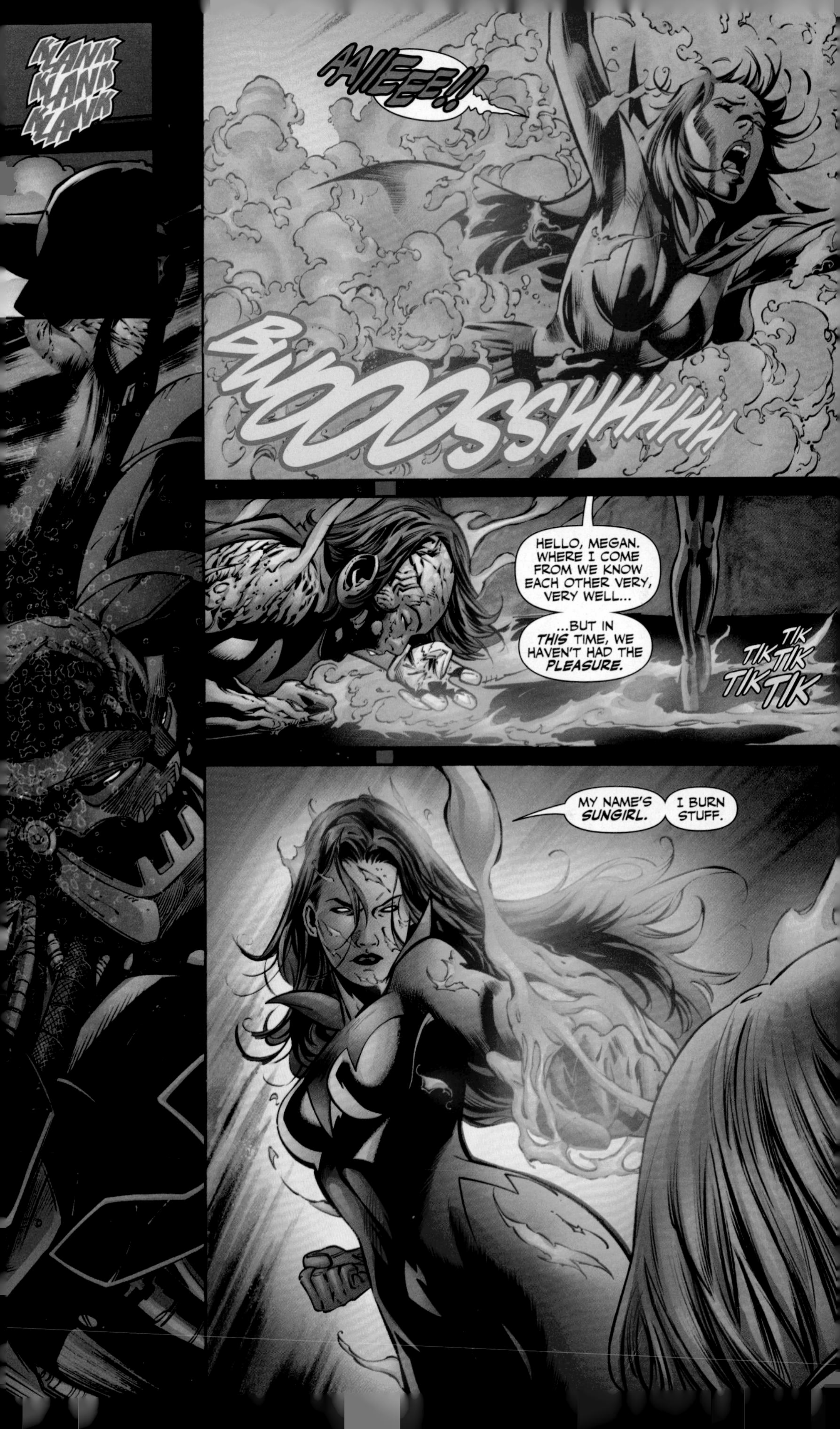
KLANK KLANK KLANK
AAIIEEEE!!
BWOOOSSHHHHH
HELLO, MEGAN. WHERE I COME FROM WE KNOW EACH OTHER VERY, VERY WELL...
...BUT IN THIS TIME, WE HAVEN'T HAD THE PLEASURE.
TIK TIK TIK TIK TIK
MY NAME'S SUNGIRL.
I BURN STUFF.

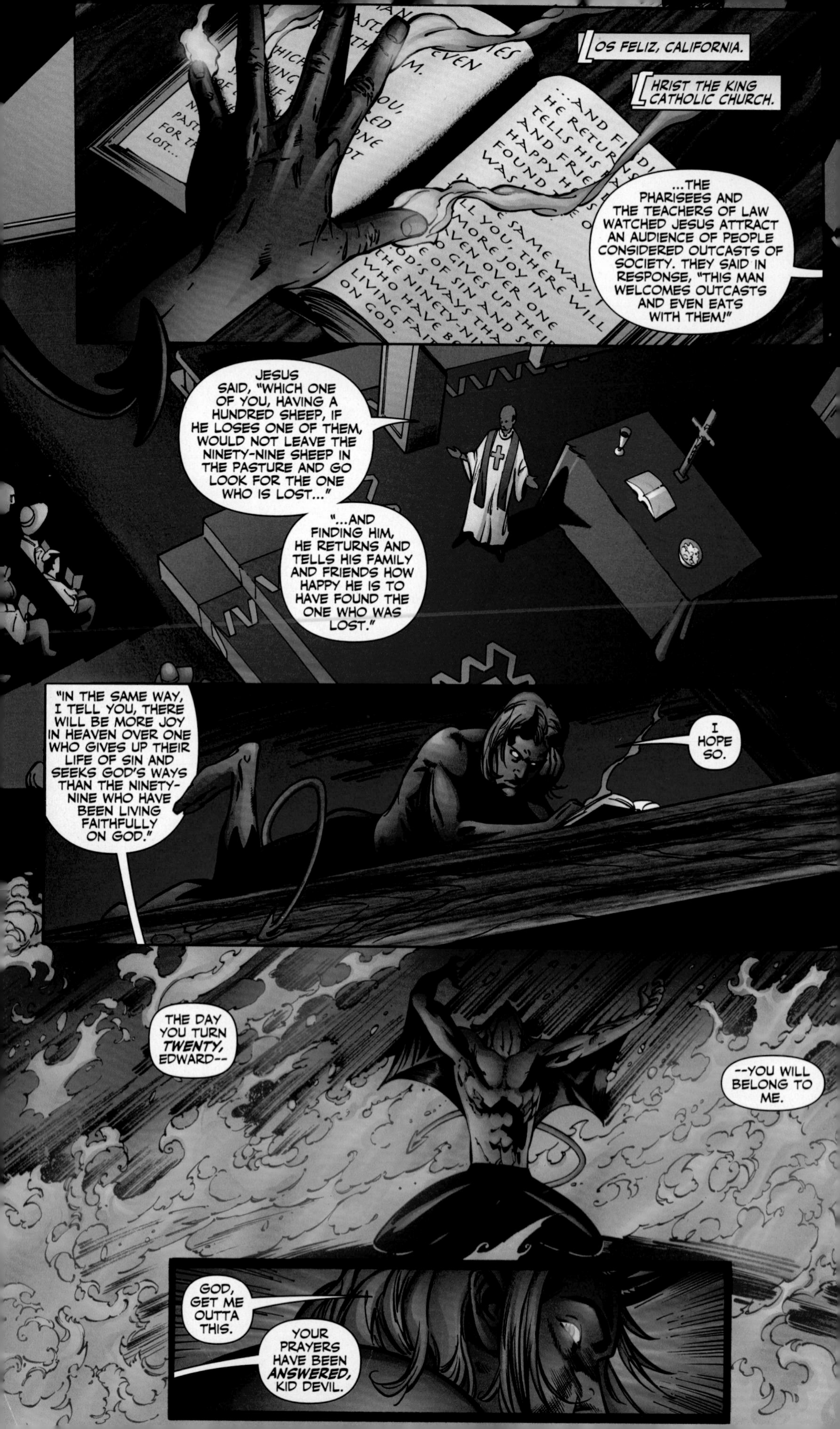

LOS FELIZ, CALIFORNIA.
CHRIST THE KING CATHOLIC CHURCH.
...THE PHARISEES AND THE TEACHERS OF LAW WATCHED JESUS ATTRACT AN AUDIENCE OF PEOPLE CONSIDERED OUTCASTS OF SOCIETY. THEY SAID IN RESPONSE, "THIS MAN WELCOMES OUTCASTS AND EVEN EATS WITH THEM!"
JESUS SAID, "WHICH ONE OF YOU, HAVING A HUNDRED SHEEP, IF HE LOSES ONE OF THEM, WOULD NOT LEAVE THE NINETY-NINE SHEEP IN THE PASTURE AND GO LOOK FOR THE ONE WHO IS LOST..."
"...AND FINDING HIM, HE RETURNS AND TELLS HIS FAMILY AND FRIENDS HOW HAPPY HE IS TO HAVE FOUND THE ONE WHO WAS LOST."
"IN THE SAME WAY, I TELL YOU, THERE WILL BE MORE JOY IN HEAVEN OVER ONE WHO GIVES UP THEIR LIFE OF SIN AND SEEKS GOD'S WAYS THAN THE NINETY-NINE WHO HAVE BEEN LIVING FAITHFULLY ON GOD."
I HOPE SO.
THE DAY YOU TURN *TWENTY,* EDWARD--
--YOU WILL BELONG TO ME.
GOD, GET ME OUTTA THIS.
YOUR PRAYERS HAVE BEEN *ANSWERED,* KID DEVIL.

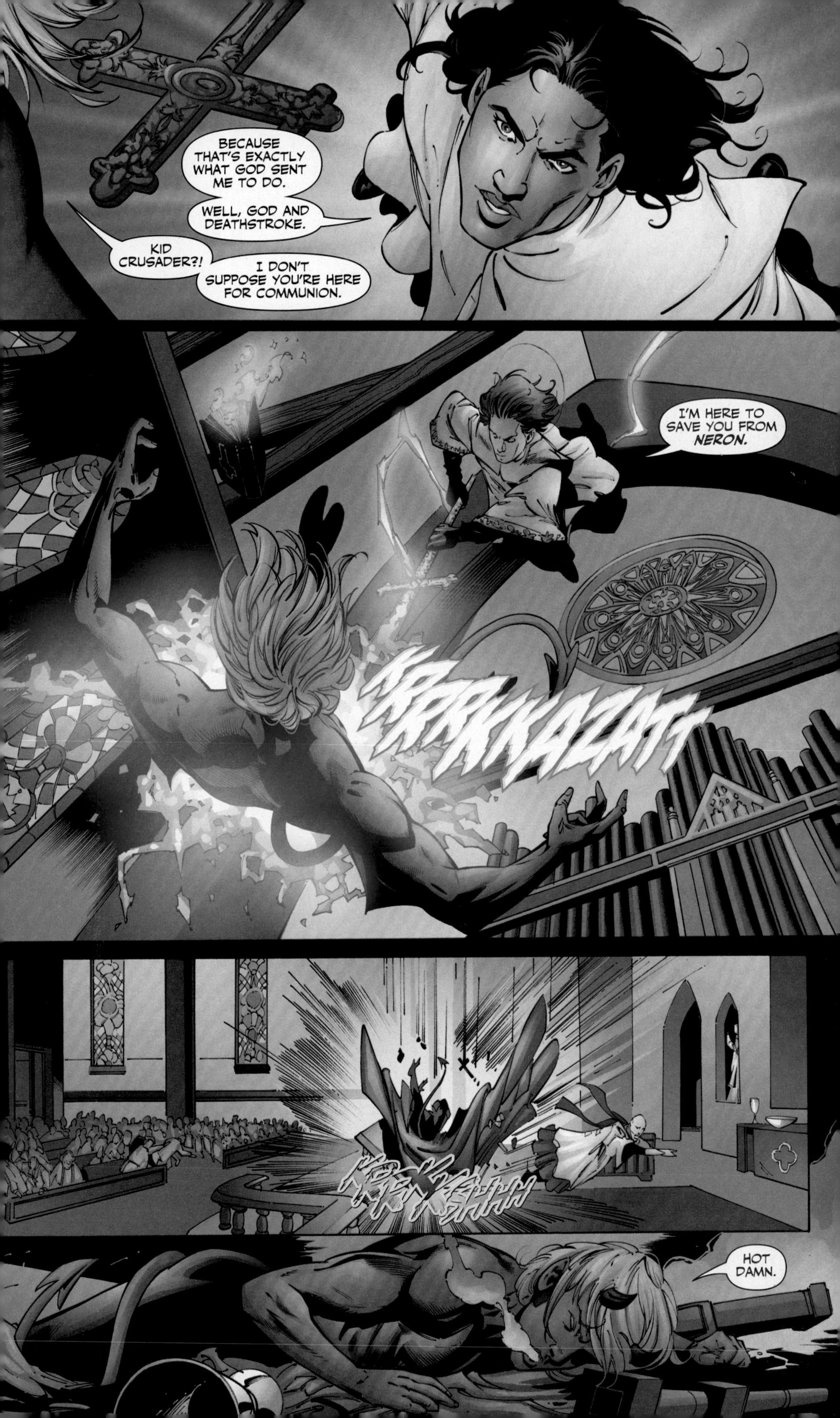
BECAUSE THAT'S EXACTLY WHAT GOD SENT ME TO DO.
WELL, GOD AND DEATHSTROKE.
KID CRUSADER?!
I DON'T SUPPOSE YOU'RE HERE FOR COMMUNION.
I'M HERE TO SAVE YOU FROM *NERON.*
HOT DAMN.

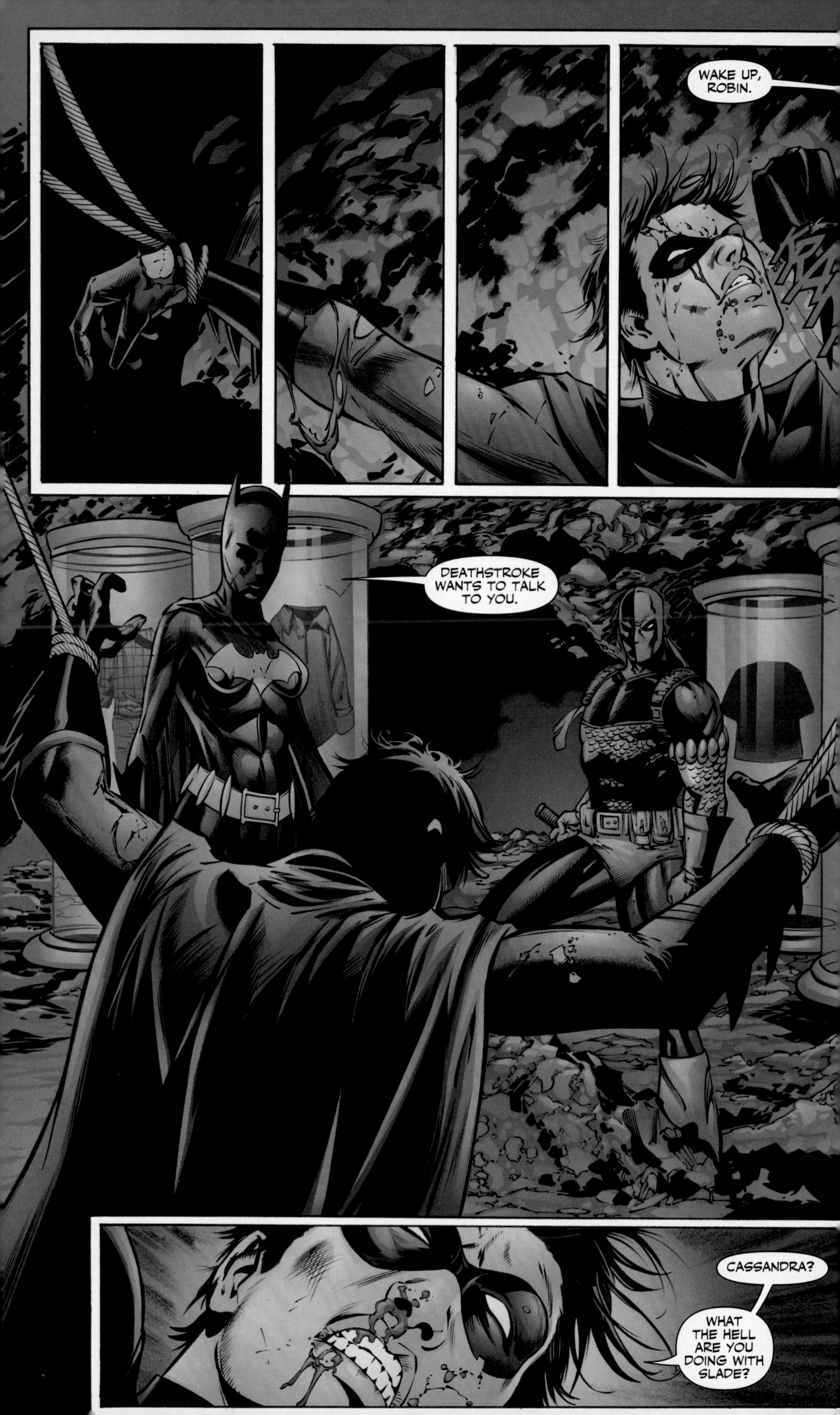
WAKE UP, ROBIN.
DEATHSTROKE WANTS TO TALK TO YOU.
CASSANDRA?
WHAT THE HELL ARE YOU DOING WITH SLADE?

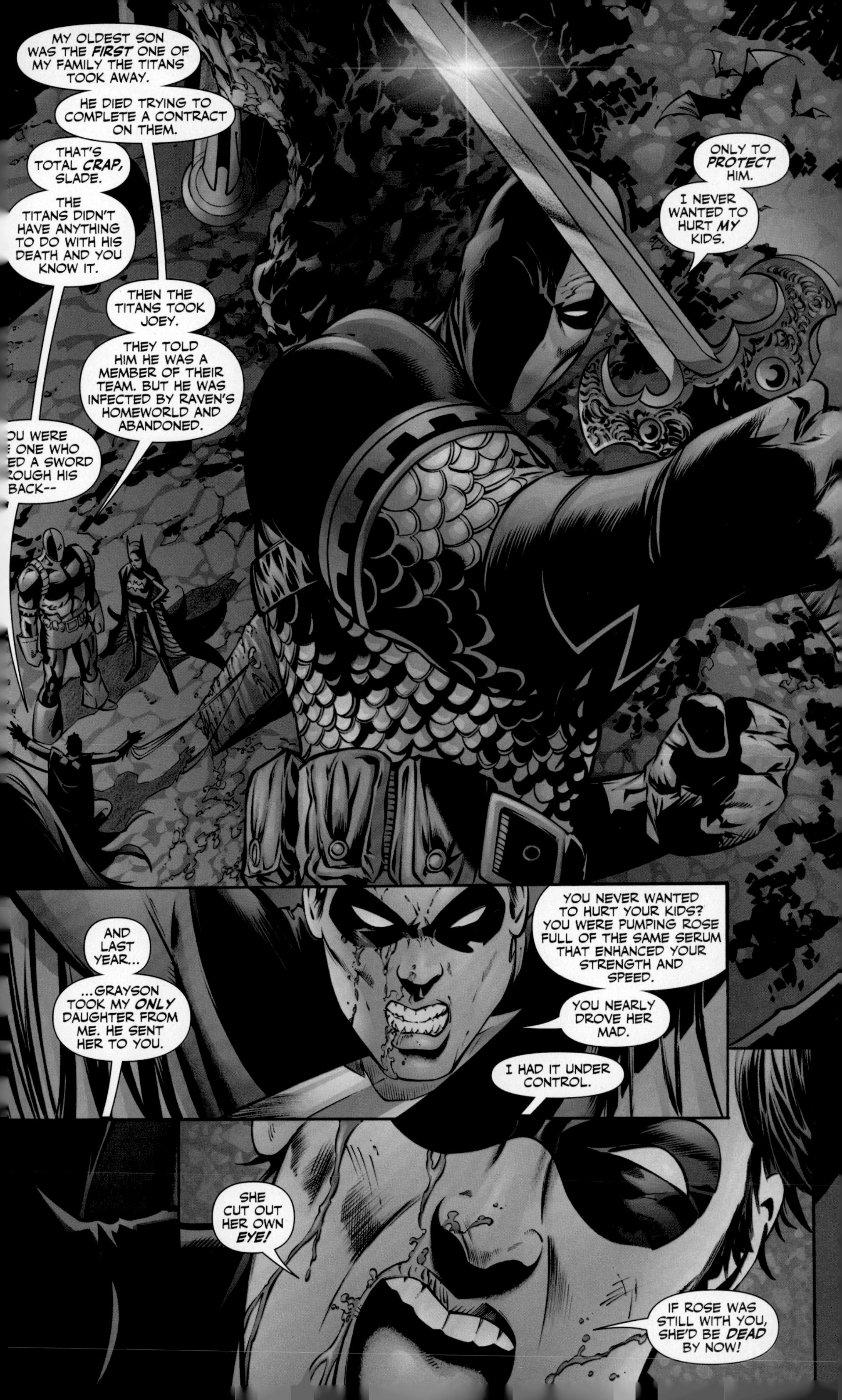
MY OLDEST SON WAS THE *FIRST* ONE OF MY FAMILY THE TITANS TOOK AWAY.
HE DIED TRYING TO COMPLETE A CONTRACT ON THEM.
THAT'S TOTAL *CRAP,* SLADE.
THE TITANS DIDN'T HAVE ANYTHING TO DO WITH HIS DEATH AND YOU KNOW IT.
THEN THE TITANS TOOK JOEY.
THEY TOLD HIM HE WAS A MEMBER OF THEIR TEAM. BUT HE WAS INFECTED BY RAVEN'S HOMEWORLD AND ABANDONED.
OU WERE E ONE WHO ED A SWORD ROUGH HIS BACK--
ONLY TO *PROTECT* HIM.
I NEVER WANTED TO HURT *MY* KIDS.
AND LAST YEAR...
...GRAYSON TOOK MY *ONLY* DAUGHTER FROM ME. HE SENT HER TO YOU.
YOU NEVER WANTED TO HURT YOUR KIDS? YOU WERE PUMPING ROSE FULL OF THE SAME SERUM THAT ENHANCED YOUR STRENGTH AND SPEED.
YOU NEARLY DROVE HER MAD.
I HAD IT UNDER CONTROL.
SHE CUT OUT HER OWN *EYE!*
IF ROSE WAS STILL WITH YOU, SHE'D BE *DEAD* BY NOW!

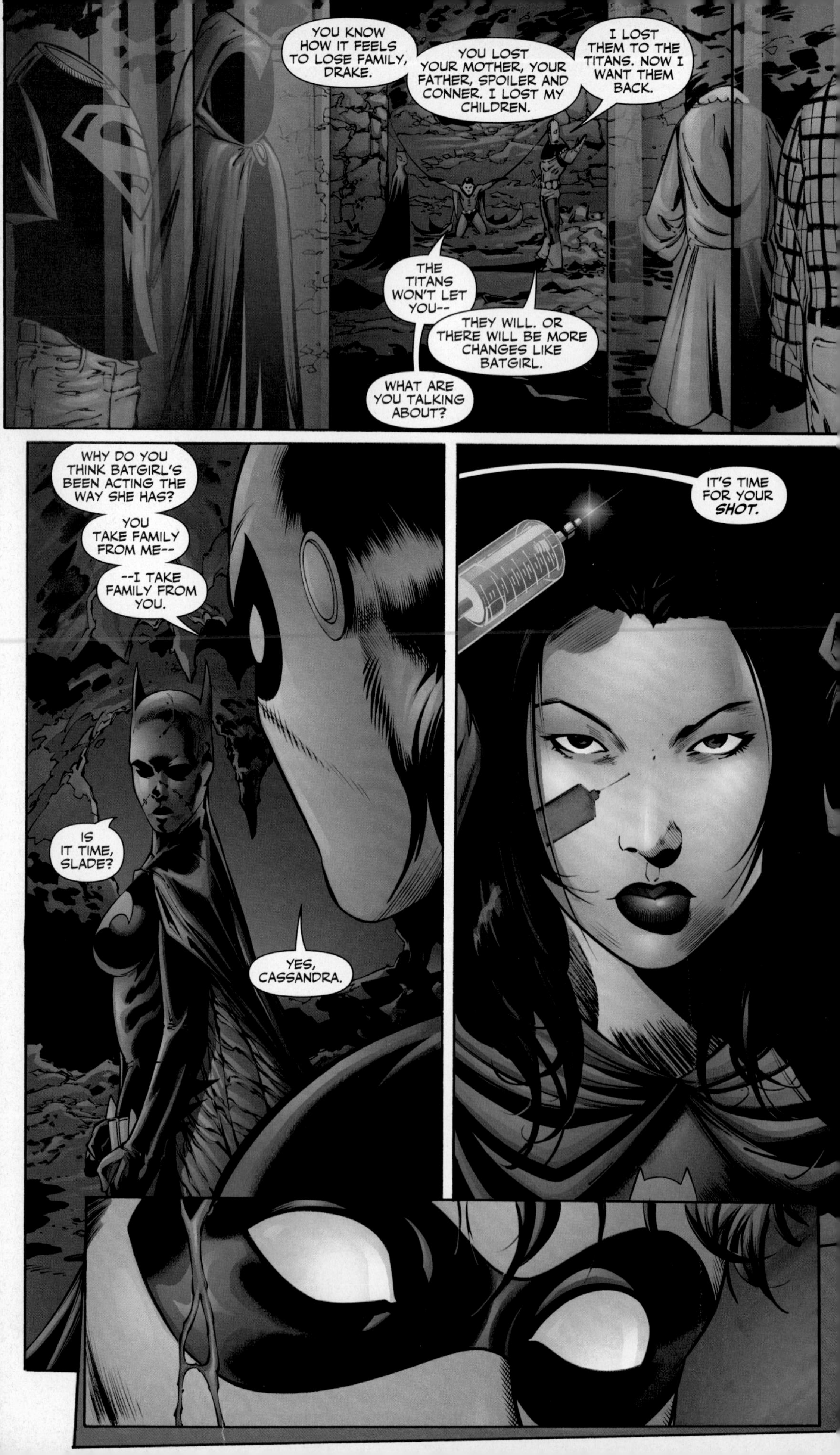

YOU KNOW HOW IT FEELS TO LOSE FAMILY, DRAKE.
YOU LOST YOUR MOTHER, YOUR FATHER, SPOILER AND CONNER. I LOST MY CHILDREN.
I LOST THEM TO THE TITANS. NOW I WANT THEM BACK.
THE TITANS WON'T LET YOU--
THEY WILL. OR THERE WILL BE MORE CHANGES LIKE BATGIRL.
WHAT ARE YOU TALKING ABOUT?
WHY DO YOU THINK BATGIRL'S BEEN ACTING THE WAY SHE HAS?
YOU TAKE FAMILY FROM ME--
--I TAKE FAMILY FROM YOU.
IS IT TIME, SLADE?
YES, CASSANDRA.
IT'S TIME FOR YOUR *SHOT.*

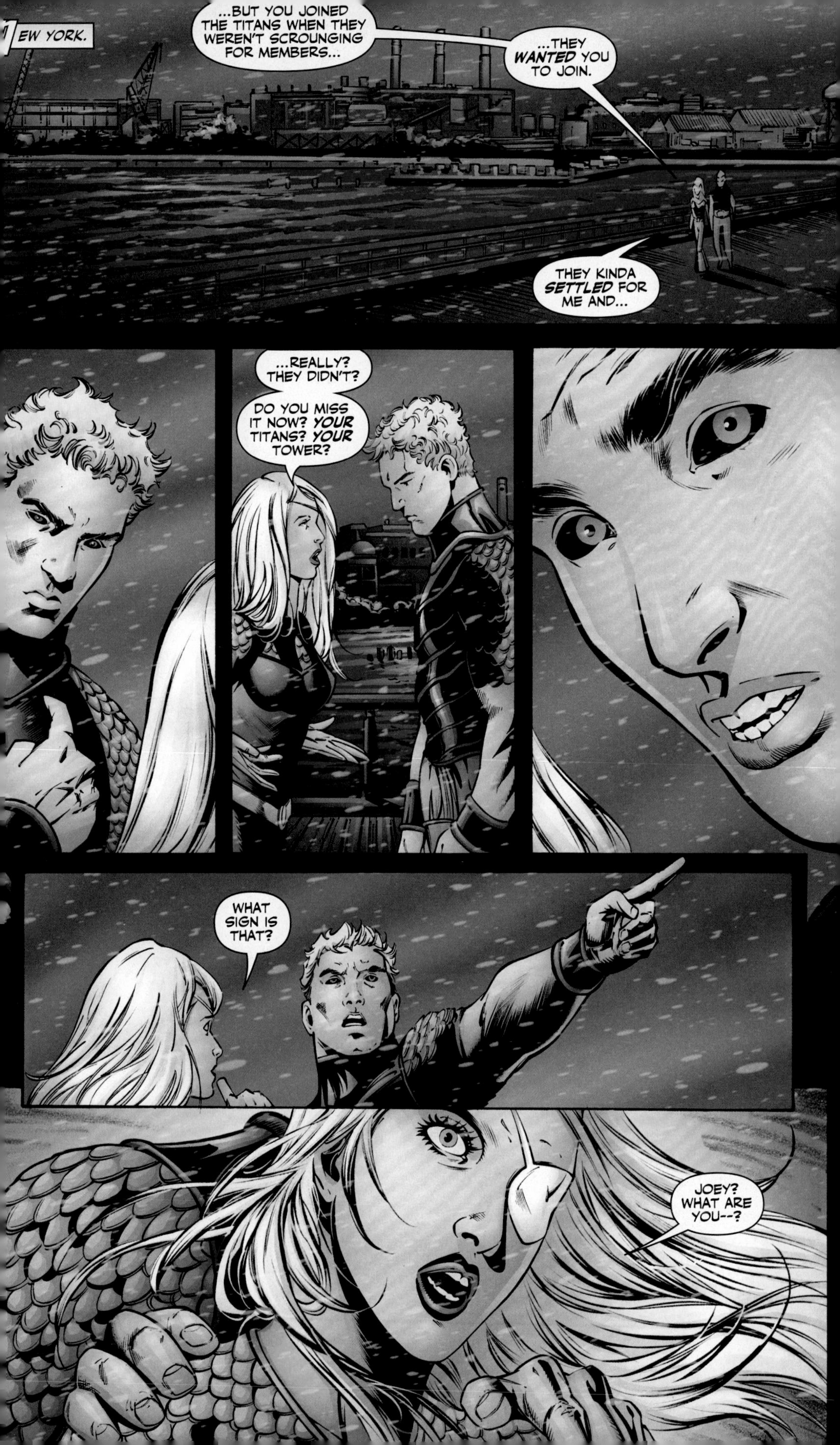

EW YORK.
...BUT YOU JOINED THE TITANS WHEN THEY WEREN'T SCROUNGING FOR MEMBERS...
...THEY WANTED YOU TO JOIN.
THEY KINDA SETTLED FOR ME AND...
...REALLY? THEY DIDN'T?
DO YOU MISS IT NOW? YOUR TITANS? YOUR TOWER?
WHAT SIGN IS THAT?
JOEY? WHAT ARE YOU--?

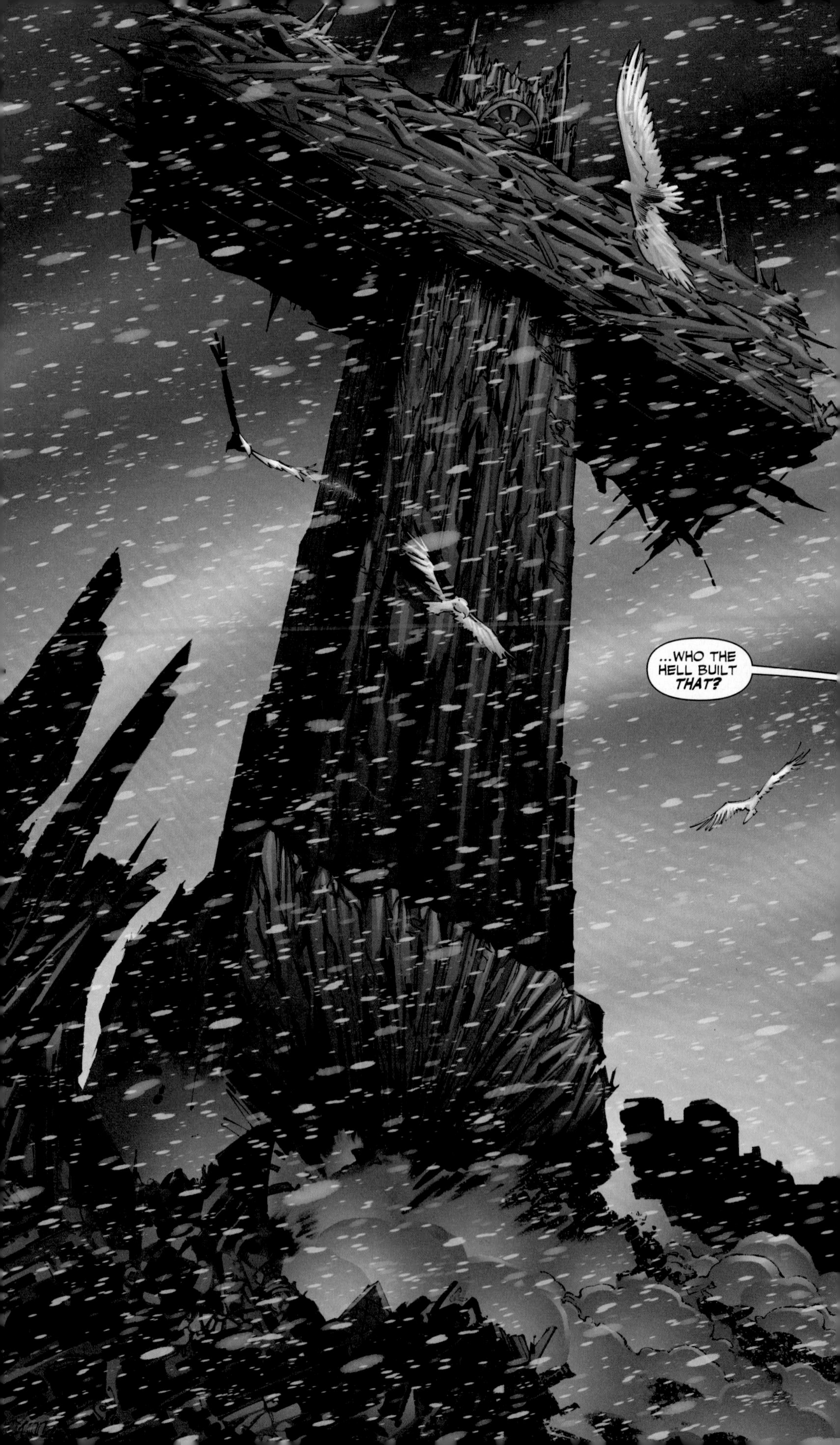
...WHO THE HELL BUILT *THAT?*

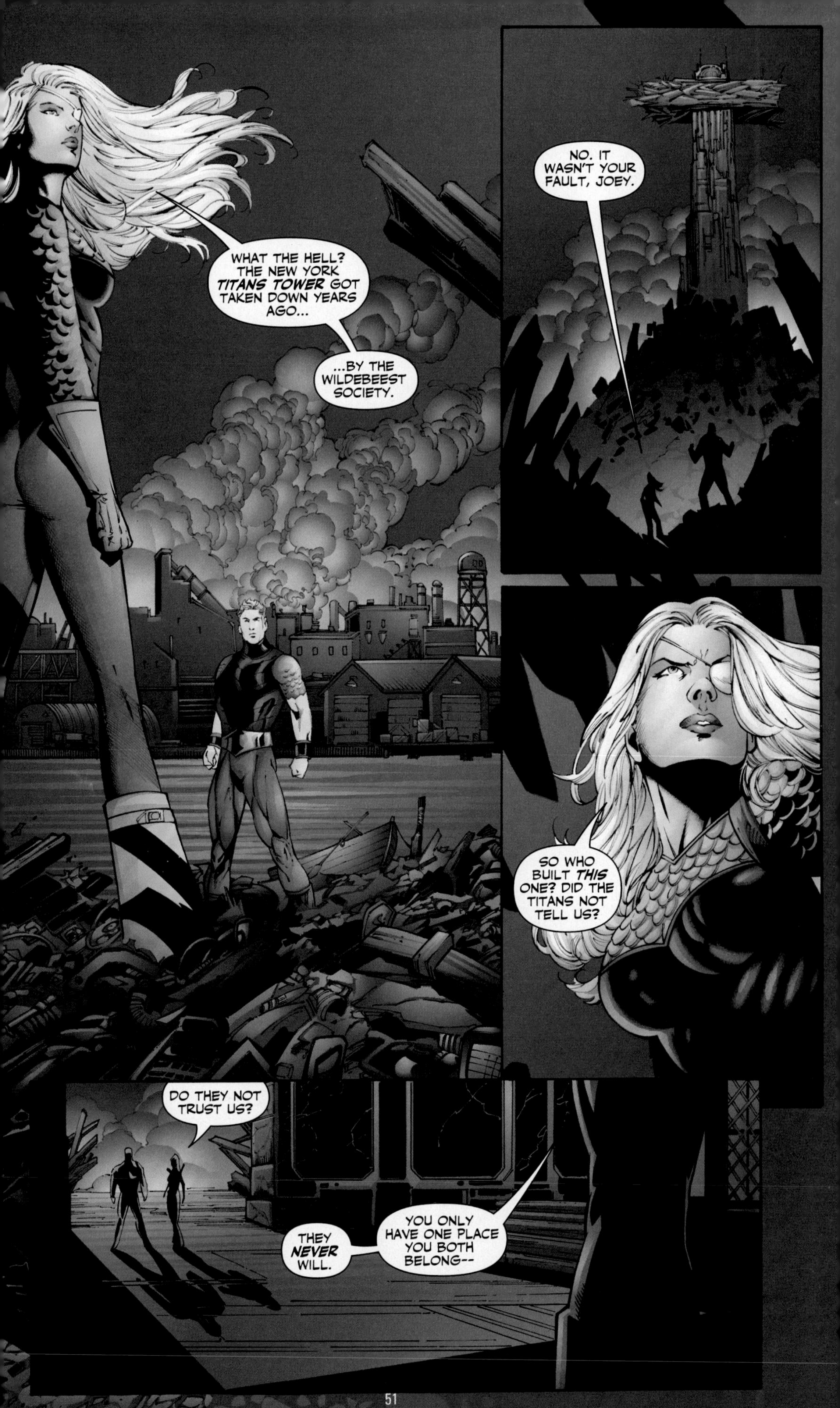
WHAT THE HELL? THE NEW YORK TITANS TOWER GOT TAKEN DOWN YEARS AGO...
...BY THE WILDEBEEST SOCIETY.
NO. IT WASN'T YOUR FAULT, JOEY.
SO WHO BUILT THIS ONE? DID THE TITANS NOT TELL US?
DO THEY NOT TRUST US?
THEY NEVER WILL.
YOU ONLY HAVE ONE PLACE YOU BOTH BELONG--

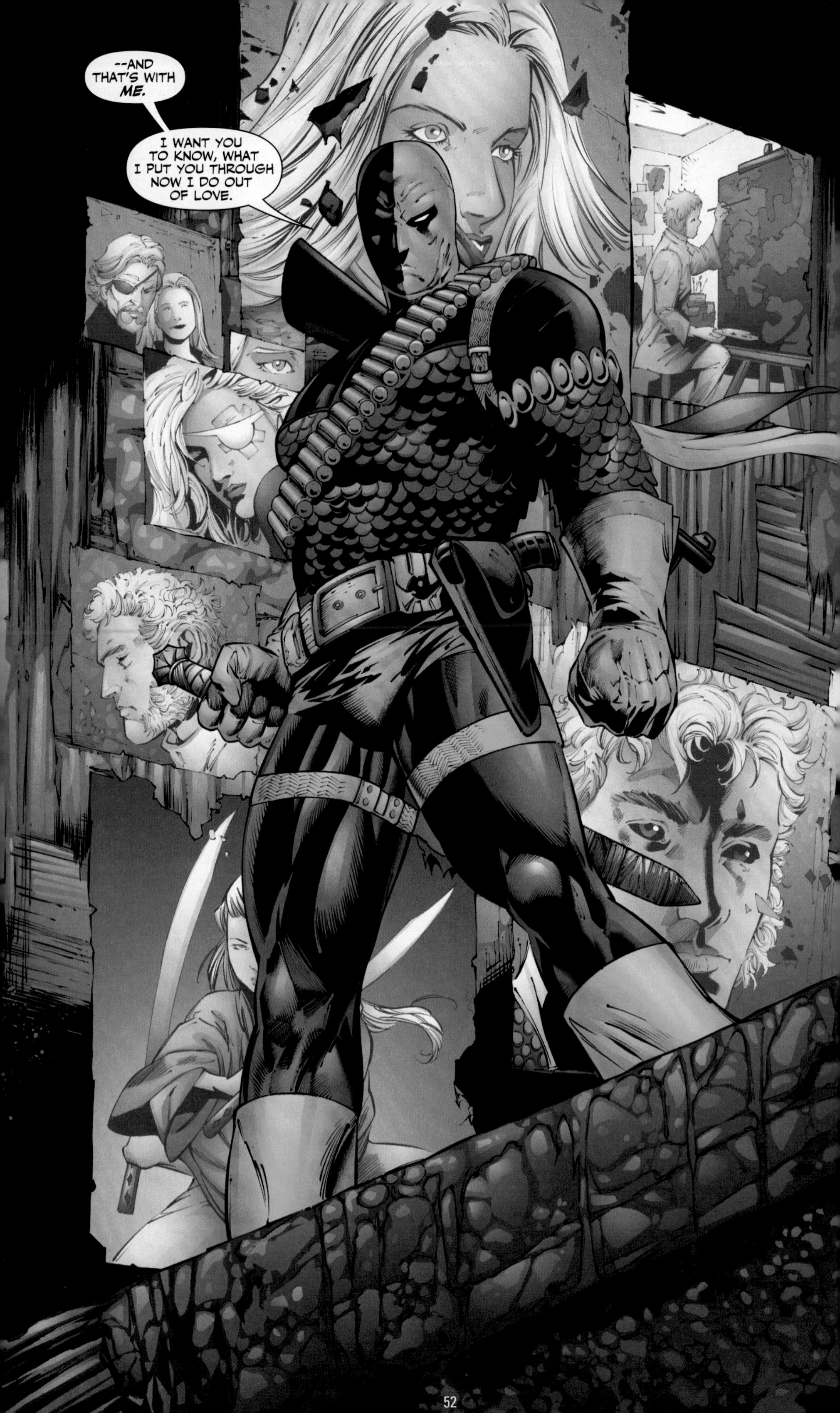
--AND THAT'S WITH ME.
I WANT YOU TO KNOW, WHAT I PUT YOU THROUGH NOW I DO OUT OF LOVE.

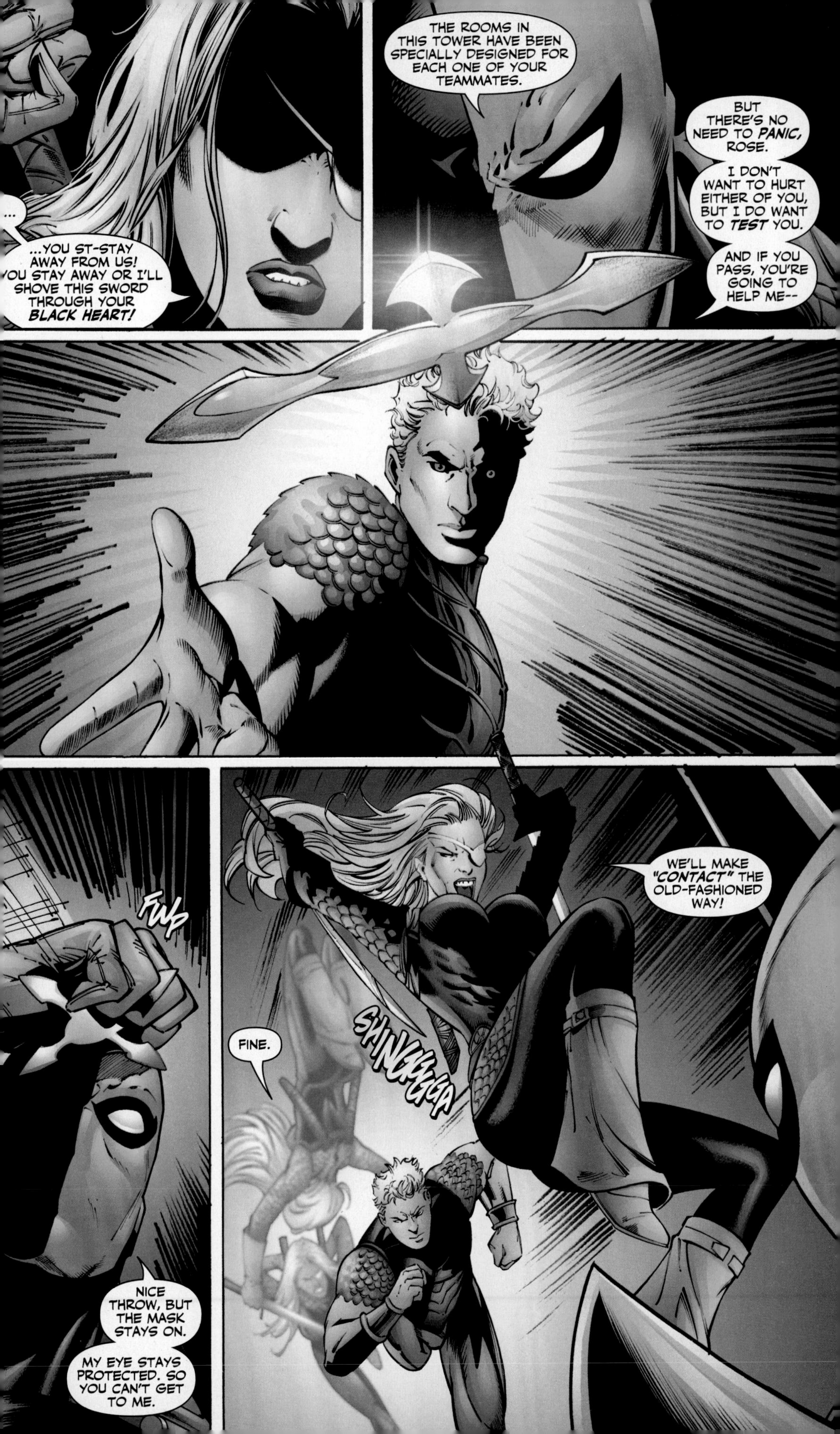

...
...YOU ST-STAY AWAY FROM US! YOU STAY AWAY OR I'LL SHOVE THIS SWORD THROUGH YOUR BLACK HEART!
THE ROOMS IN THIS TOWER HAVE BEEN SPECIALLY DESIGNED FOR EACH ONE OF YOUR TEAMMATES.
BUT THERE'S NO NEED TO PANIC, ROSE.
I DON'T WANT TO HURT EITHER OF YOU, BUT I DO WANT TO TEST YOU.
AND IF YOU PASS, YOU'RE GOING TO HELP ME--
FWP
NICE THROW, BUT THE MASK STAYS ON.
MY EYE STAYS PROTECTED. SO YOU CAN'T GET TO ME.
WE'LL MAKE "CONTACT" THE OLD-FASHIONED WAY!
SHINGGGGA
FINE.

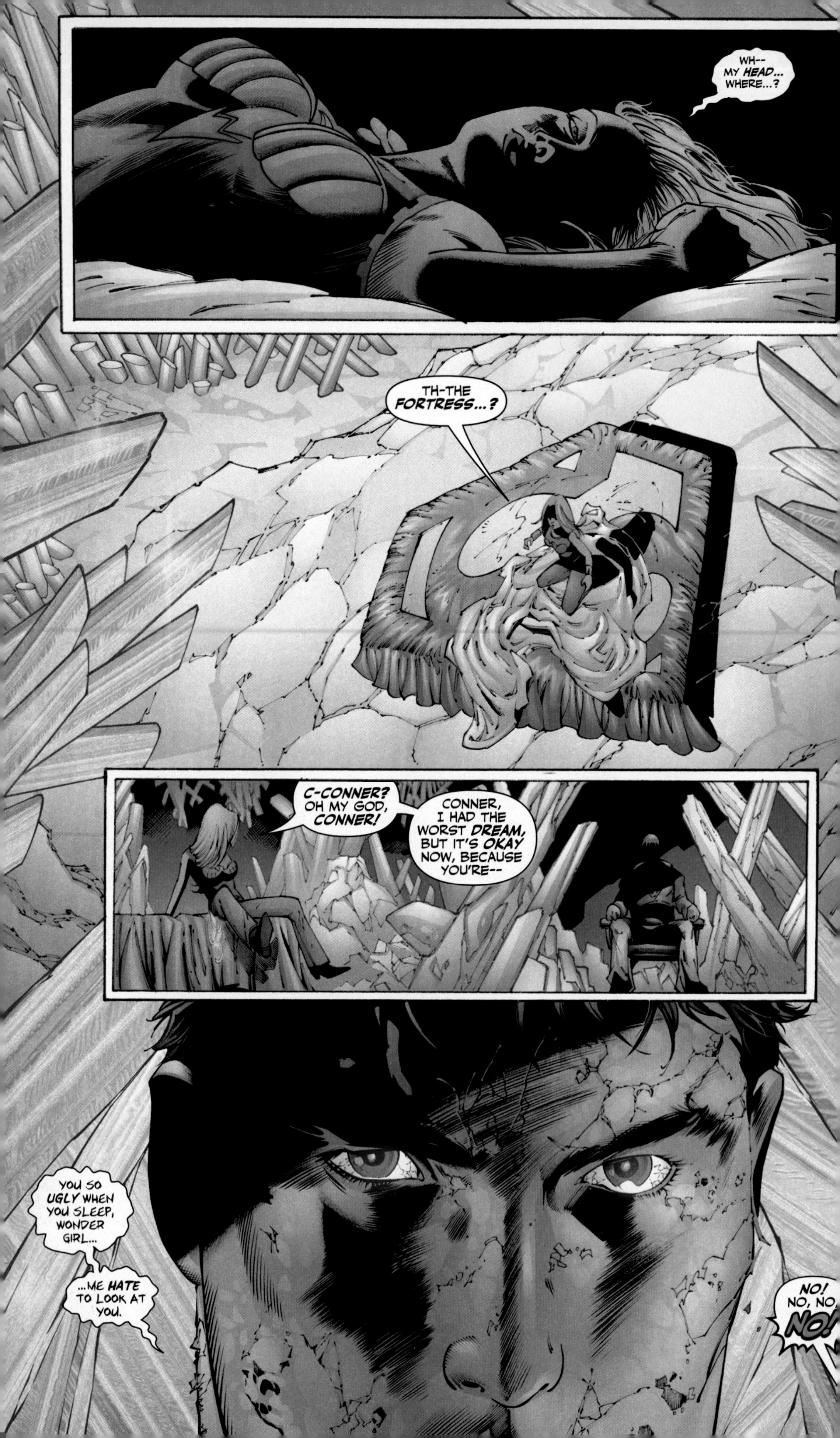
WH-- MY HEAD... WHERE...?
TH-THE FORTRESS...?
C-CONNER? OH MY GOD, CONNER!
CONNER, I HAD THE WORST DREAM, BUT IT'S OKAY NOW, BECAUSE YOU'RE--
YOU SO UGLY WHEN YOU SLEEP, WONDER GIRL...
...ME HATE TO LOOK AT YOU.
NO! NO, NO, NO!

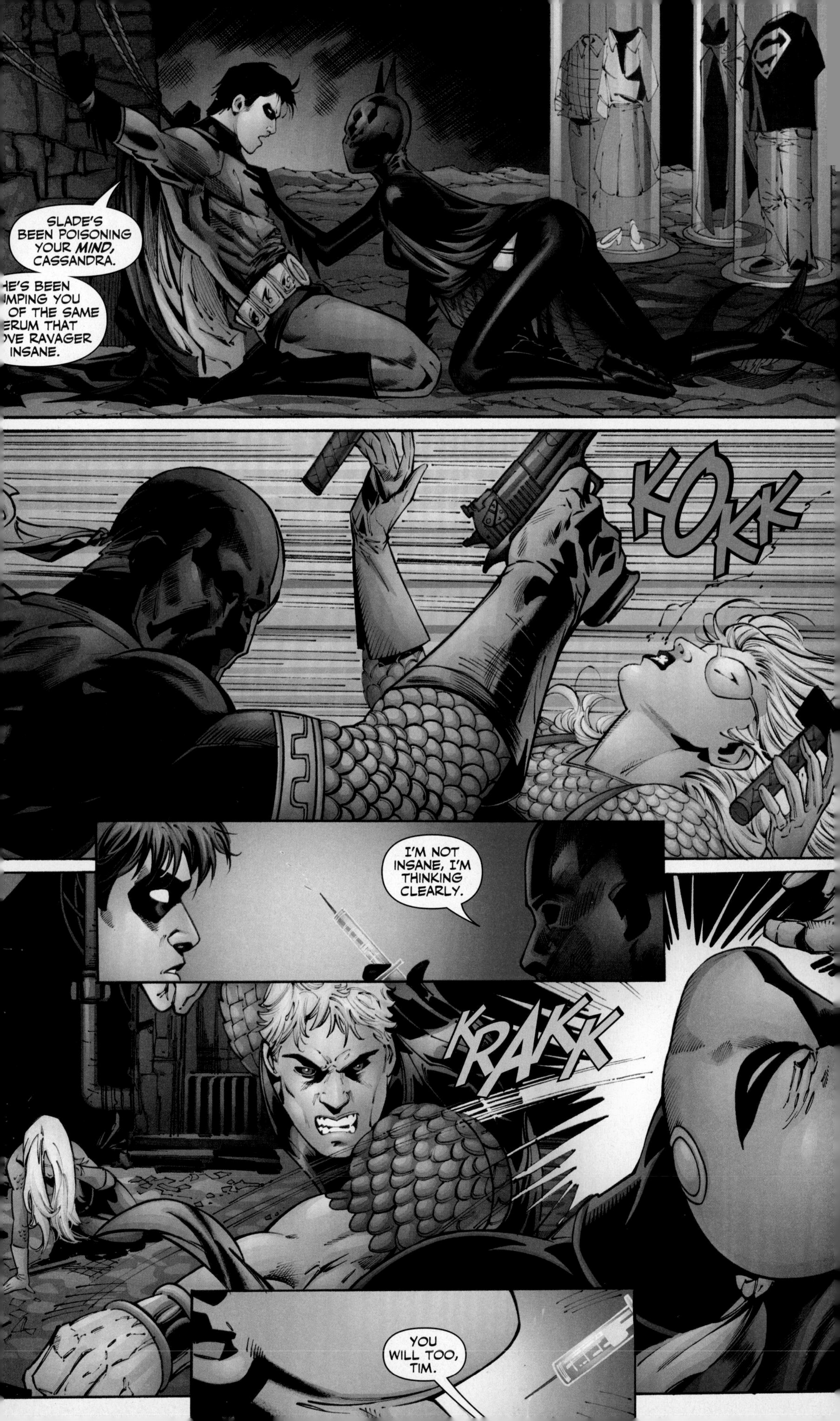
SLADE'S BEEN POISONING YOUR *MIND,* CASSANDRA.
HE'S BEEN
UMPING YOU
OF THE SAME
ERUM THAT
OVE RAVAGER
INSANE.
KOKK
I'M NOT INSANE, I'M THINKING CLEARLY.
KRAKK
YOU WILL TOO, TIM.

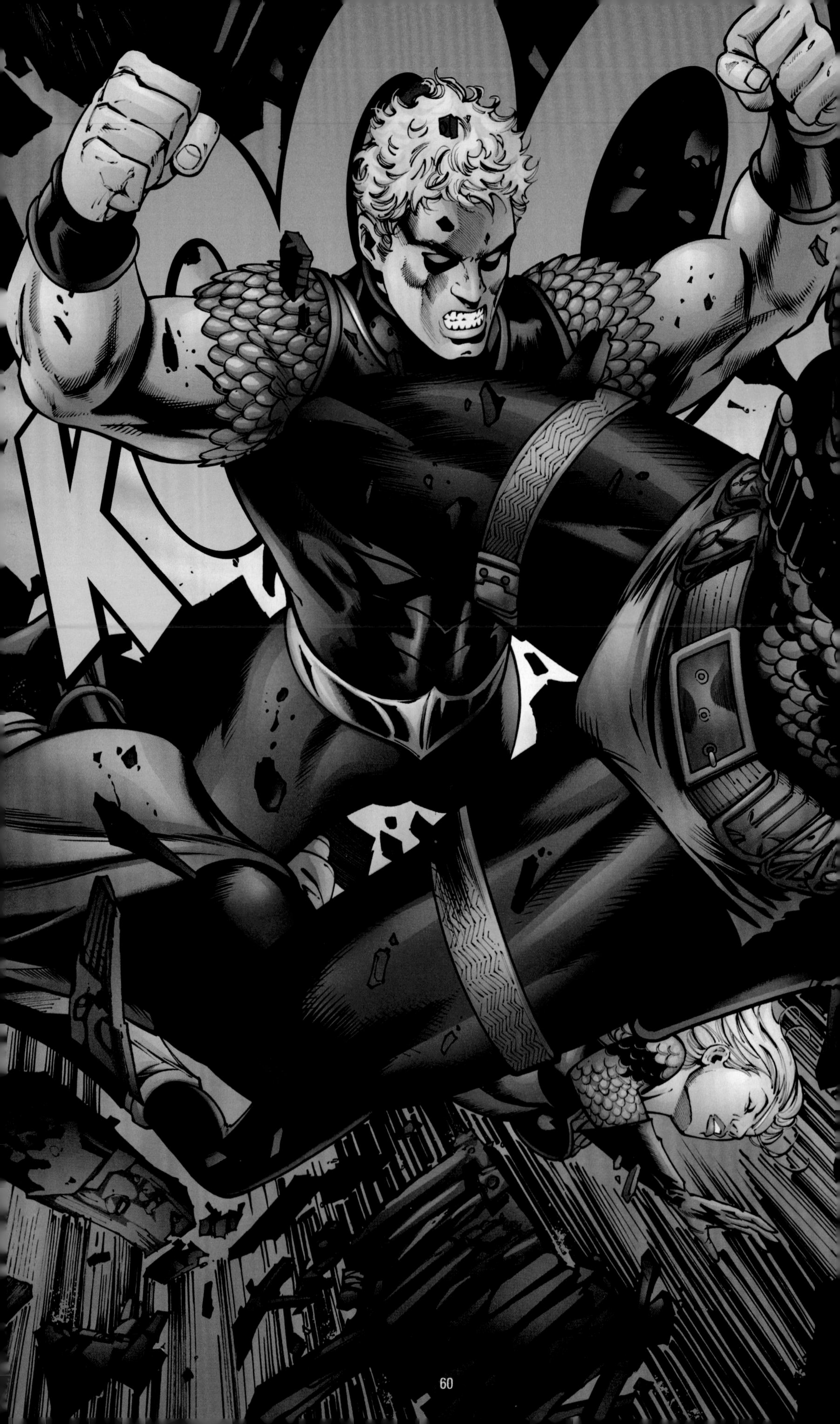

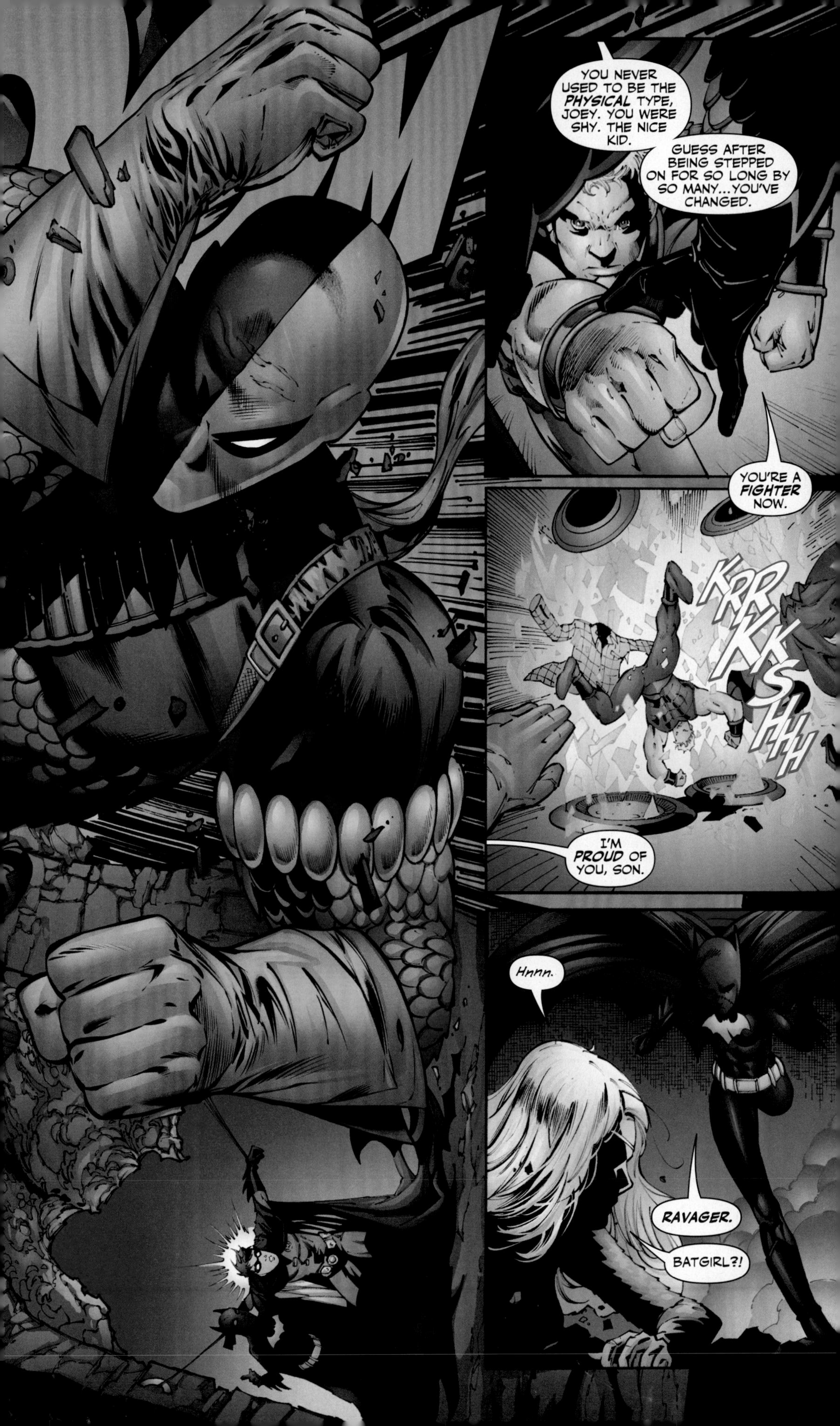

YOU NEVER USED TO BE THE PHYSICAL TYPE, JOEY. YOU WERE SHY. THE NICE KID.
GUESS AFTER BEING STEPPED ON FOR SO LONG BY SO MANY...YOU'VE CHANGED.
YOU'RE A FIGHTER NOW.
KRRKKKSHHH
I'M PROUD OF YOU, SON.
Hnnn.
RAVAGER.
BATGIRL?!

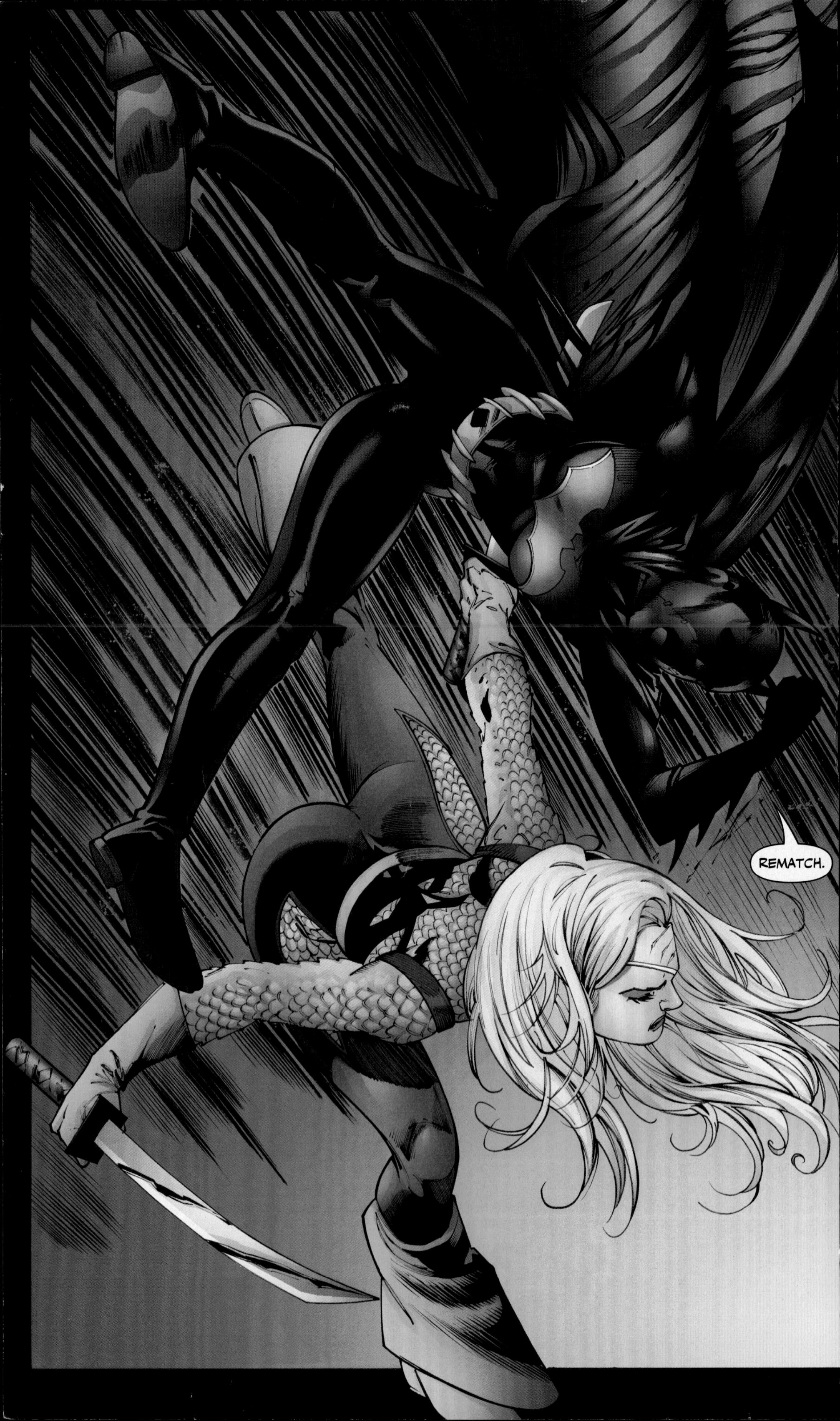
REMATCH.

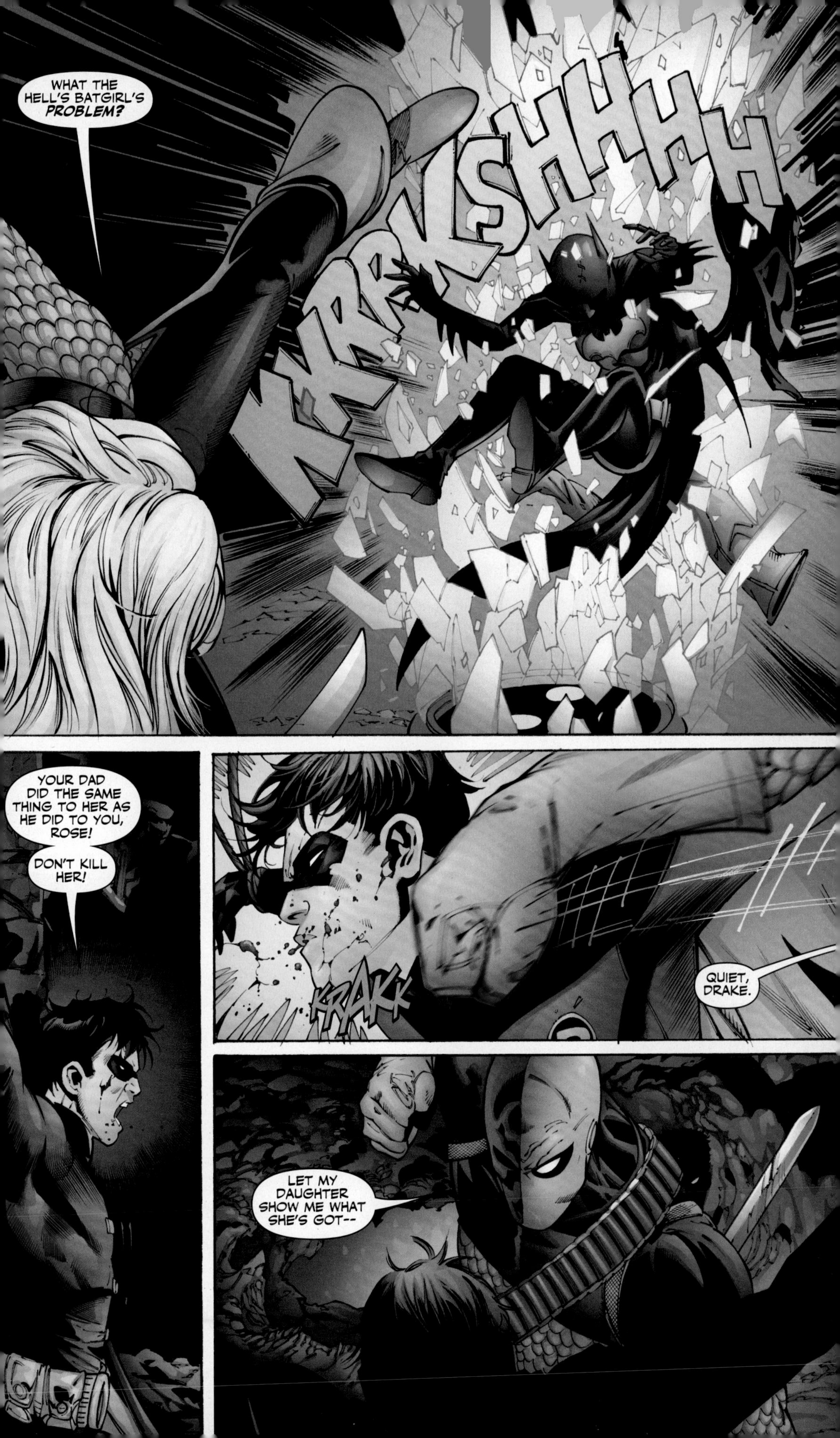
WHAT THE HELL'S BATGIRL'S PROBLEM?
KRRKSHHHHH
YOUR DAD DID THE SAME THING TO HER AS HE DID TO YOU, ROSE!
DON'T KILL HER!
KRAKK
QUIET, DRAKE.
LET MY DAUGHTER SHOW ME WHAT SHE'S GOT--

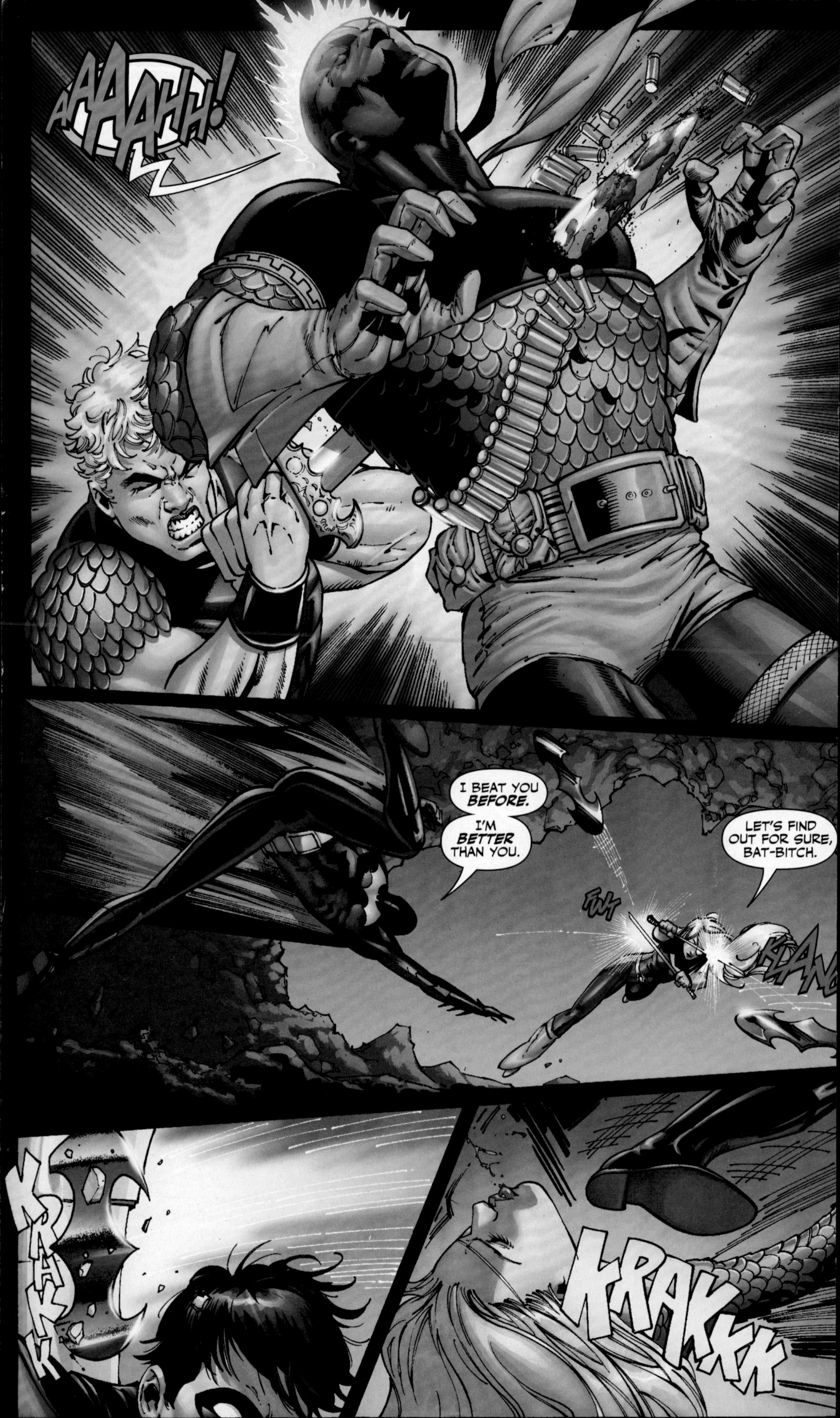

AAAAHH!
I BEAT YOU BEFORE.
I'M BETTER THAN YOU.
LET'S FIND OUT FOR SURE, BAT-BITCH.
FUK
KLANG
KRAKK
KRAKKK

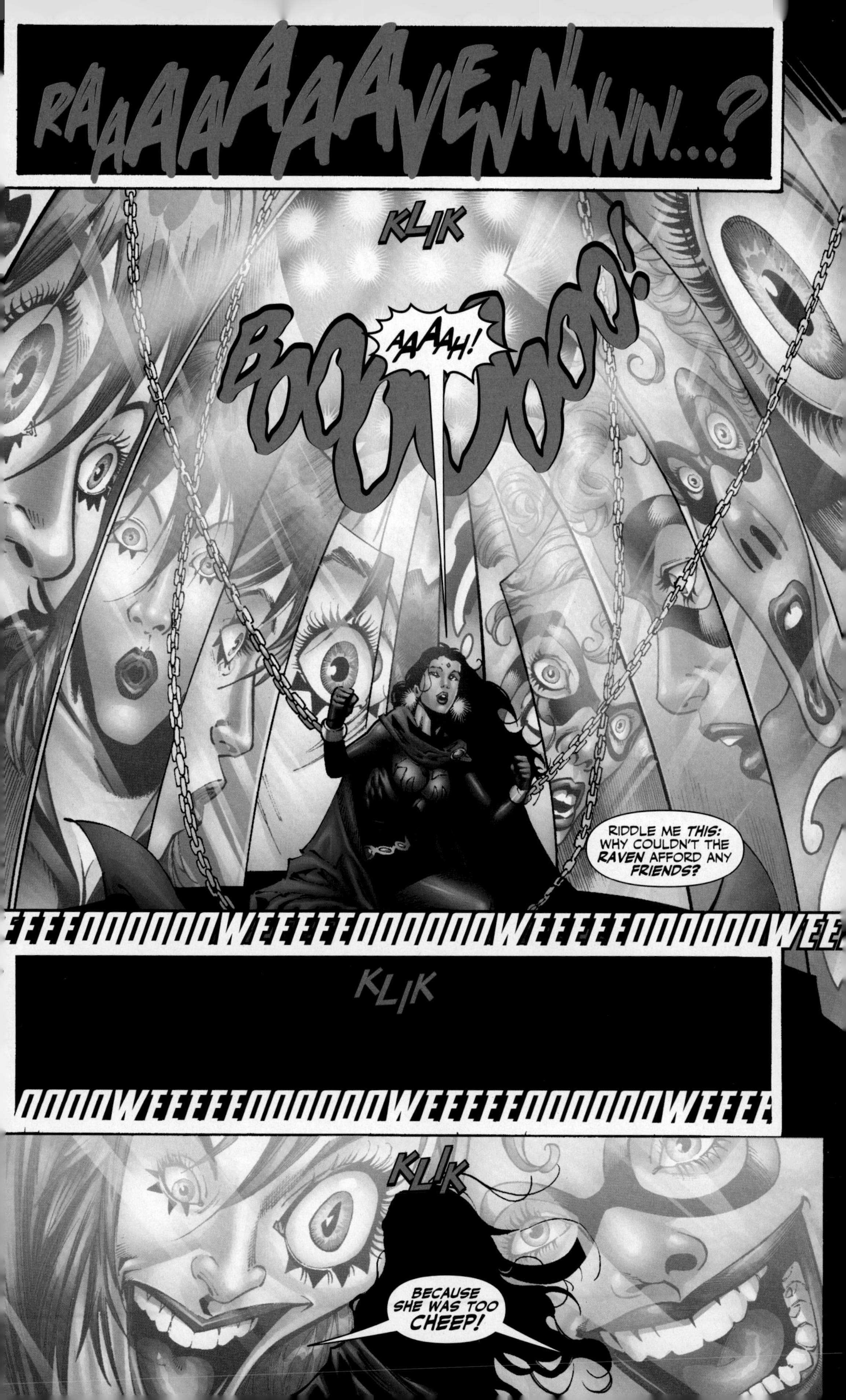
RAAAAAAAAVENNNNNN...?
KLIK
BOOOOOOOOM!
AAAAH!
RIDDLE ME THIS: WHY COULDN'T THE RAVEN AFFORD ANY FRIENDS?
EEEEOOOOOOOWEEEEEEOOOOOOOWEEEEEEOOOOOOOWEE
KLIK
OOOOWEEEEEOOOOOOOWEEEEEEOOOOOOOWEEEE
KLIK
BECAUSE SHE WAS TOO CHEEP!

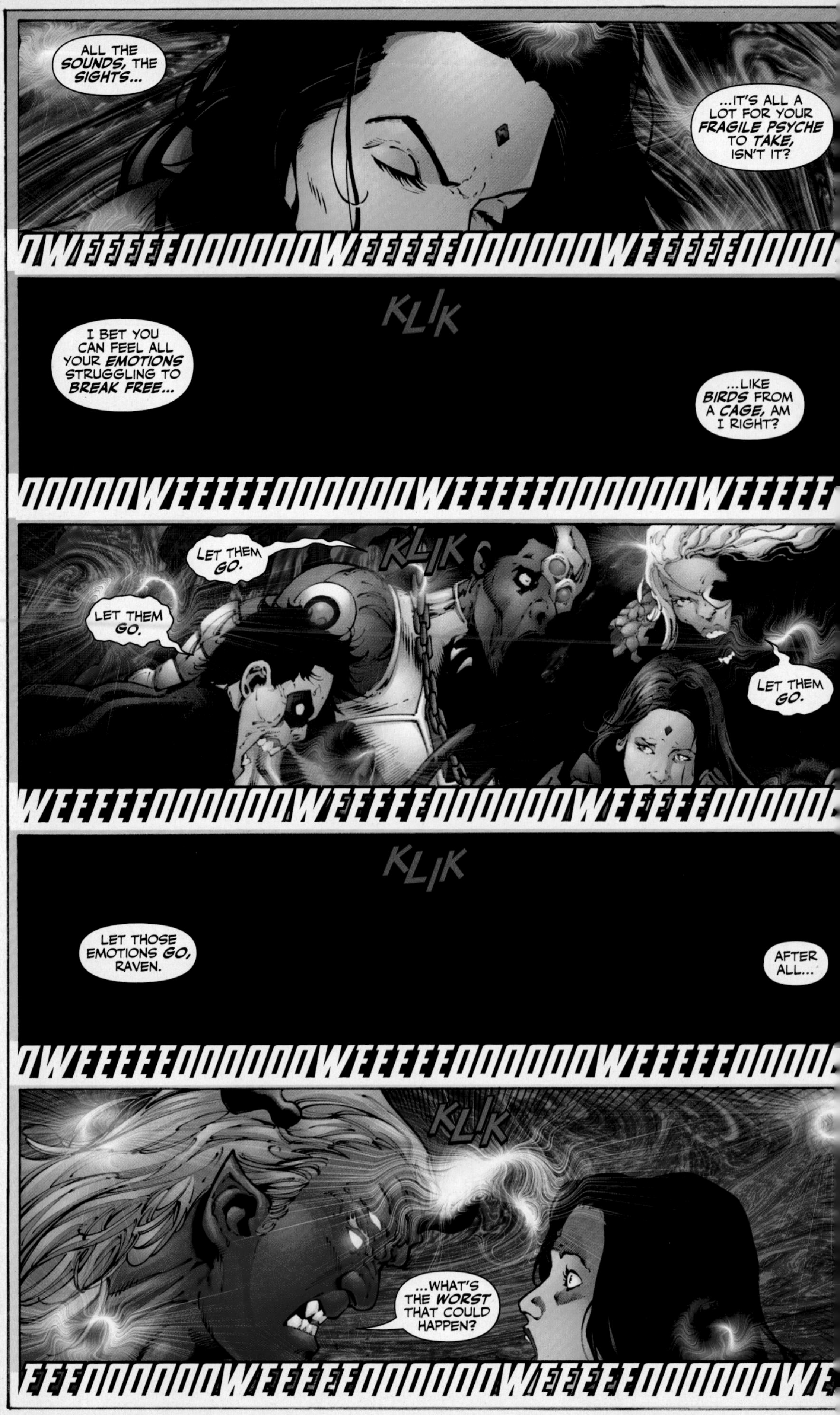
ALL THE SOUNDS, THE SIGHTS...
...IT'S ALL A LOT FOR YOUR FRAGILE PSYCHE TO TAKE, ISN'T IT?
KLIK
I BET YOU CAN FEEL ALL YOUR EMOTIONS STRUGGLING TO BREAK FREE...
...LIKE BIRDS FROM A CAGE, AM I RIGHT?
KLIK
LET THEM GO.
LET THEM GO.
LET THEM GO.
KLIK
LET THOSE EMOTIONS GO, RAVEN.
AFTER ALL...
KLIK
...WHAT'S THE WORST THAT COULD HAPPEN?

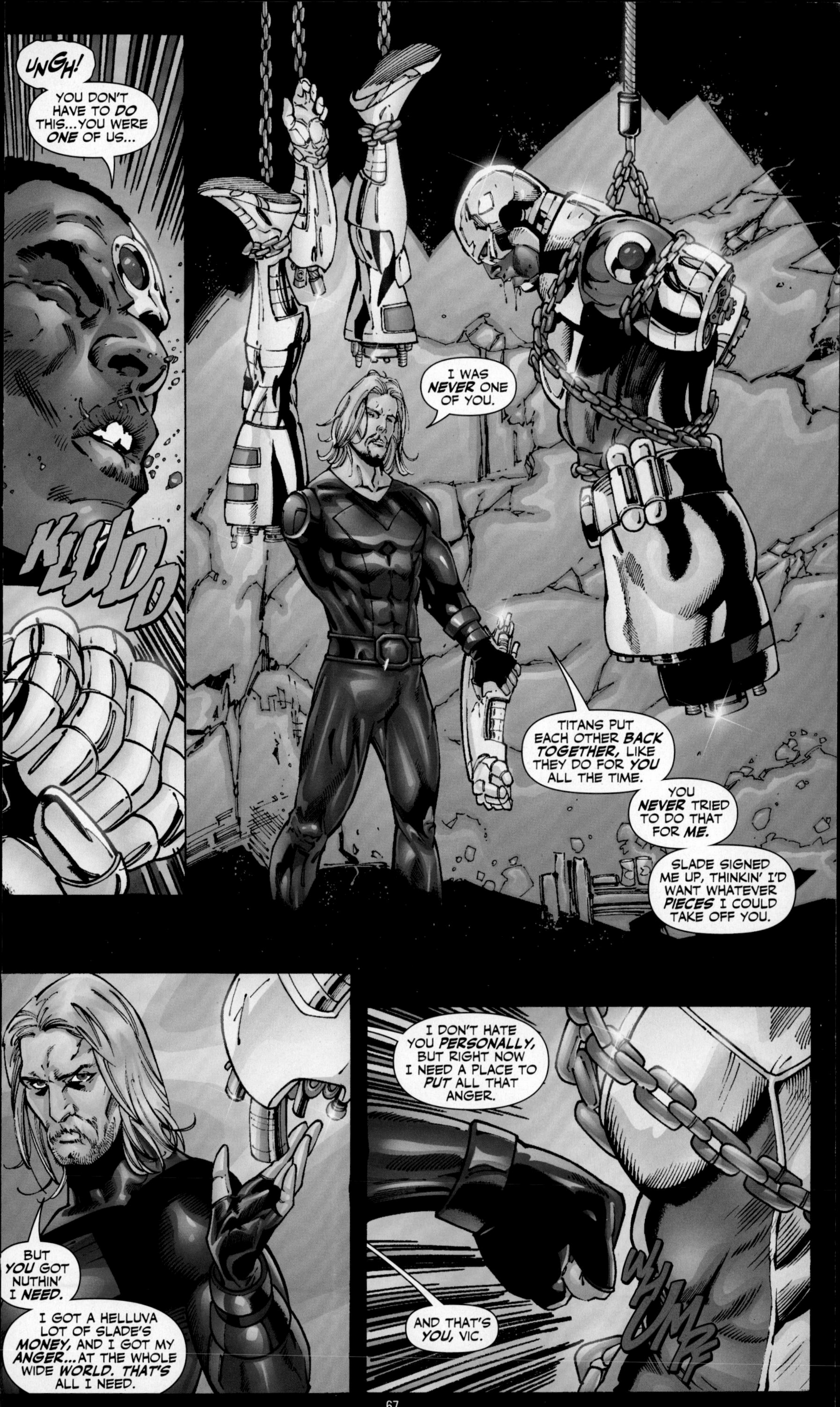

UNGH!
YOU DON'T HAVE TO DO THIS...YOU WERE ONE OF US...
KLUDD
I WAS NEVER ONE OF YOU.
TITANS PUT EACH OTHER BACK TOGETHER, LIKE THEY DO FOR YOU ALL THE TIME.
YOU NEVER TRIED TO DO THAT FOR ME.
SLADE SIGNED ME UP, THINKIN' I'D WANT WHATEVER PIECES I COULD TAKE OFF YOU.
BUT YOU GOT NUTHIN' I NEED.
I GOT A HELLUVA LOT OF SLADE'S MONEY, AND I GOT MY ANGER...AT THE WHOLE WIDE WORLD. THAT'S ALL I NEED.
I DON'T HATE YOU PERSONALLY, BUT RIGHT NOW I NEED A PLACE TO PUT ALL THAT ANGER.
AND THAT'S YOU, VIC.

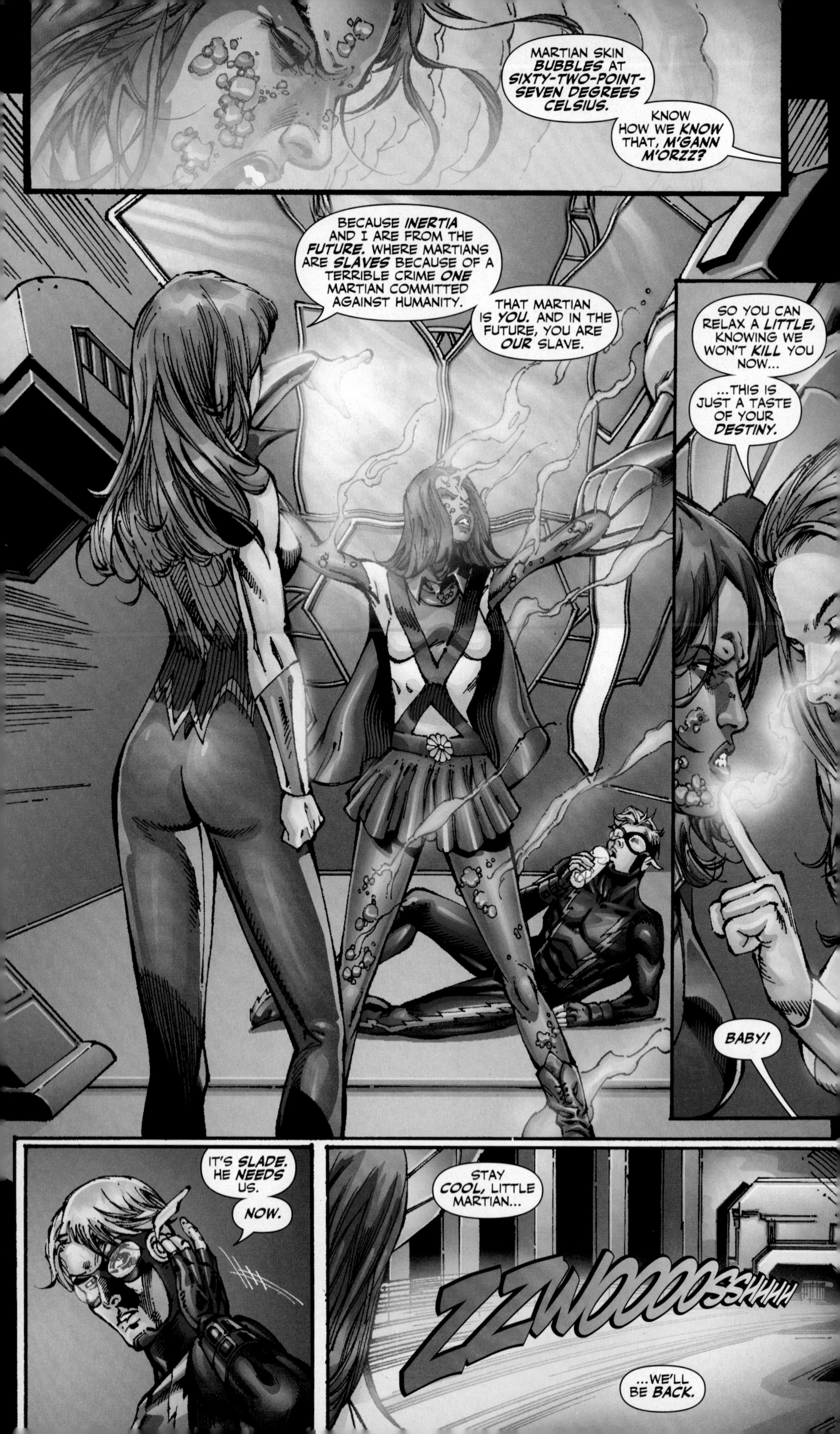

MARTIAN SKIN BUBBLES AT SIXTY-TWO-POINT-SEVEN DEGREES CELSIUS.
KNOW HOW WE KNOW THAT, M'GANN M'ORZZ?
BECAUSE INERTIA AND I ARE FROM THE FUTURE. WHERE MARTIANS ARE SLAVES BECAUSE OF A TERRIBLE CRIME ONE MARTIAN COMMITTED AGAINST HUMANITY.
THAT MARTIAN IS YOU. AND IN THE FUTURE, YOU ARE OUR SLAVE.
SO YOU CAN RELAX A LITTLE, KNOWING WE WON'T KILL YOU NOW...
...THIS IS JUST A TASTE OF YOUR DESTINY.
BABY!
IT'S SLADE. HE NEEDS US.
NOW.
STAY COOL, LITTLE MARTIAN...
ZZWOOOOSHHHH
...WE'LL BE BACK.

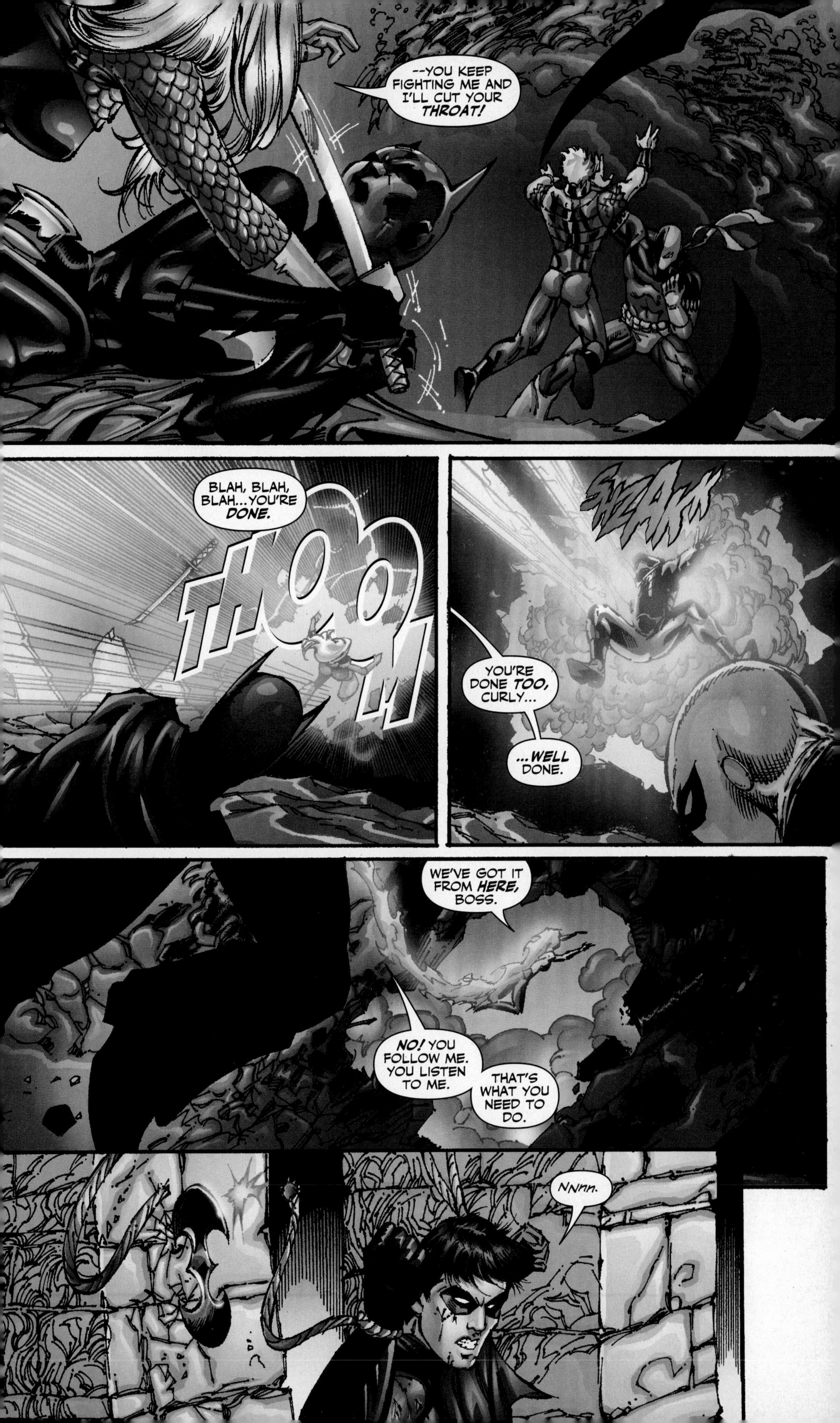
--YOU KEEP FIGHTING ME AND I'LL CUT YOUR *THROAT!*
BLAH, BLAH, BLAH...YOU'RE *DONE.*
THOOM
SHZAKK
YOU'RE DONE *TOO,* CURLY...
...WELL DONE.
WE'VE GOT IT FROM *HERE,* BOSS.
NO! YOU FOLLOW ME. YOU LISTEN TO ME.
THAT'S WHAT YOU NEED TO DO.
Nnnn.

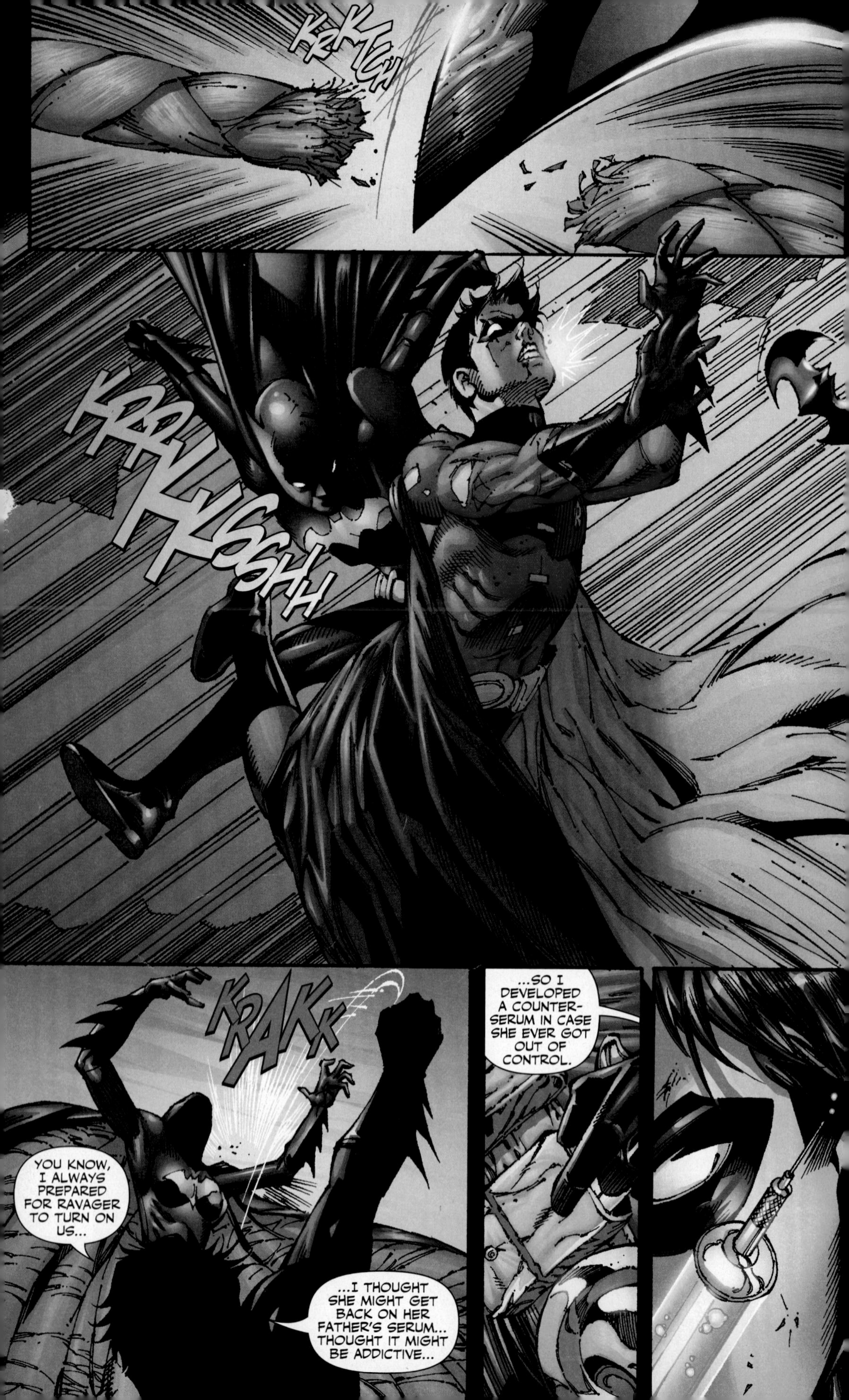
KRKTCH
KRRKKSSHH
KRAKK
YOU KNOW, I ALWAYS PREPARED FOR RAVAGER TO TURN ON US...
...I THOUGHT SHE MIGHT GET BACK ON HER FATHER'S SERUM... THOUGHT IT MIGHT BE ADDICTIVE...
...SO I DEVELOPED A COUNTER-SERUM IN CASE SHE EVER GOT OUT OF CONTROL.

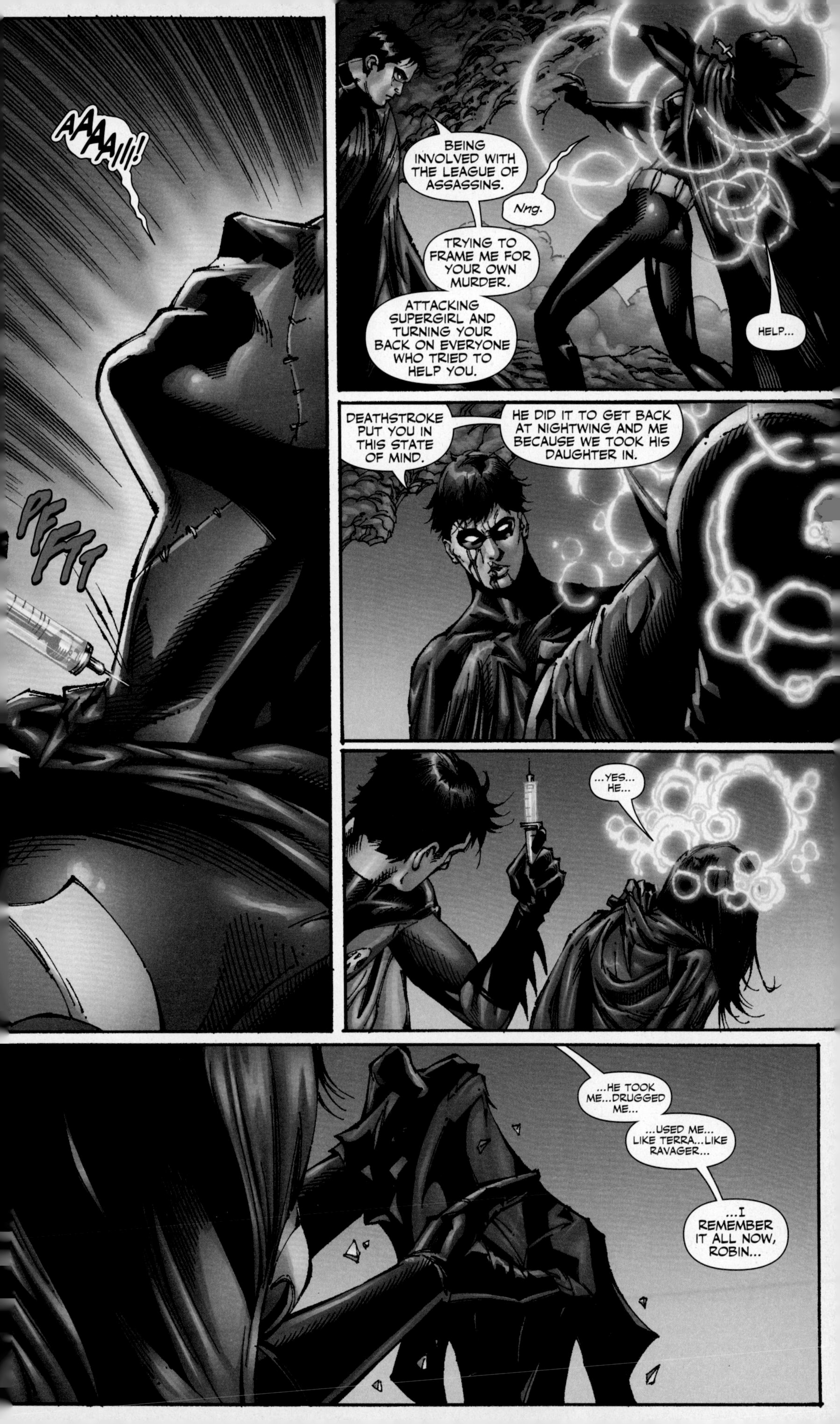
AAAAiii!
PFFT
BEING INVOLVED WITH THE LEAGUE OF ASSASSINS.
Nng.
TRYING TO FRAME ME FOR YOUR OWN MURDER.
ATTACKING SUPERGIRL AND TURNING YOUR BACK ON EVERYONE WHO TRIED TO HELP YOU.
HELP...
DEATHSTROKE PUT YOU IN THIS STATE OF MIND.
HE DID IT TO GET BACK AT NIGHTWING AND ME BECAUSE WE TOOK HIS DAUGHTER IN.
...YES... HE...
...HE TOOK ME...DRUGGED ME...
...USED ME... LIKE TERRA...LIKE RAVAGER...
...I REMEMBER IT ALL NOW, ROBIN...

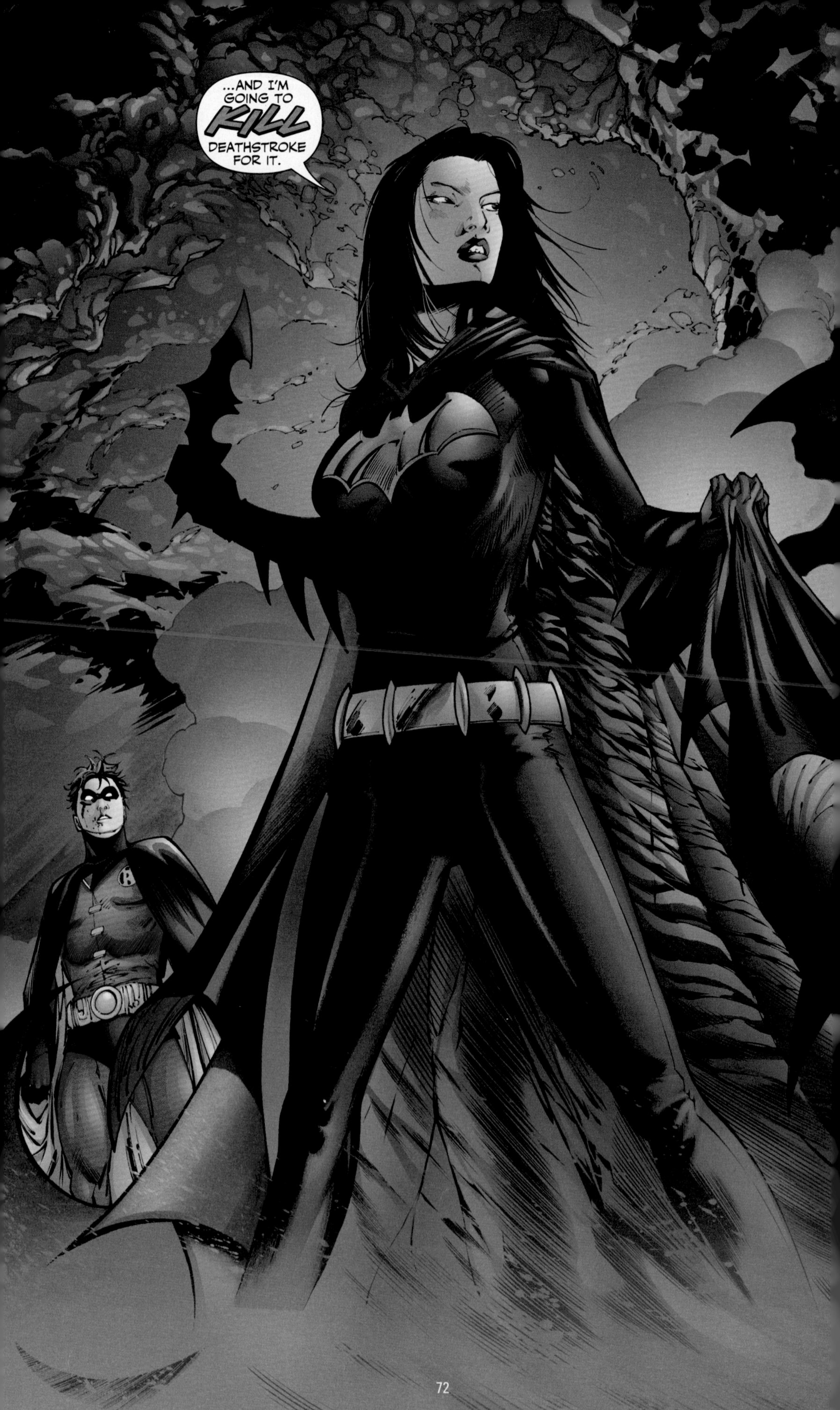
...AND I'M GOING TO KILL DEATHSTROKE FOR IT.

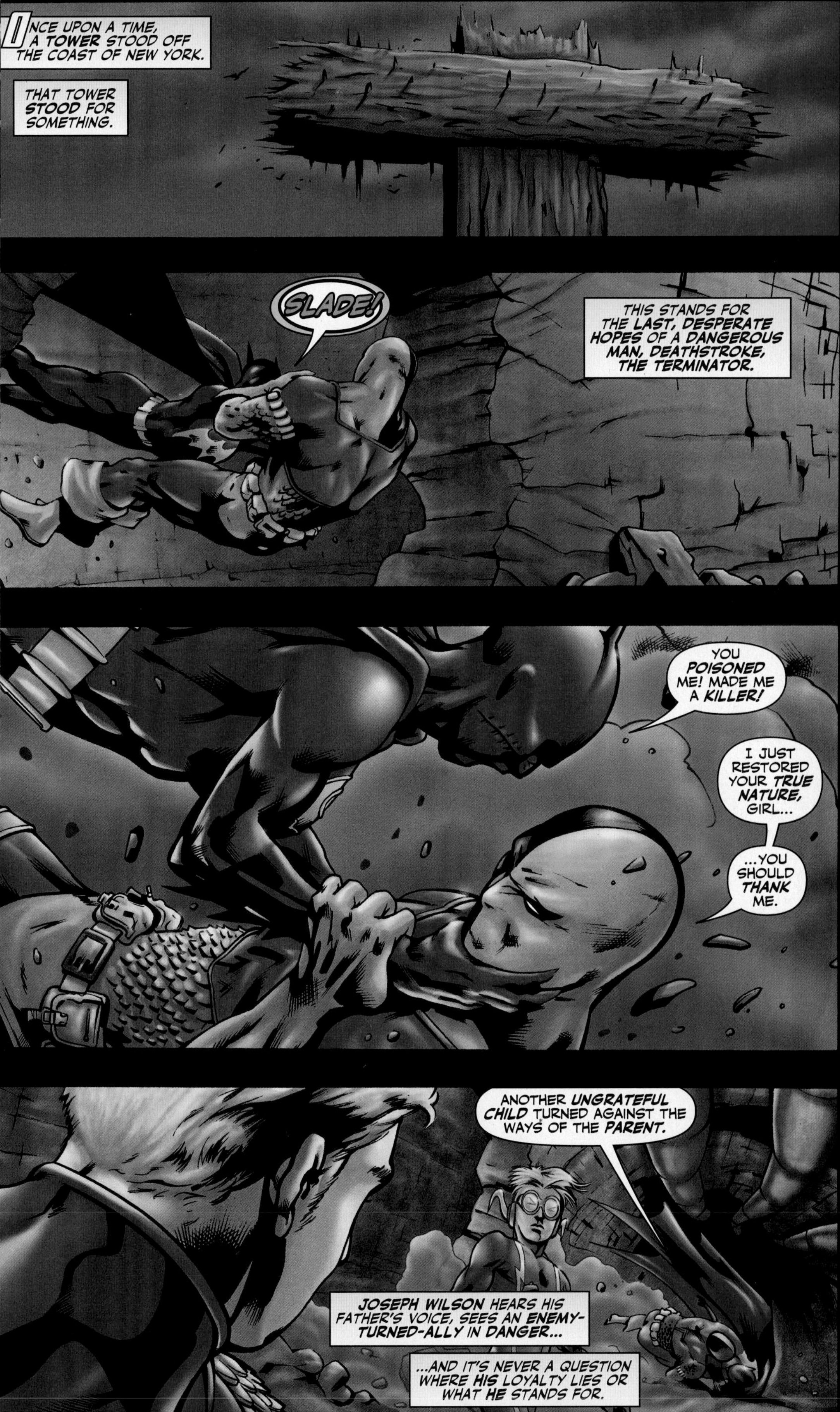
ONCE UPON A TIME, A TOWER STOOD OFF THE COAST OF NEW YORK.
THAT TOWER STOOD FOR SOMETHING.
SLADE!
THIS STANDS FOR THE LAST, DESPERATE HOPES OF A DANGEROUS MAN, DEATHSTROKE, THE TERMINATOR.
YOU POISONED ME! MADE ME A KILLER!
I JUST RESTORED YOUR TRUE NATURE, GIRL...
...YOU SHOULD THANK ME.
ANOTHER UNGRATEFUL CHILD TURNED AGAINST THE WAYS OF THE PARENT.
JOSEPH WILSON HEARS HIS FATHER'S VOICE, SEES AN ENEMY-TURNED-ALLY IN DANGER...
...AND IT'S NEVER A QUESTION WHERE HIS LOYALTY LIES OR WHAT HE STANDS FOR.

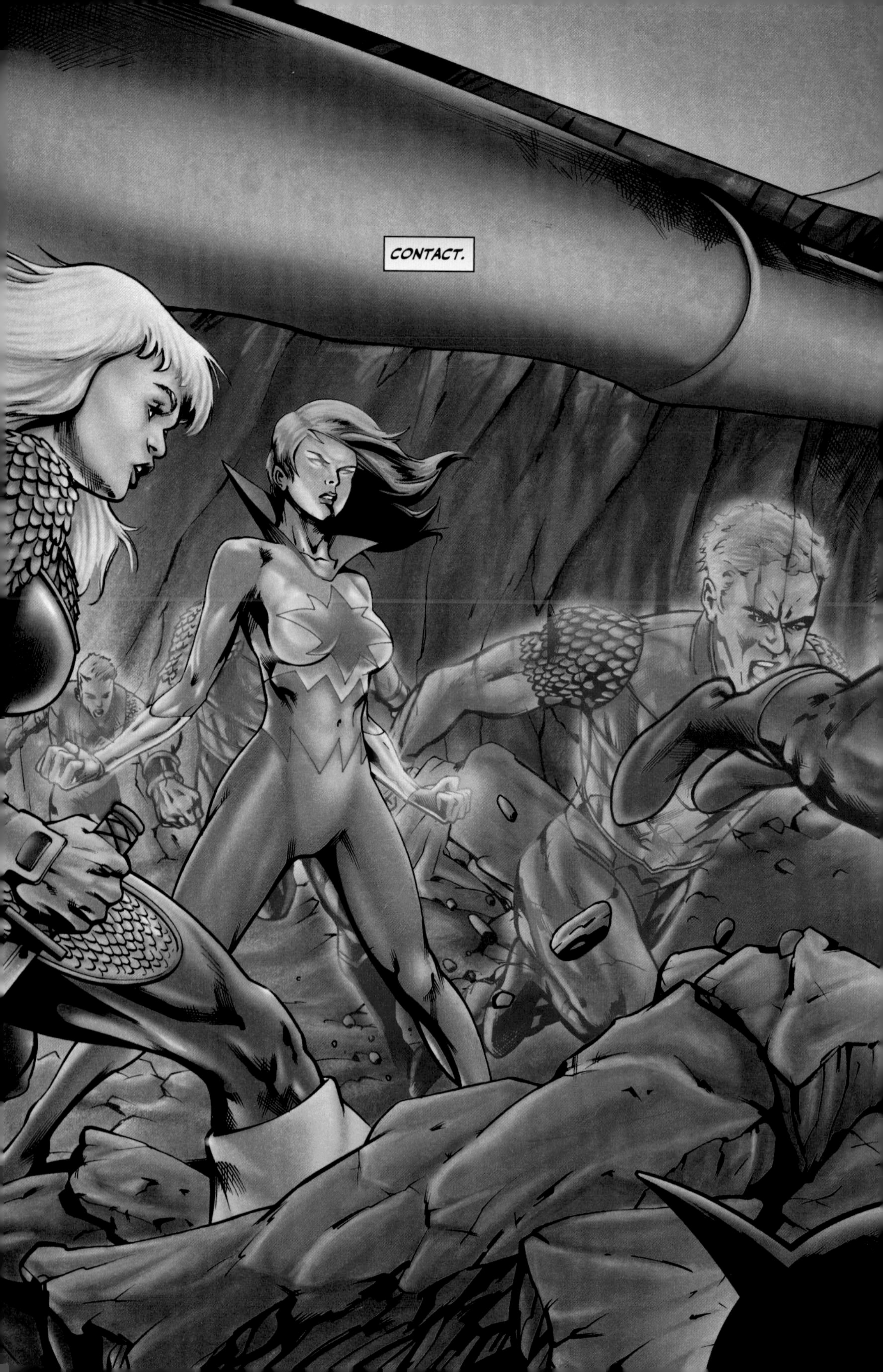
CONTACT.

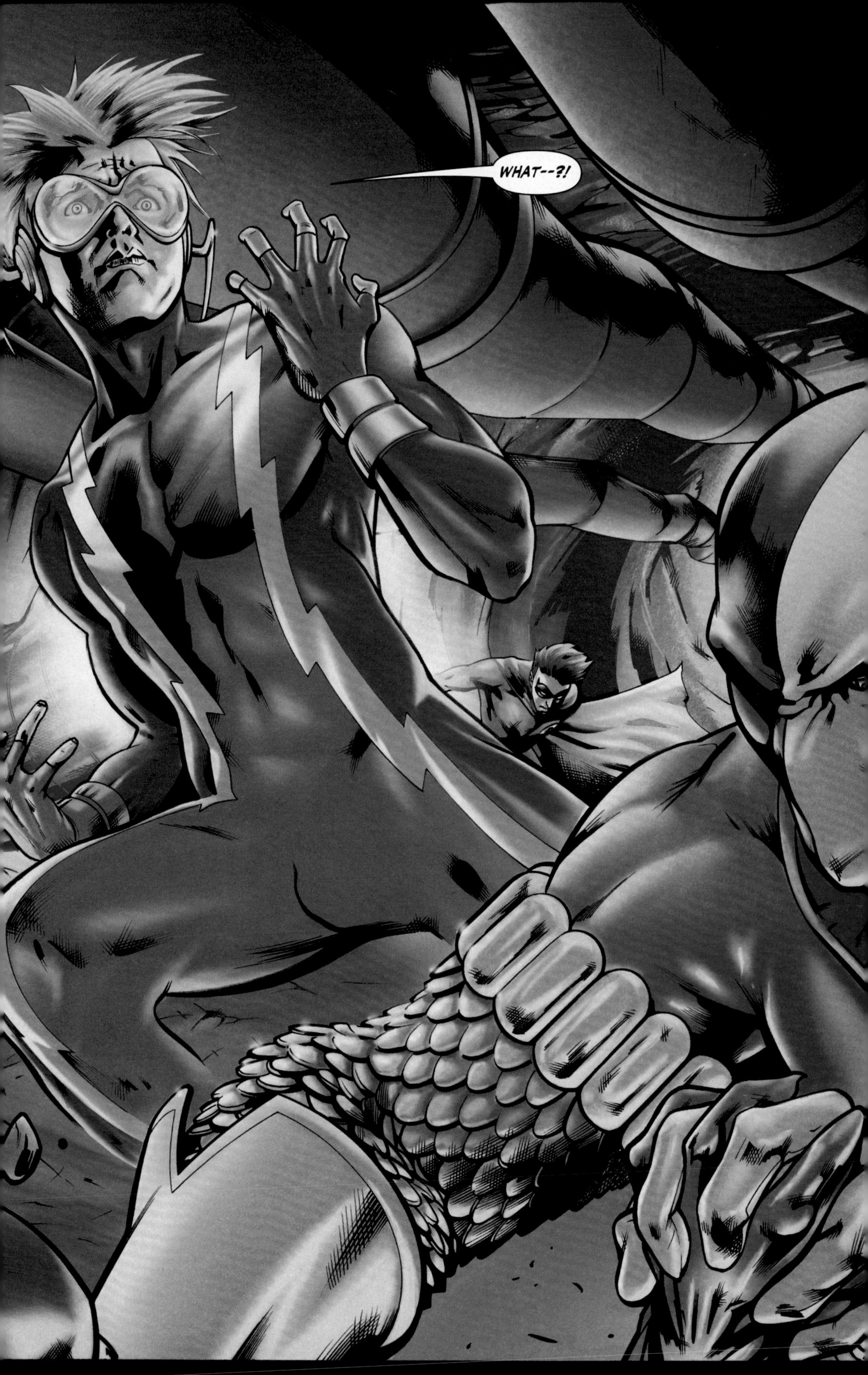
WHAT--?!

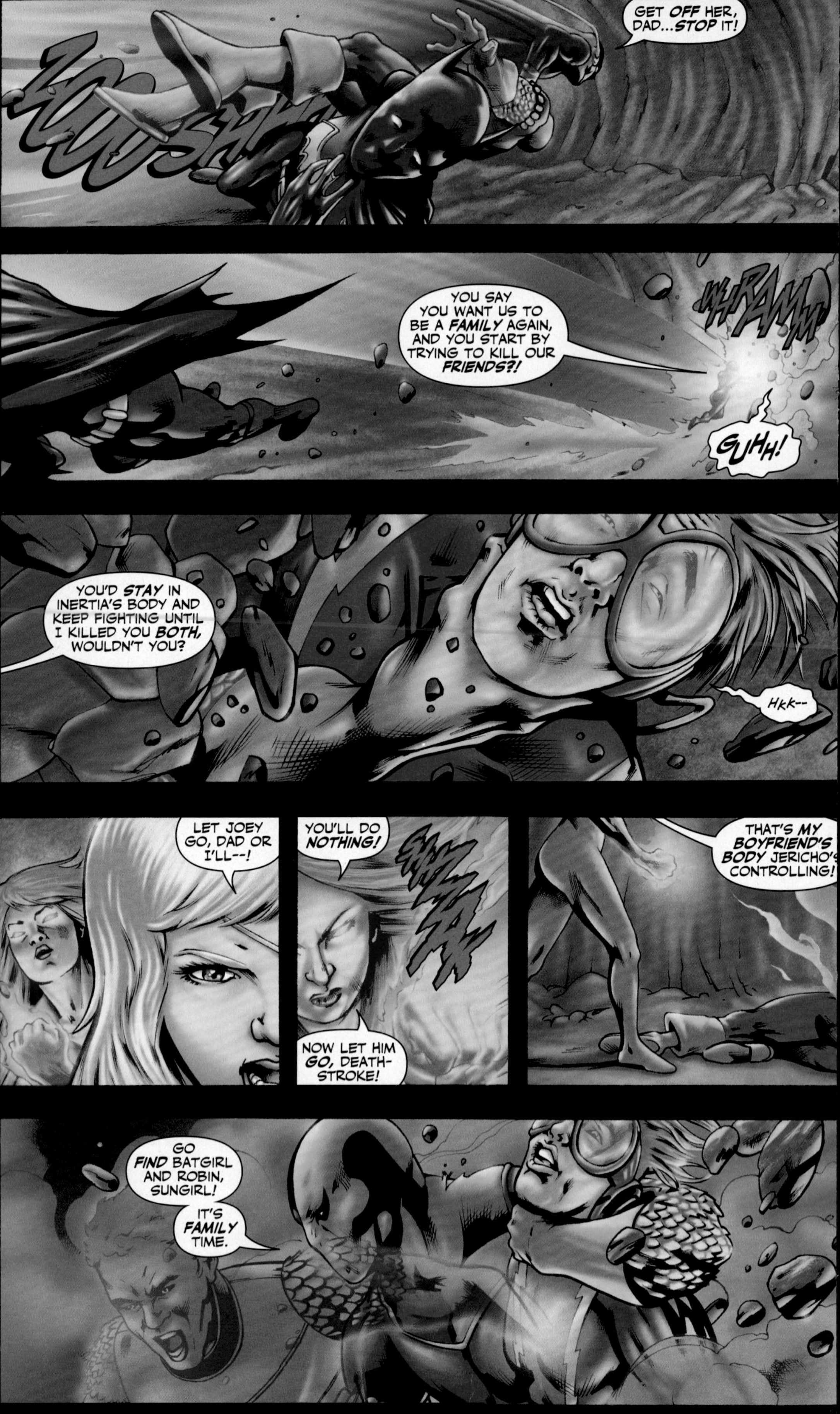
GET OFF HER, DAD...STOP IT!
ZOOOSHHH
YOU SAY YOU WANT US TO BE A FAMILY AGAIN, AND YOU START BY TRYING TO KILL OUR FRIENDS?!
WHRAMM
GUHH!
YOU'D STAY IN INERTIA'S BODY AND KEEP FIGHTING UNTIL I KILLED YOU BOTH, WOULDN'T YOU?
HKK--
LET JOEY GO, DAD OR I'LL--!
YOU'LL DO NOTHING!
NOW LET HIM GO, DEATH-STROKE!
THAT'S MY BOYFRIEND'S BODY JERICHO'S CONTROLLING!
GO FIND BATGIRL AND ROBIN, SUNGIRL!
IT'S FAMILY TIME.

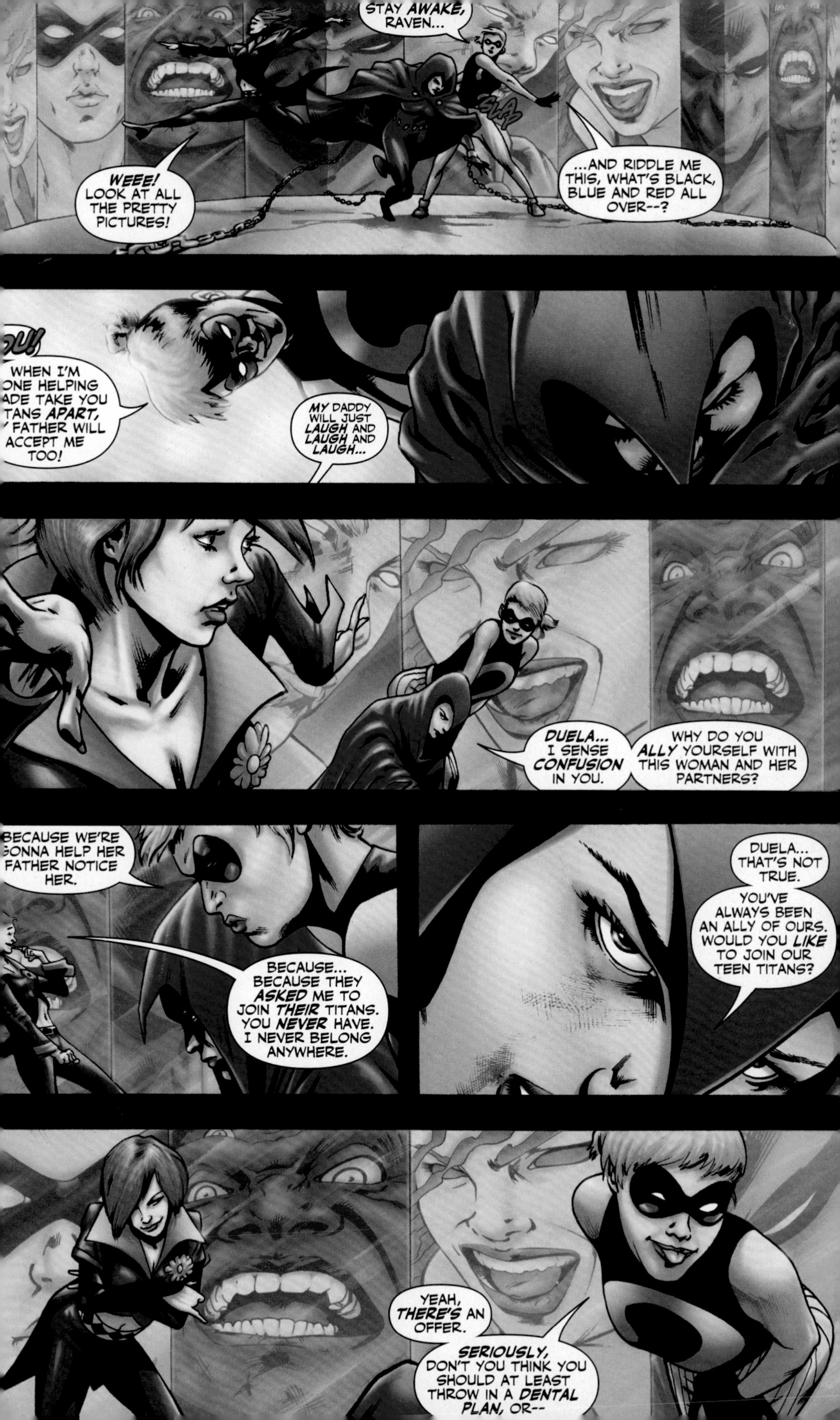
STAY *AWAKE*, RAVEN...
WEEE! LOOK AT ALL THE PRETTY PICTURES!
...AND RIDDLE ME THIS, WHAT'S BLACK, BLUE AND RED ALL OVER--?
WHEN I'M ONE HELPING ADE TAKE YOU TANS *APART,* FATHER WILL ACCEPT ME TOO!
MY DADDY WILL JUST *LAUGH* AND *LAUGH* AND *LAUGH*...
DUELA... I SENSE *CONFUSION* IN YOU.
WHY DO YOU *ALLY* YOURSELF WITH THIS WOMAN AND HER PARTNERS?
BECAUSE WE'RE GONNA HELP HER FATHER NOTICE HER.
BECAUSE... BECAUSE THEY *ASKED* ME TO JOIN *THEIR* TITANS. YOU *NEVER* HAVE. I NEVER BELONG ANYWHERE.
DUELA... THAT'S NOT TRUE.
YOU'VE ALWAYS BEEN AN ALLY OF OURS. WOULD YOU *LIKE* TO JOIN OUR TEEN TITANS?
YEAH, *THERE'S* AN OFFER.
SERIOUSLY, DON'T YOU THINK YOU SHOULD AT LEAST THROW IN A *DENTAL PLAN,* OR--

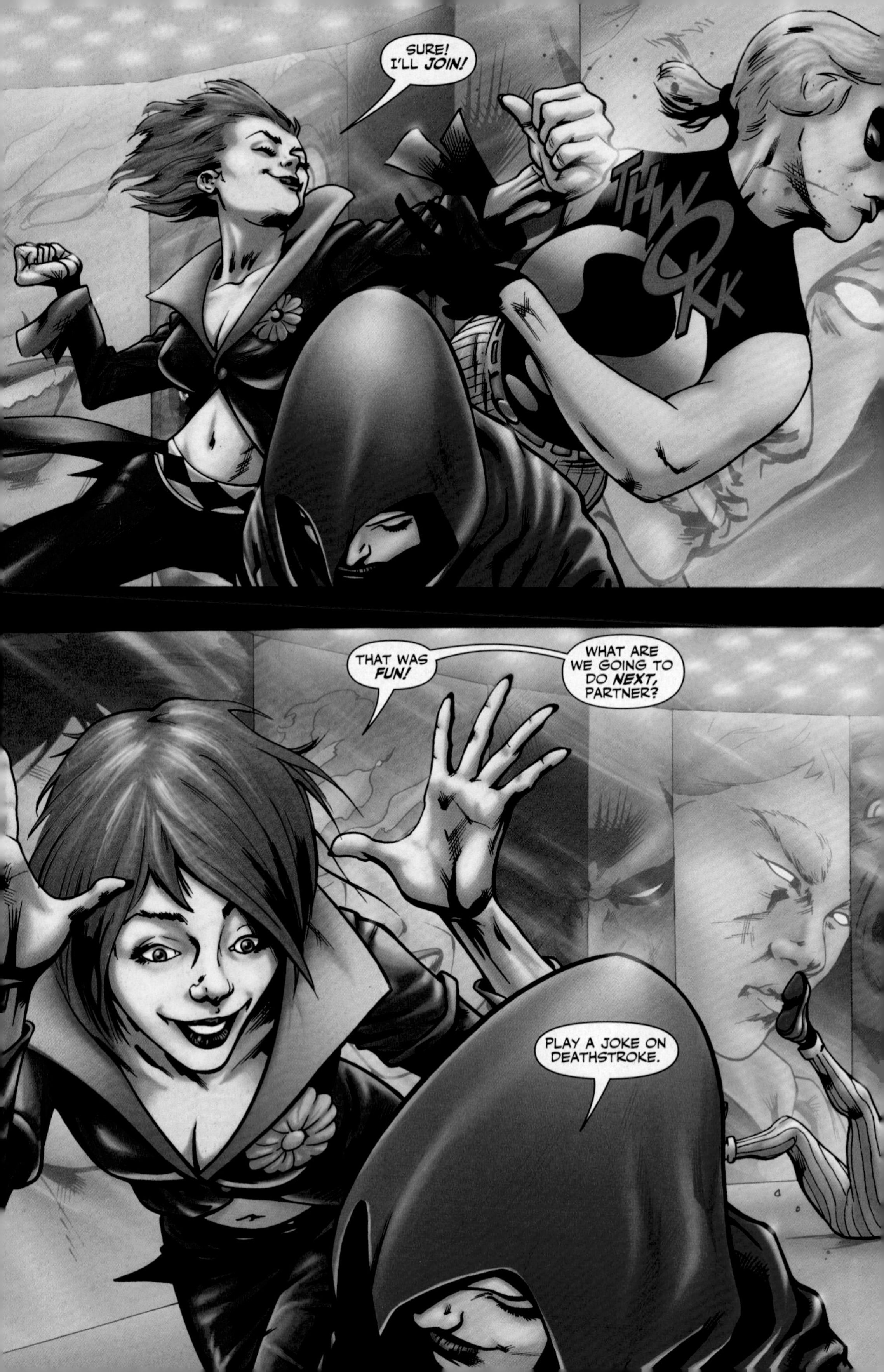
SURE! I'LL JOIN!
THWOKK
THAT WAS FUN!
WHAT ARE WE GOING TO DO NEXT, PARTNER?
PLAY A JOKE ON DEATHSTROKE.

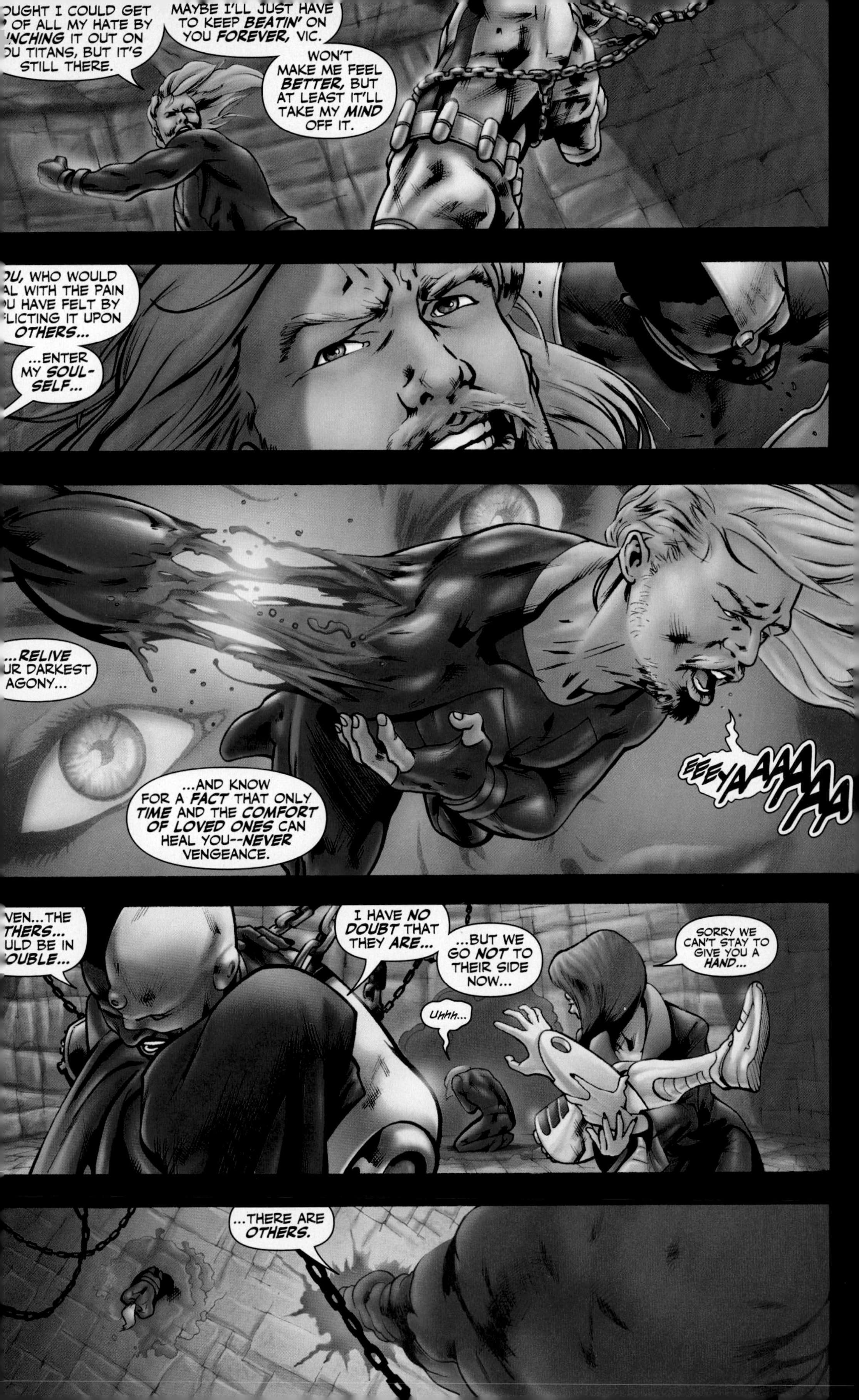
OUGHT I COULD GET
OF ALL MY HATE BY
UNCHING IT OUT ON
OU TITANS, BUT IT'S
STILL THERE.
MAYBE I'LL JUST HAVE TO KEEP BEATIN' ON YOU FOREVER, VIC.
WON'T MAKE ME FEEL BETTER, BUT AT LEAST IT'LL TAKE MY MIND OFF IT.
OU, WHO WOULD
AL WITH THE PAIN
OU HAVE FELT BY
FLICTING IT UPON
OTHERS...
...ENTER MY SOUL-SELF...
...RELIVE
UR DARKEST
AGONY...
...AND KNOW FOR A FACT THAT ONLY TIME AND THE COMFORT OF LOVED ONES CAN HEAL YOU--NEVER VENGEANCE.
EEEYAAAAAAAA
VEN...THE
THERS...
ULD BE IN
OUBLE...
I HAVE NO DOUBT THAT THEY ARE...
...BUT WE GO NOT TO THEIR SIDE NOW...
SORRY WE CAN'T STAY TO GIVE YOU A HAND...
Uhhh...
...THERE ARE OTHERS.

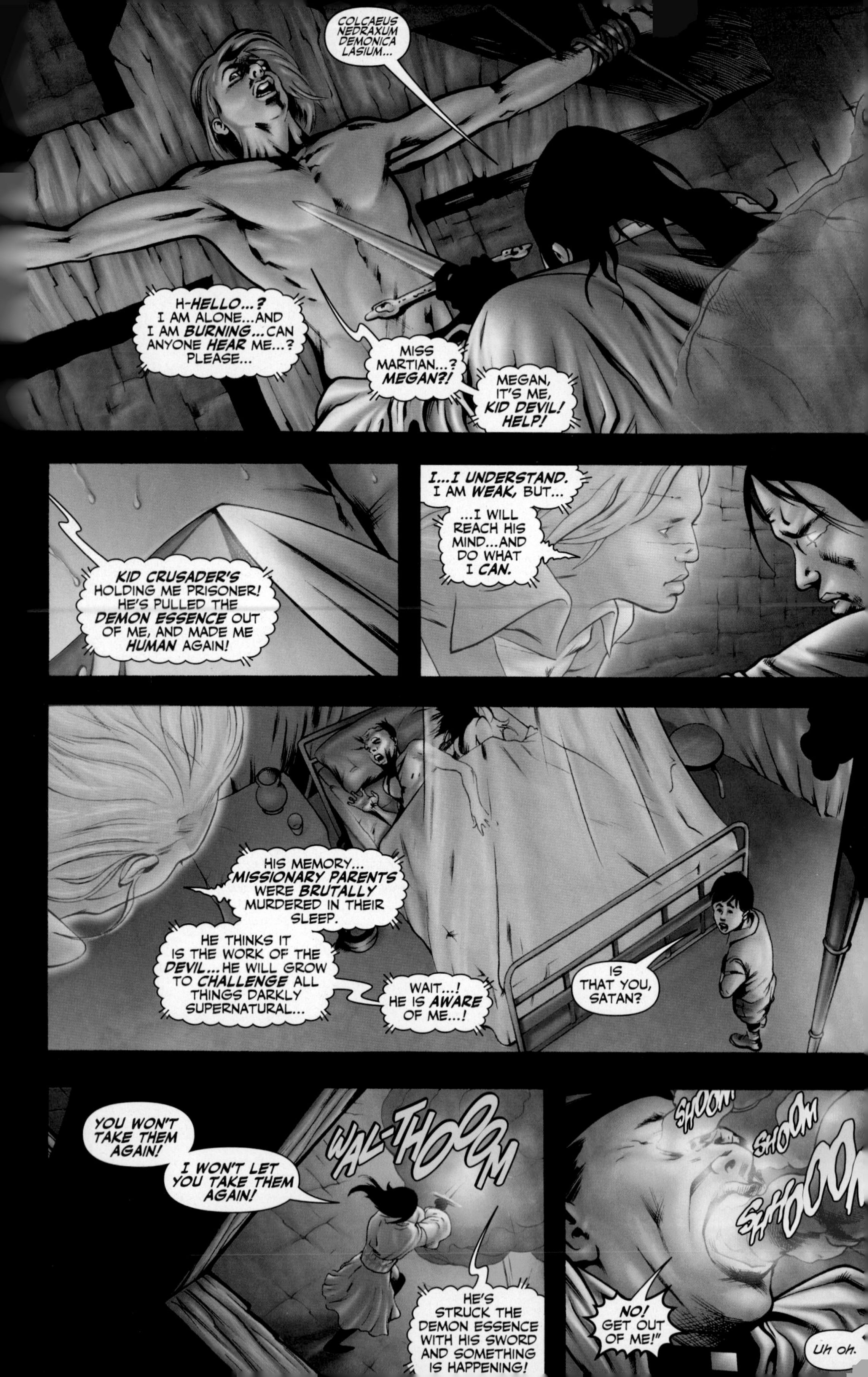
COLCAEUS NEDRAXUM DEMONICA LASIUM...
H-HELLO...? I AM ALONE...AND I AM BURNING...CAN ANYONE HEAR ME...? PLEASE...
MISS MARTIAN...? MEGAN?!
MEGAN, IT'S ME, KID DEVIL! HELP!
KID CRUSADER'S HOLDING ME PRISONER! HE'S PULLED THE DEMON ESSENCE OUT OF ME, AND MADE ME HUMAN AGAIN!
I...I UNDERSTAND. I AM WEAK, BUT...
...I WILL REACH HIS MIND...AND DO WHAT I CAN.
HIS MEMORY... MISSIONARY PARENTS WERE BRUTALLY MURDERED IN THEIR SLEEP.
HE THINKS IT IS THE WORK OF THE DEVIL...HE WILL GROW TO CHALLENGE ALL THINGS DARKLY SUPERNATURAL...
WAIT...! HE IS AWARE OF ME...!
IS THAT YOU, SATAN?
YOU WON'T TAKE THEM AGAIN!
I WON'T LET YOU TAKE THEM AGAIN!
WAL-THOOOM
HE'S STRUCK THE DEMON ESSENCE WITH HIS SWORD AND SOMETHING IS HAPPENING!
SHOOM
SHOOM
SHOOOM
NO! GET OUT OF ME!"
Uh oh.

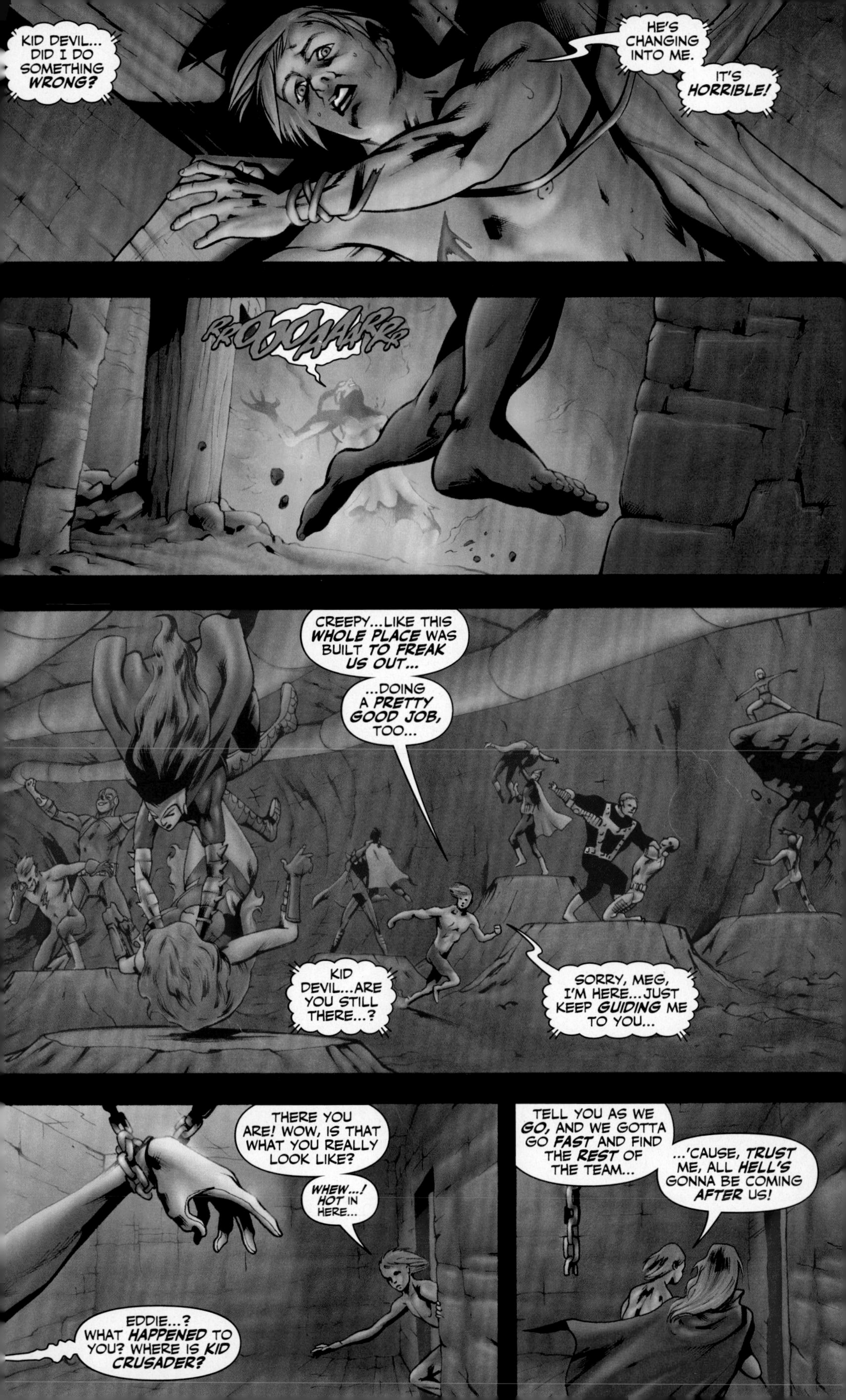
KID DEVIL... DID I DO SOMETHING WRONG?
HE'S CHANGING INTO ME.
IT'S HORRIBLE!
RRROOOAAARRR
CREEPY...LIKE THIS WHOLE PLACE WAS BUILT TO FREAK US OUT...
...DOING A PRETTY GOOD JOB, TOO...
KID DEVIL...ARE YOU STILL THERE...?
SORRY, MEG, I'M HERE...JUST KEEP GUIDING ME TO YOU...
THERE YOU ARE! WOW, IS THAT WHAT YOU REALLY LOOK LIKE?
WHEW...! HOT IN HERE...
EDDIE...? WHAT HAPPENED TO YOU? WHERE IS KID CRUSADER?
TELL YOU AS WE GO, AND WE GOTTA GO FAST AND FIND THE REST OF THE TEAM...
...'CAUSE, TRUST ME, ALL HELL'S GONNA BE COMING AFTER US!

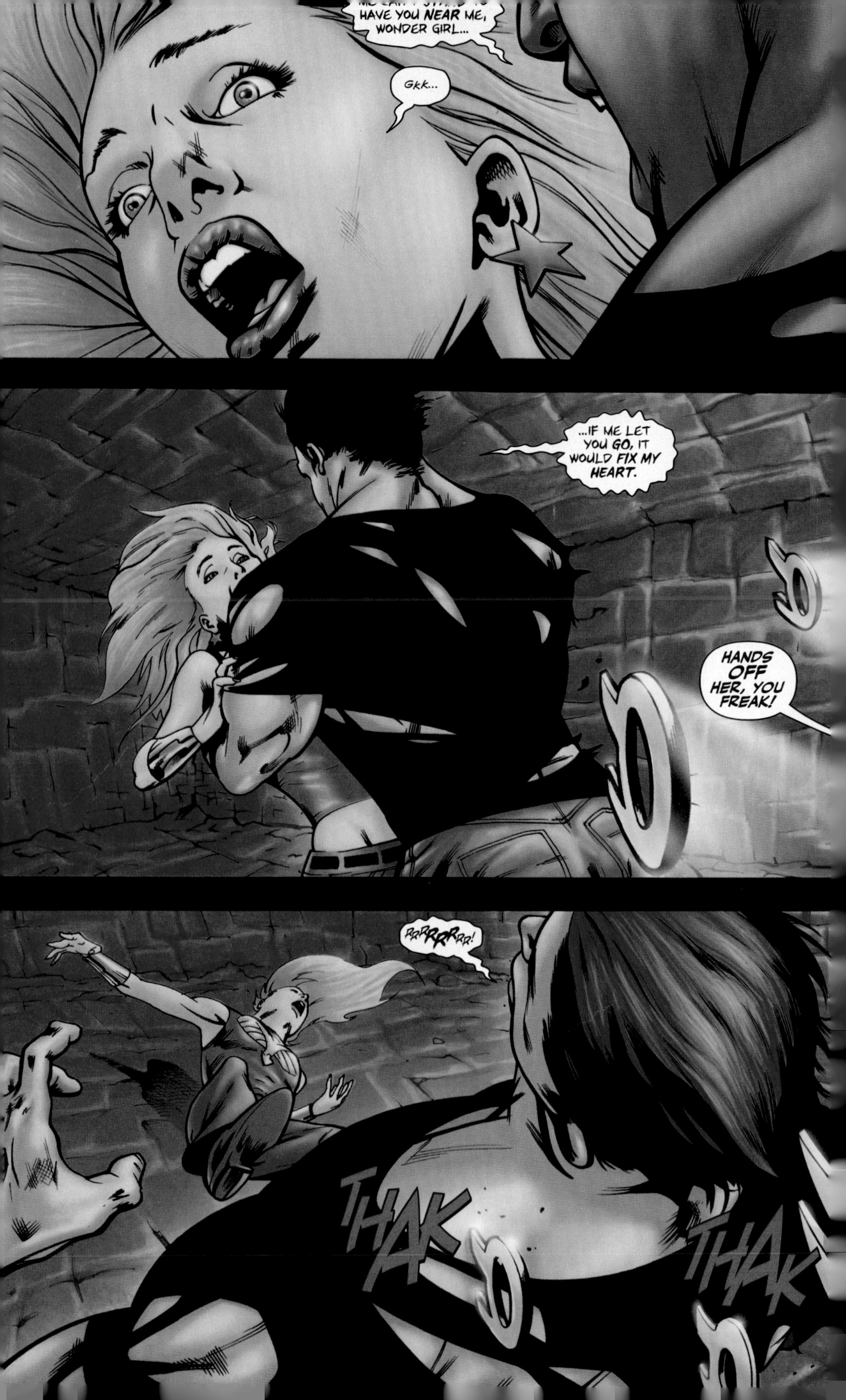
HAVE YOU NEAR ME, WONDER GIRL...
GKK...
...IF ME LET YOU GO, IT WOULD FIX MY HEART.
HANDS OFF HER, YOU FREAK!
RRRRRRRRR!
THAK
THAK

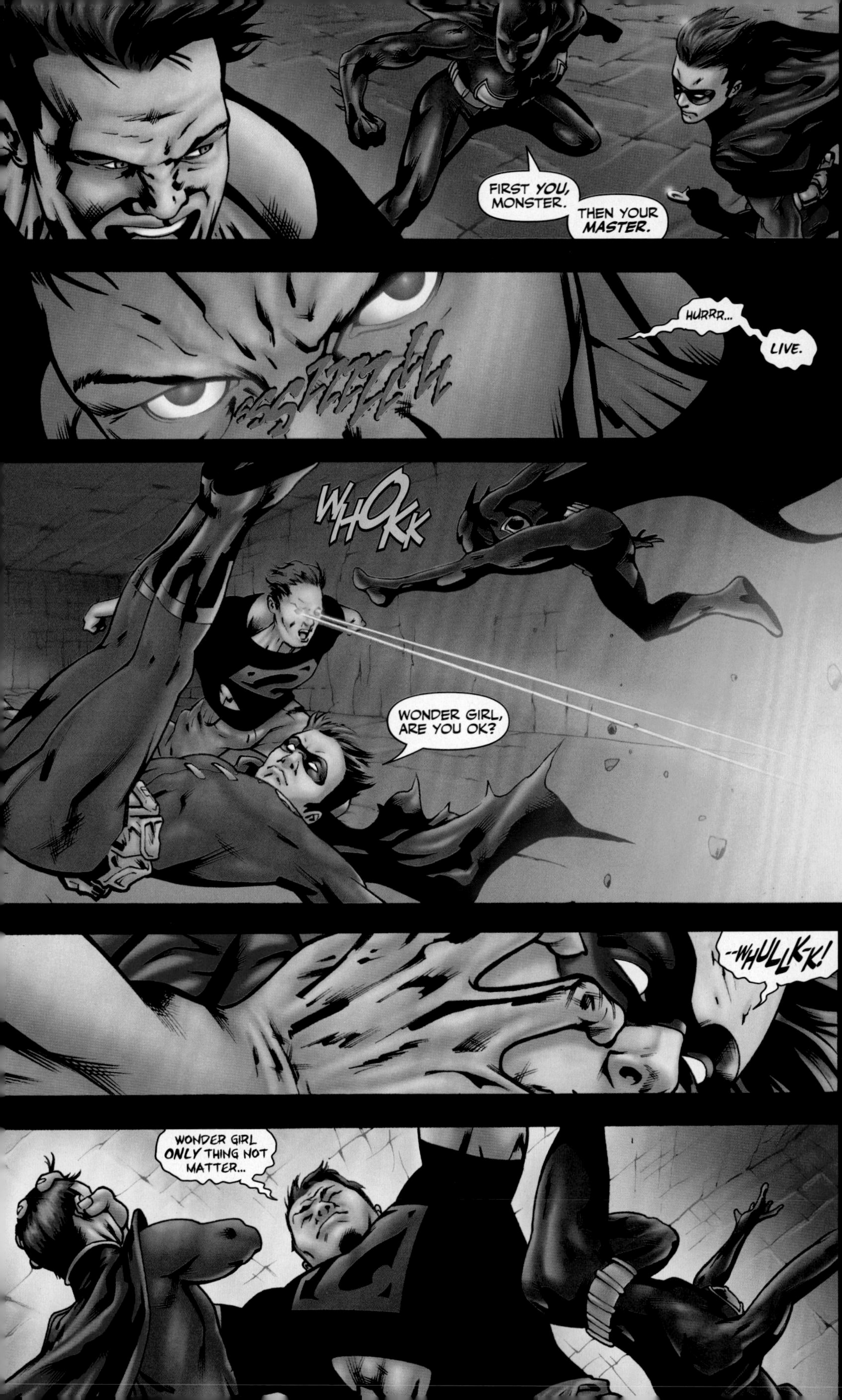

FIRST YOU, MONSTER.
THEN YOUR MASTER.
HURRR...
LIVE.
SSSZZZZZHHH
WHOKK
WONDER GIRL, ARE YOU OK?
--WHULLK-K!
WONDER GIRL ONLY THING NOT MATTER...

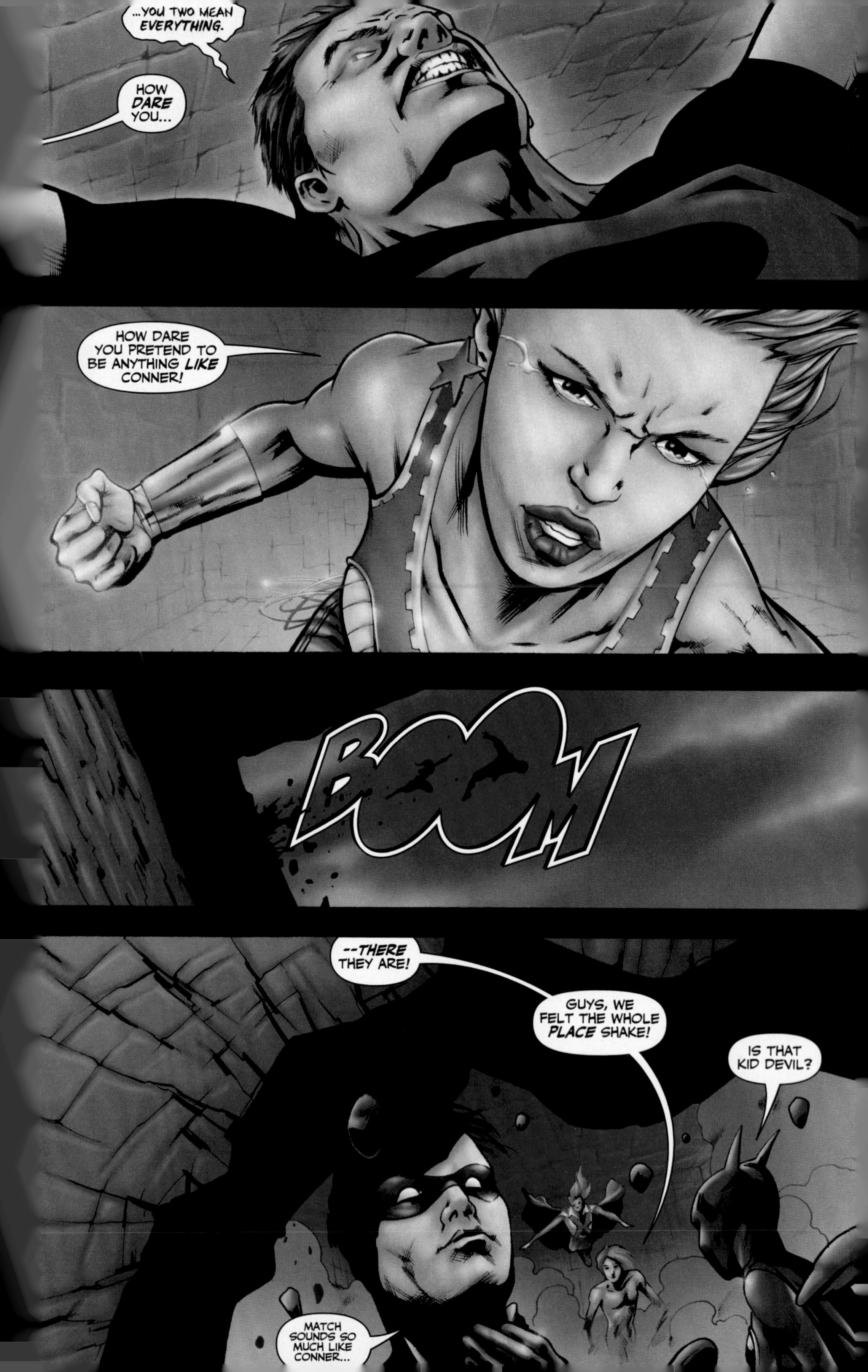

...YOU TWO MEAN EVERYTHING.
HOW DARE YOU...
HOW DARE YOU PRETEND TO BE ANYTHING LIKE CONNER!
BOOM
--THERE THEY ARE!
GUYS, WE FELT THE WHOLE PLACE SHAKE!
IS THAT KID DEVIL?
MATCH SOUNDS SO MUCH LIKE CONNER...

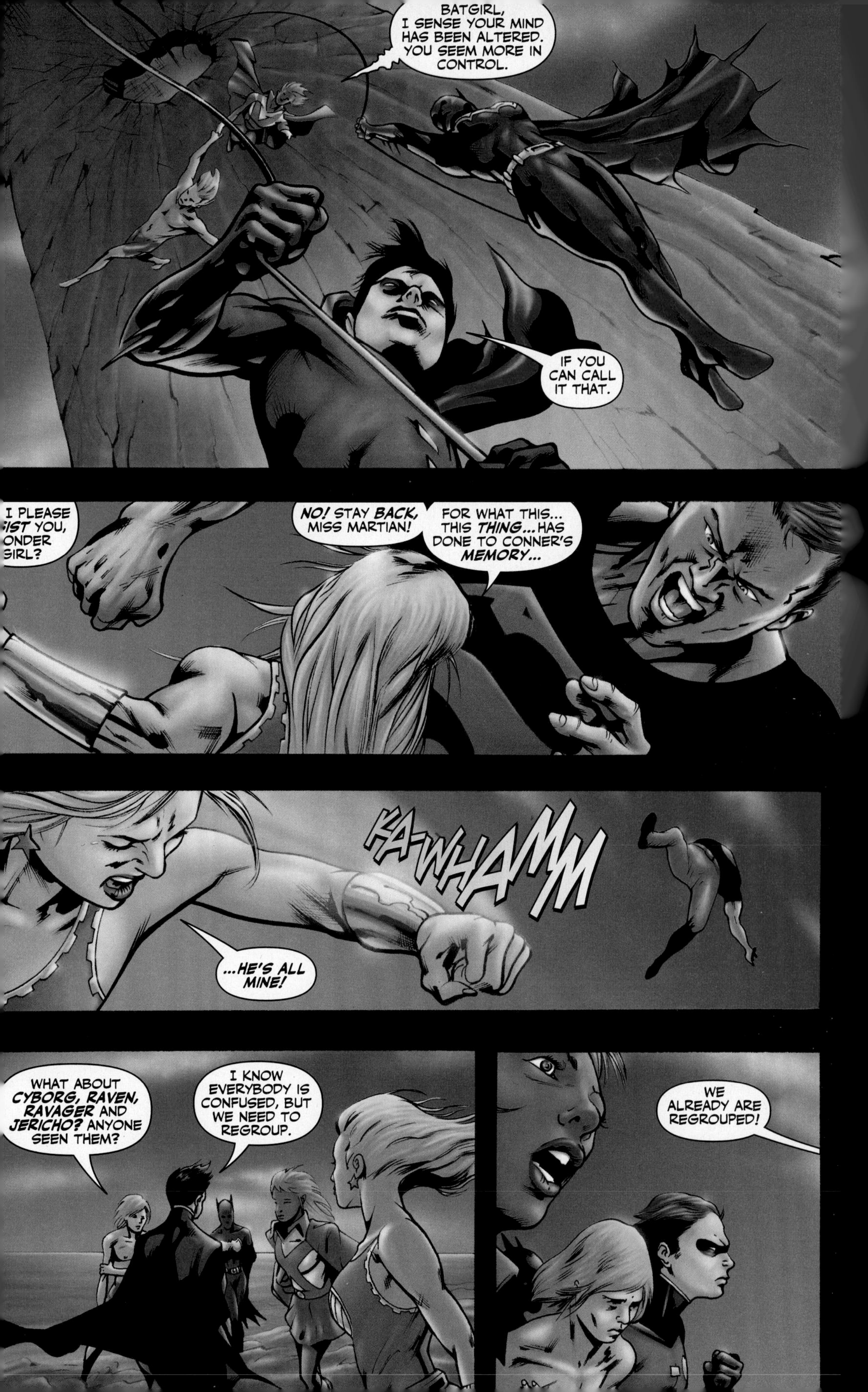
BATGIRL, I SENSE YOUR MIND HAS BEEN ALTERED. YOU SEEM MORE IN CONTROL.
IF YOU CAN CALL IT THAT.
I PLEASE ᵴIST YOU, ONDER GIRL?
NO! STAY BACK, MISS MARTIAN!
FOR WHAT THIS... THIS THING... HAS DONE TO CONNER'S MEMORY...
KA-WHAMM
...HE'S ALL MINE!
WHAT ABOUT CYBORG, RAVEN, RAVAGER AND JERICHO? ANYONE SEEN THEM?
I KNOW EVERYBODY IS CONFUSED, BUT WE NEED TO REGROUP.
WE ALREADY ARE REGROUPED!

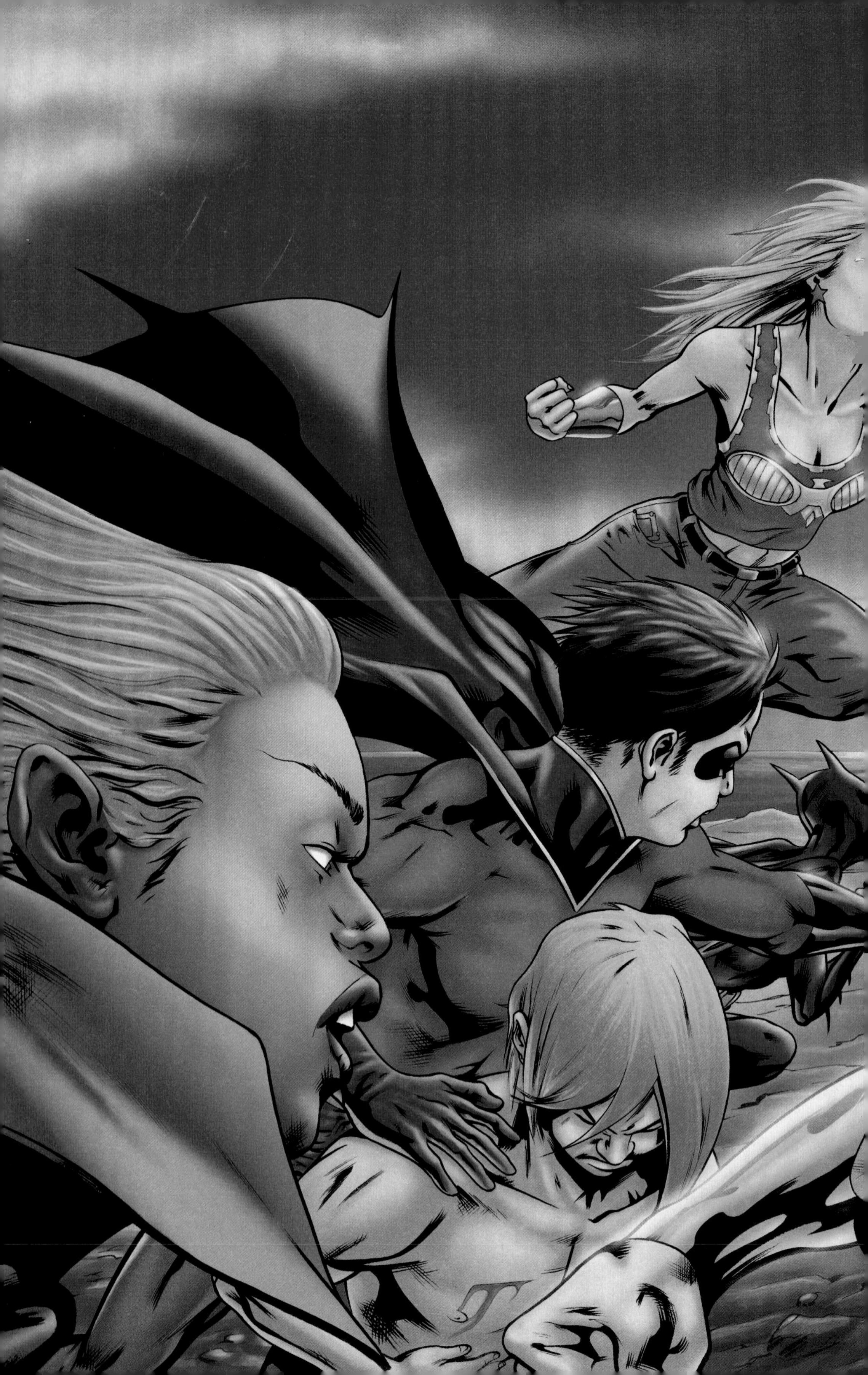

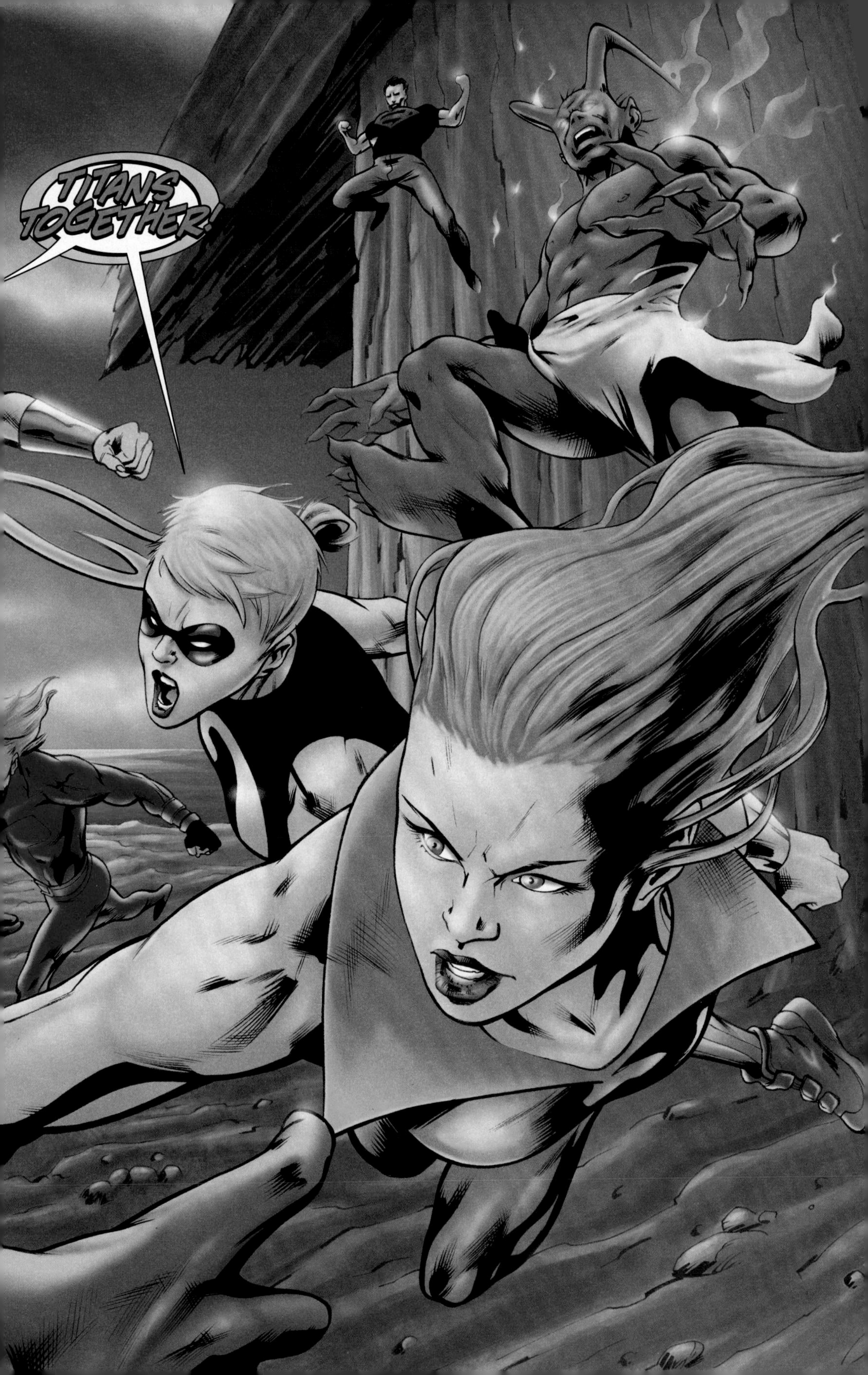
TITANS TOGETHER!

HE'S SO MUCH LIKE CONNER.

I KNOW.

WONDER GIRL, *STOP!* YOU CAN'T BEAT MATCH WITH *BRUTE FORCE!*

THEY *OUT-POWER* US! IF WE DON'T WORK AS A *TEAM*, WE'LL--

RIDDLE ME *THIS:* WHAT GAME WILL THE *REST* OF THE TITANS PLAY AFTER I KILL ROBIN?

ANSWER: FOLLOW THE LEA--

OMPH!

I GUESS YOUR GOT ALL THE *RIDDLE* TALENT IN THE FA**ENIGMA**...

SWOOSH

TELL ME, SUN GIRL! TELL ME WHAT YOU THINK I'M GOING TO *DO* TO YOUR FUTURE, AND I SWEAR I WILL *NOT* DO IT!

SsszZH

TRUST ME, GREEN SLIME...

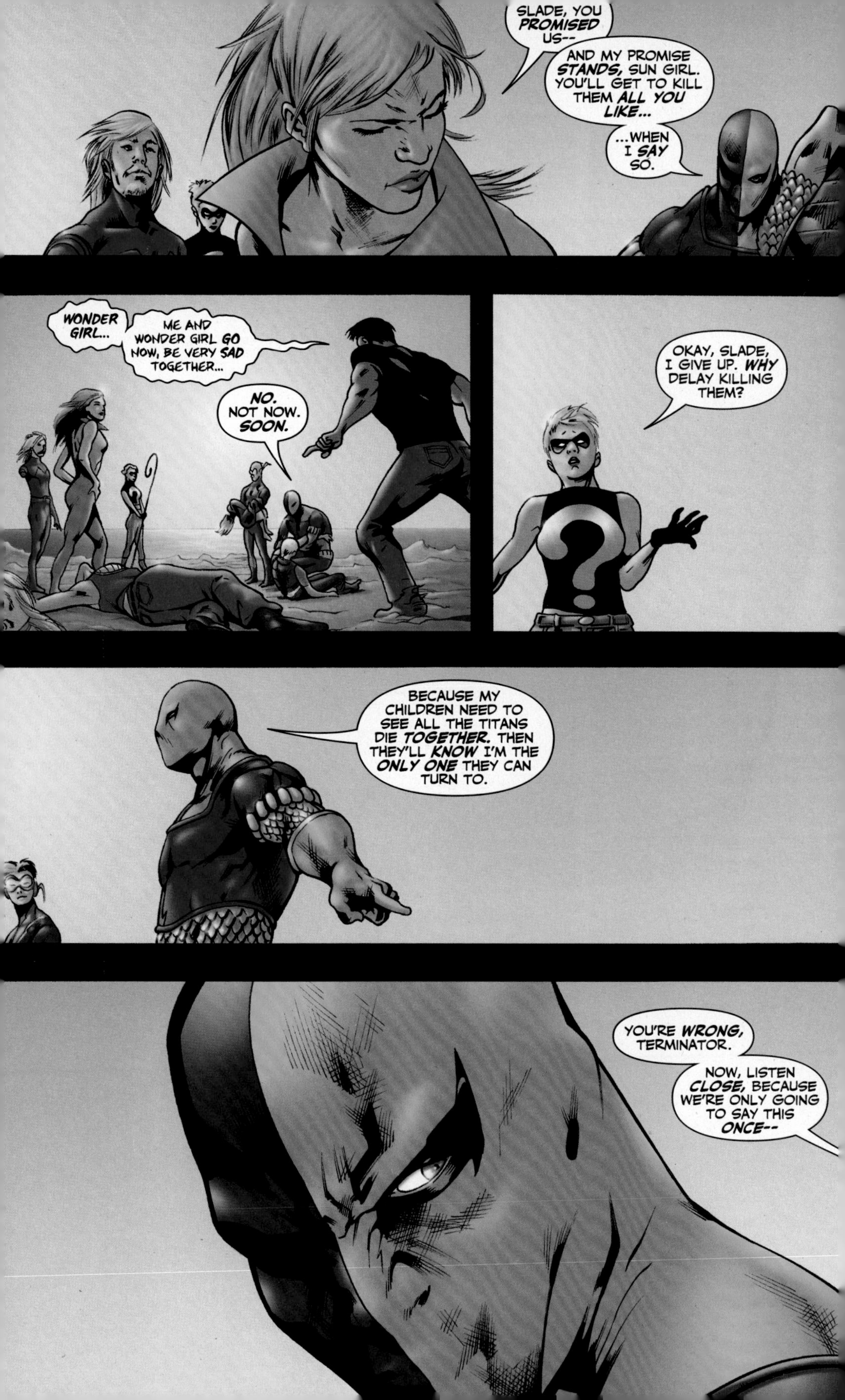
SLADE, YOU PROMISED US--
AND MY PROMISE STANDS, SUN GIRL. YOU'LL GET TO KILL THEM ALL YOU LIKE...
...WHEN I SAY SO.
WONDER GIRL...
ME AND WONDER GIRL GO NOW, BE VERY SAD TOGETHER...
NO. NOT NOW. SOON.
OKAY, SLADE, I GIVE UP. WHY DELAY KILLING THEM?
BECAUSE MY CHILDREN NEED TO SEE ALL THE TITANS DIE TOGETHER. THEN THEY'LL KNOW I'M THE ONLY ONE THEY CAN TURN TO.
YOU'RE WRONG, TERMINATOR.
NOW, LISTEN CLOSE, BECAUSE WE'RE ONLY GOING TO SAY THIS ONCE--

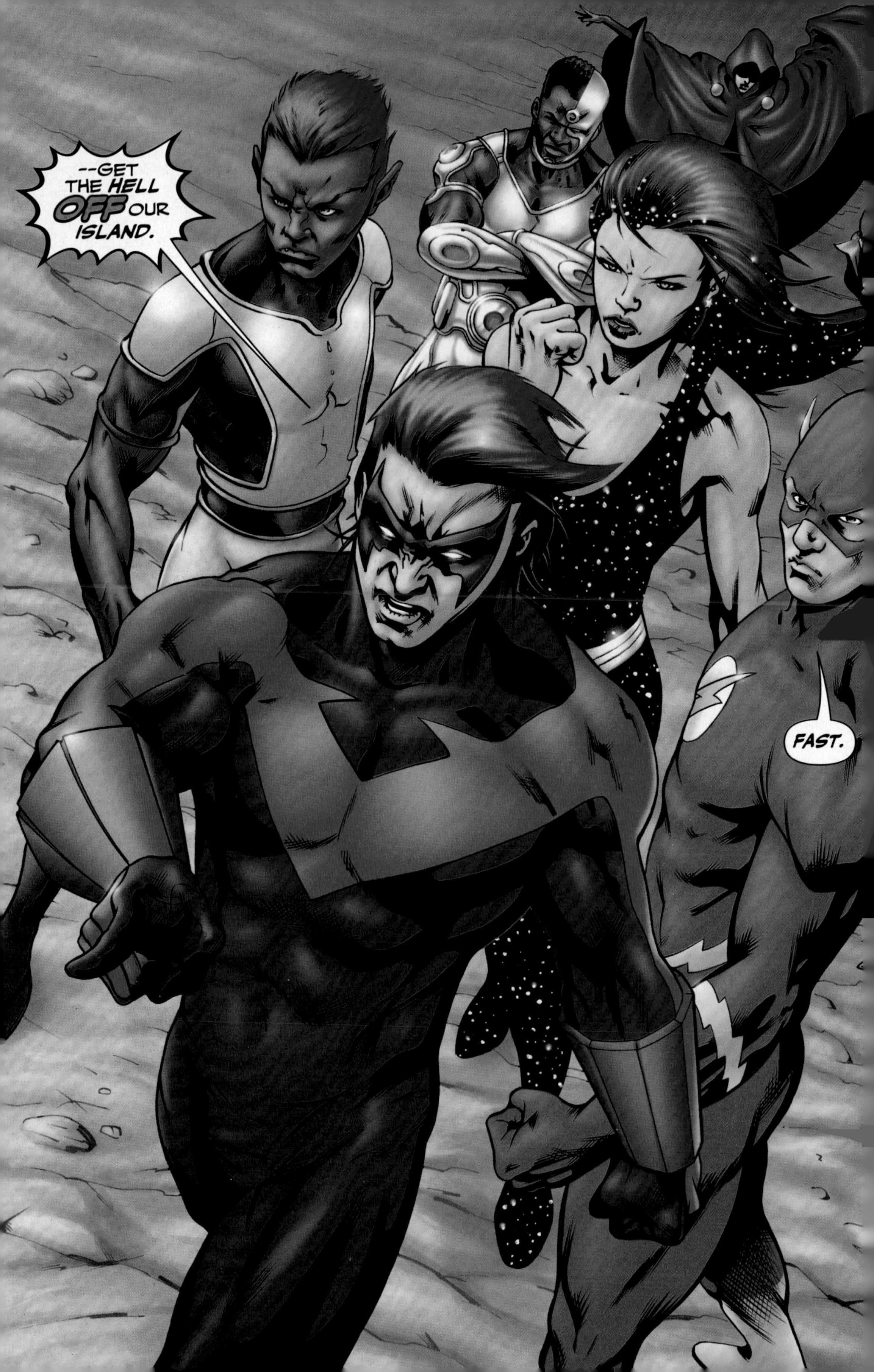
--GET THE HELL OFF OUR ISLAND.
FAST.

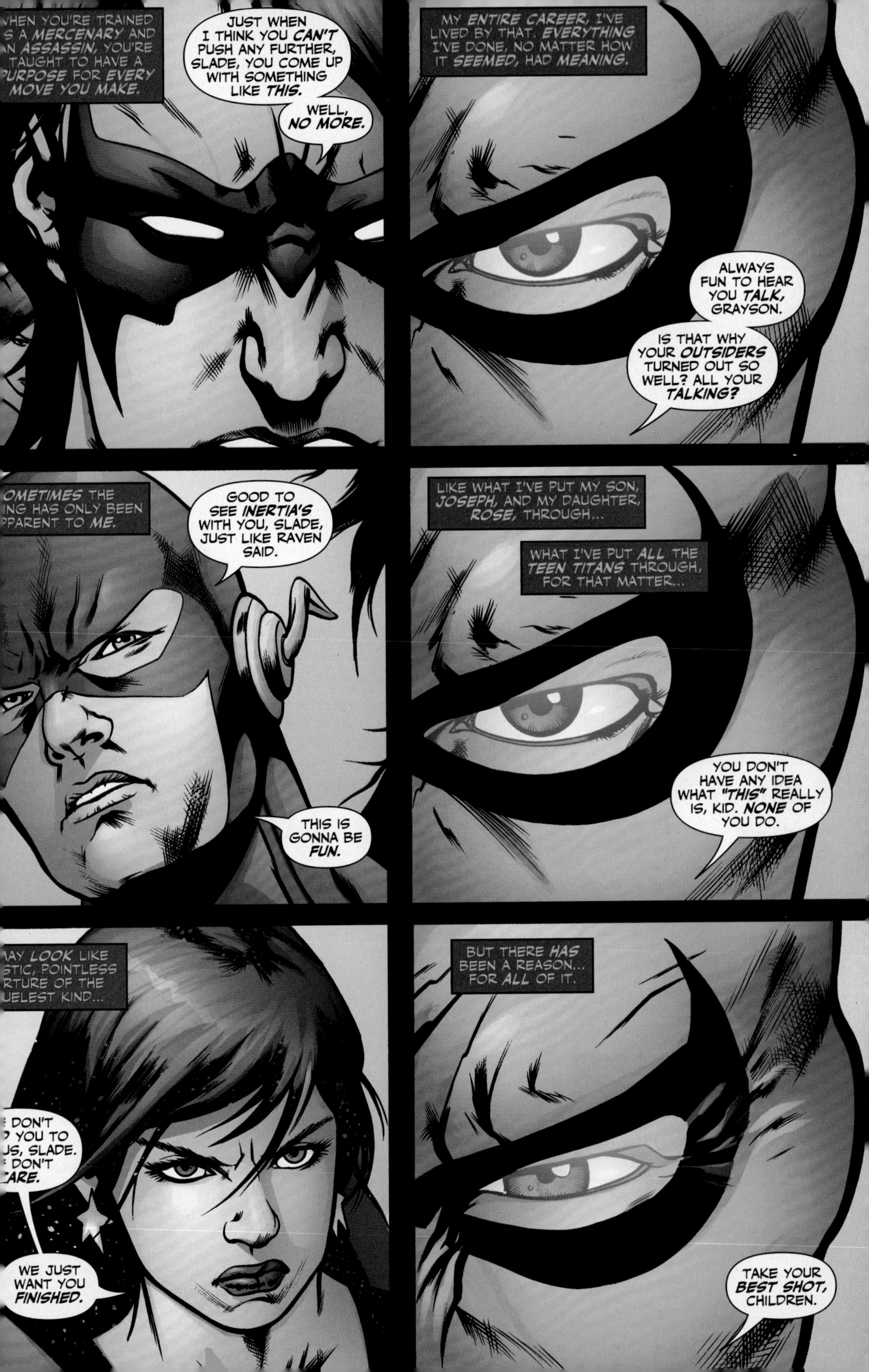
WHEN YOU'RE TRAINED
S A MERCENARY AND
N ASSASSIN, YOU'RE
TAUGHT TO HAVE A
PURPOSE FOR EVERY
MOVE YOU MAKE.
JUST WHEN I THINK YOU CAN'T PUSH ANY FURTHER, SLADE, YOU COME UP WITH SOMETHING LIKE THIS.
WELL, NO MORE.
MY ENTIRE CAREER, I'VE LIVED BY THAT. EVERYTHING I'VE DONE, NO MATTER HOW IT SEEMED, HAD MEANING.
ALWAYS FUN TO HEAR YOU TALK, GRAYSON.
IS THAT WHY YOUR OUTSIDERS TURNED OUT SO WELL? ALL YOUR TALKING?
OMETIMES THE
ING HAS ONLY BEEN
PPARENT TO ME.
GOOD TO SEE INERTIA'S WITH YOU, SLADE, JUST LIKE RAVEN SAID.
THIS IS GONNA BE FUN.
LIKE WHAT I'VE PUT MY SON, JOSEPH, AND MY DAUGHTER, ROSE, THROUGH...
WHAT I'VE PUT ALL THE TEEN TITANS THROUGH, FOR THAT MATTER...
YOU DON'T HAVE ANY IDEA WHAT "THIS" REALLY IS, KID. NONE OF YOU DO.
AY LOOK LIKE
STIC, POINTLESS
RTURE OF THE
UELEST KIND...
DON'T
YOU TO
US, SLADE.
DON'T
ARE.
WE JUST WANT YOU FINISHED.
BUT THERE HAS BEEN A REASON... FOR ALL OF IT.
TAKE YOUR BEST SHOT, CHILDREN.

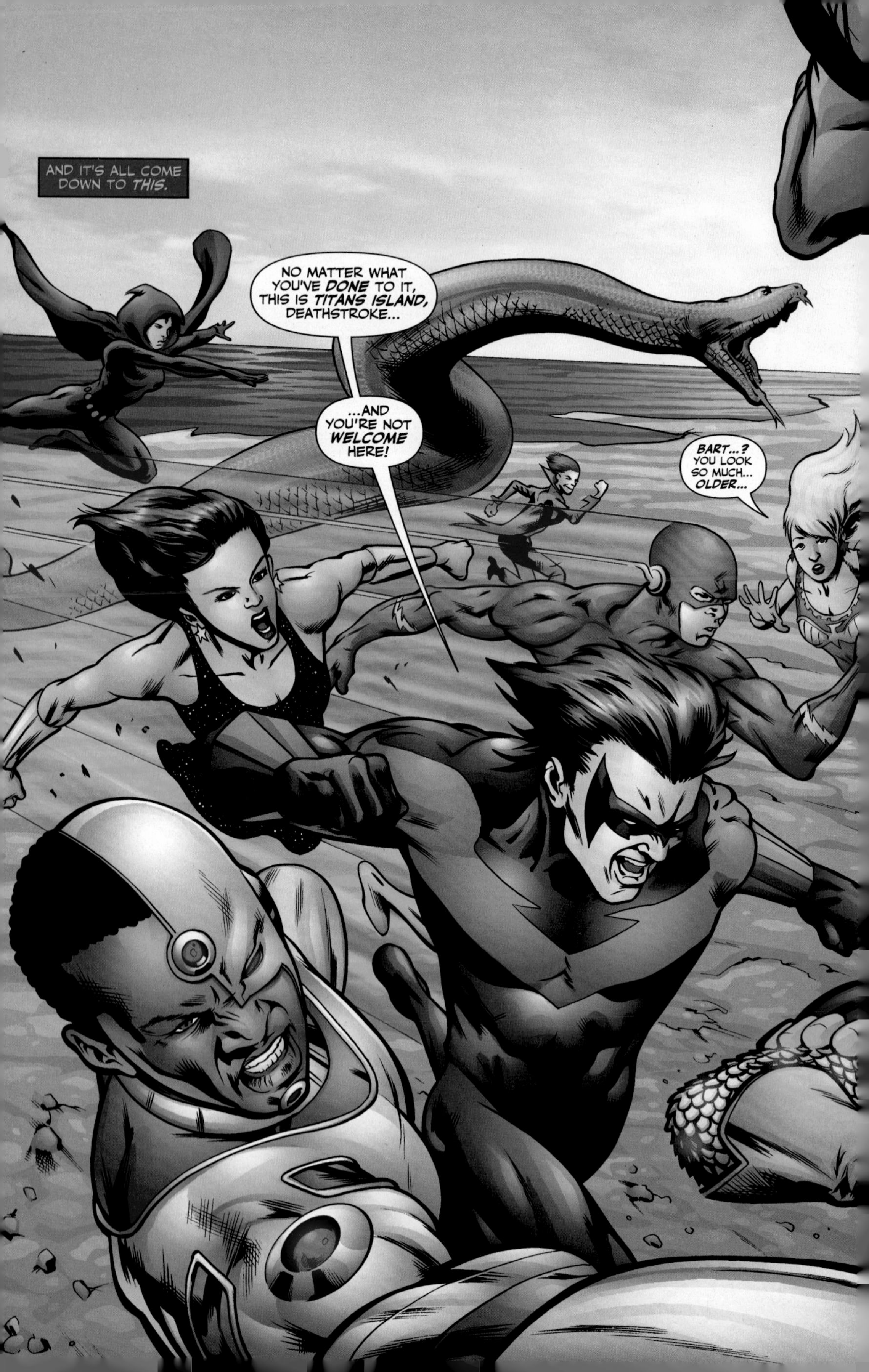
AND IT'S ALL COME DOWN TO *THIS.*
NO MATTER WHAT YOU'VE *DONE* TO IT, THIS IS *TITANS ISLAND,* DEATHSTROKE...
...AND YOU'RE NOT ***WELCOME*** HERE!
BART...? YOU LOOK SO MUCH... *OLDER...*

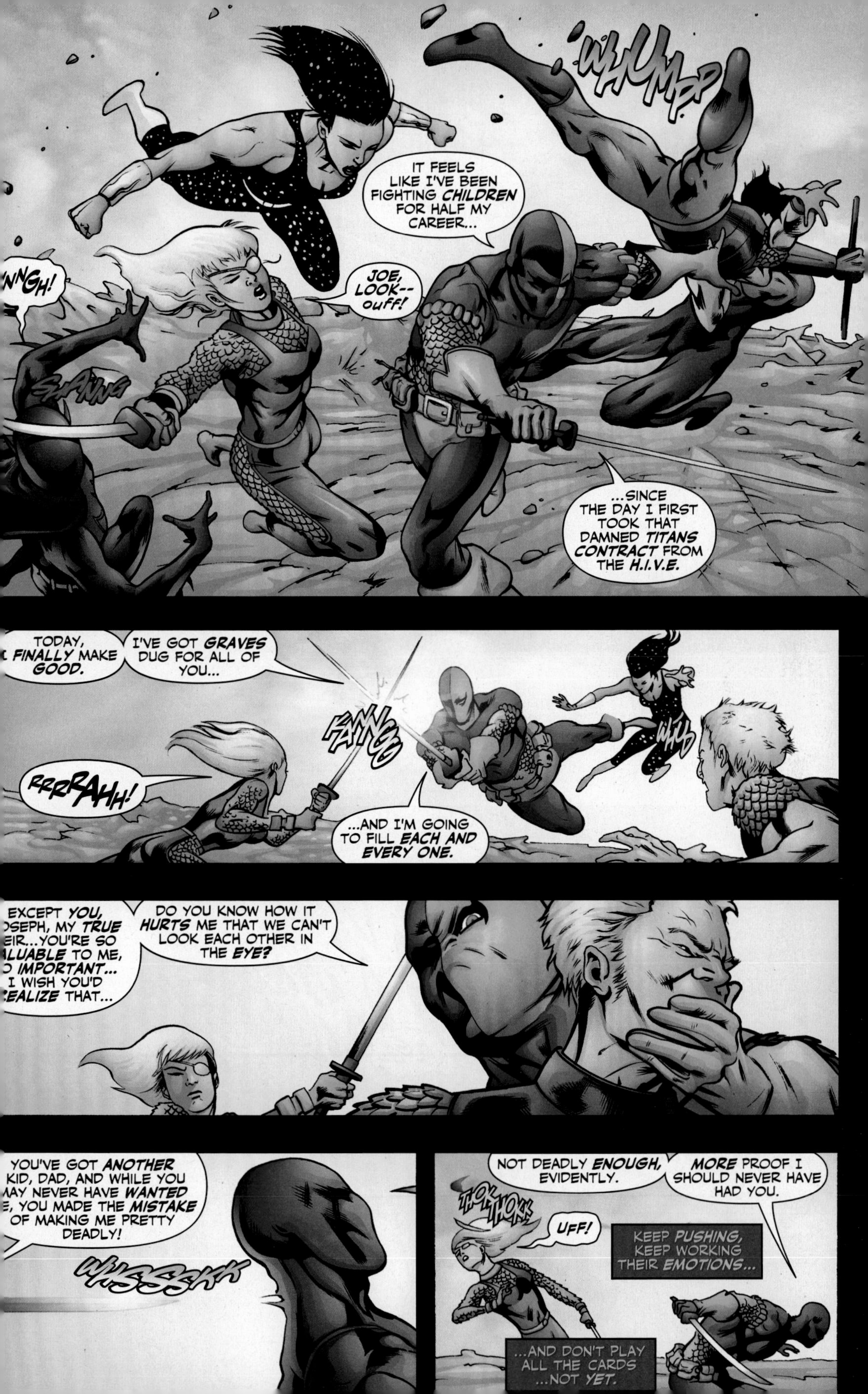
WHUMP!
IT FEELS LIKE I'VE BEEN FIGHTING CHILDREN FOR HALF MY CAREER...
NNGH!
JOE, LOOK-- ouff!
SHANNG
...SINCE THE DAY I FIRST TOOK THAT DAMNED TITANS CONTRACT FROM THE H.I.V.E.
TODAY, I FINALLY MAKE GOOD.
I'VE GOT GRAVES DUG FOR ALL OF YOU...
KANNGG
WHUD
RRRRAHH!
...AND I'M GOING TO FILL EACH AND EVERY ONE.
EXCEPT YOU, JOSEPH, MY TRUE HEIR...YOU'RE SO VALUABLE TO ME, SO IMPORTANT... I WISH YOU'D REALIZE THAT...
DO YOU KNOW HOW IT HURTS ME THAT WE CAN'T LOOK EACH OTHER IN THE EYE?
YOU'VE GOT ANOTHER KID, DAD, AND WHILE YOU MAY NEVER HAVE WANTED ME, YOU MADE THE MISTAKE OF MAKING ME PRETTY DEADLY!
WHSSSHKK
NOT DEADLY ENOUGH, EVIDENTLY.
MORE PROOF I SHOULD NEVER HAVE HAD YOU.
THOK THOK!
UFF!
KEEP PUSHING, KEEP WORKING THEIR EMOTIONS...
...AND DON'T PLAY ALL THE CARDS ...NOT YET.

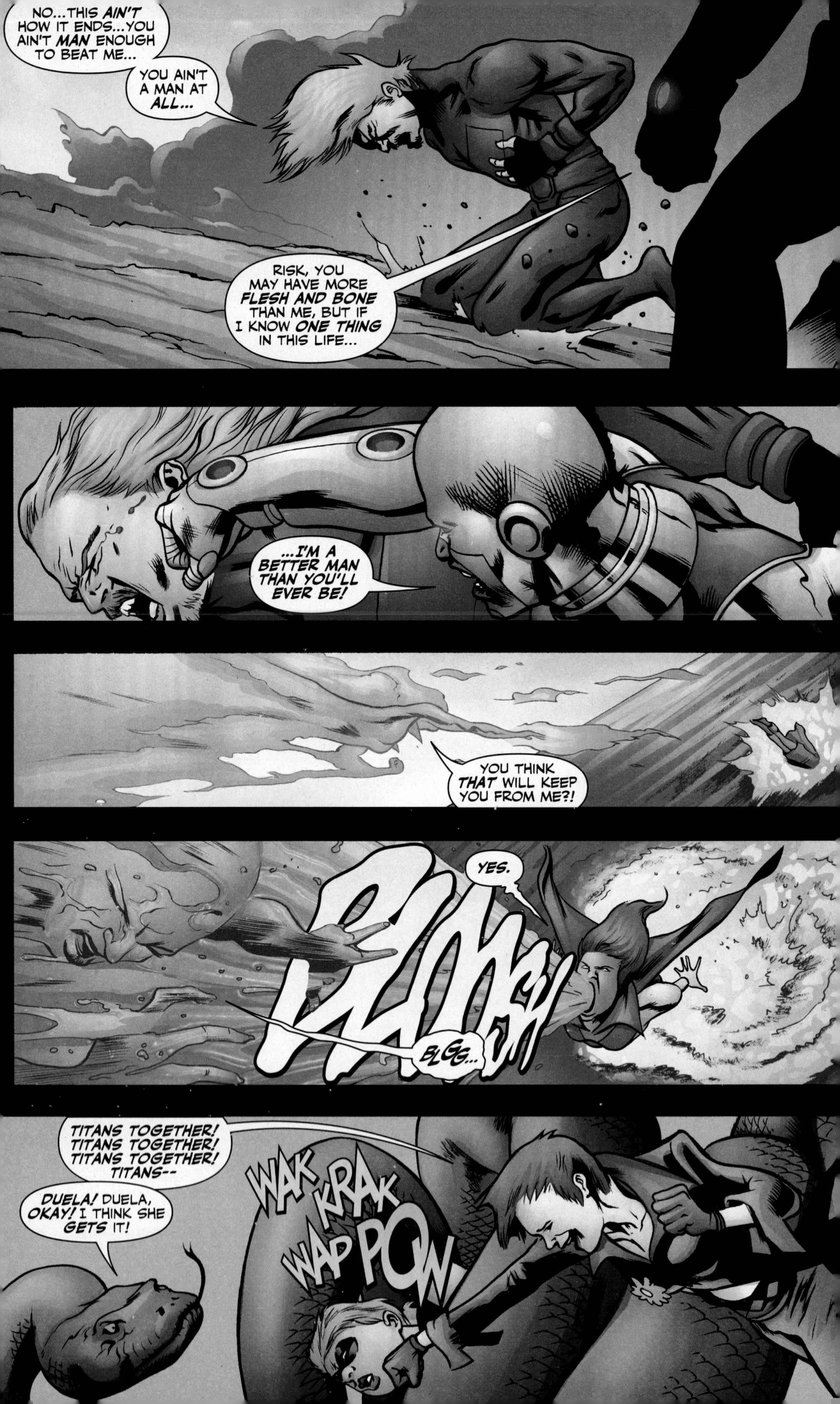
NO...THIS AIN'T HOW IT ENDS...YOU AIN'T MAN ENOUGH TO BEAT ME...
YOU AIN'T A MAN AT ALL...
RISK, YOU MAY HAVE MORE FLESH AND BONE THAN ME, BUT IF I KNOW ONE THING IN THIS LIFE...
...I'M A BETTER MAN THAN YOU'LL EVER BE!
YOU THINK THAT WILL KEEP YOU FROM ME?!
YES.
BLMSH
BLGG...
TITANS TOGETHER! TITANS TOGETHER! TITANS TOGETHER! TITANS--
DUELA! DUELA, OKAY! I THINK SHE GETS IT!
WAK KRAK WAP POW

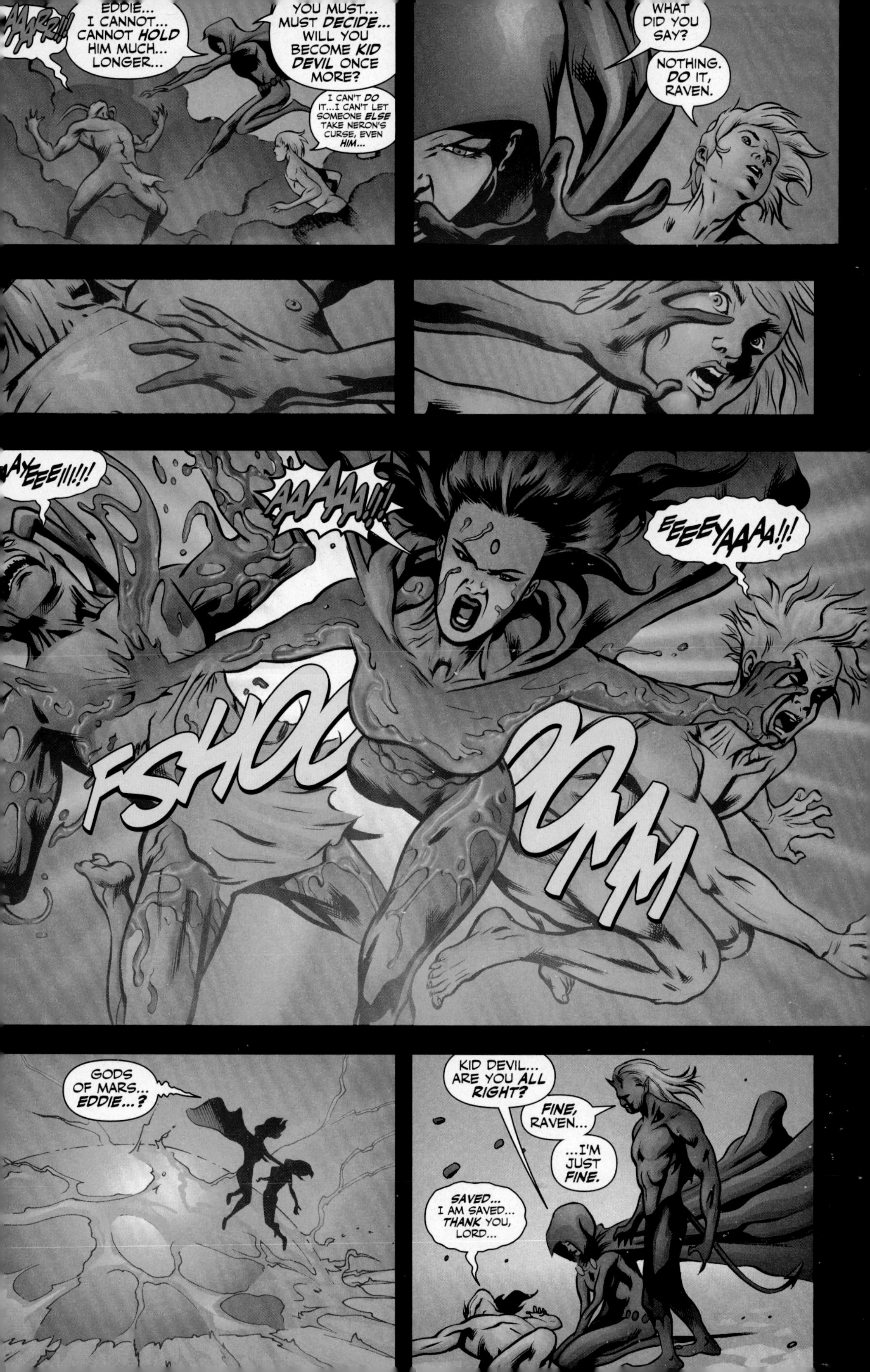
AAARR!!!
EDDIE... I CANNOT... CANNOT HOLD HIM MUCH... LONGER...
YOU MUST... MUST DECIDE... WILL YOU BECOME KID DEVIL ONCE MORE?
I CAN'T DO IT...I CAN'T LET SOMEONE ELSE TAKE NERON'S CURSE, EVEN HIM...
WHAT DID YOU SAY?
NOTHING. DO IT, RAVEN.
AYEEE!!!!!
AAAAA!!!
EEEEYAAAA!!!
FSHOOOOMM
GODS OF MARS... EDDIE...?
KID DEVIL... ARE YOU ALL RIGHT?
FINE, RAVEN...
...I'M JUST FINE.
SAVED... I AM SAVED... THANK YOU, LORD...

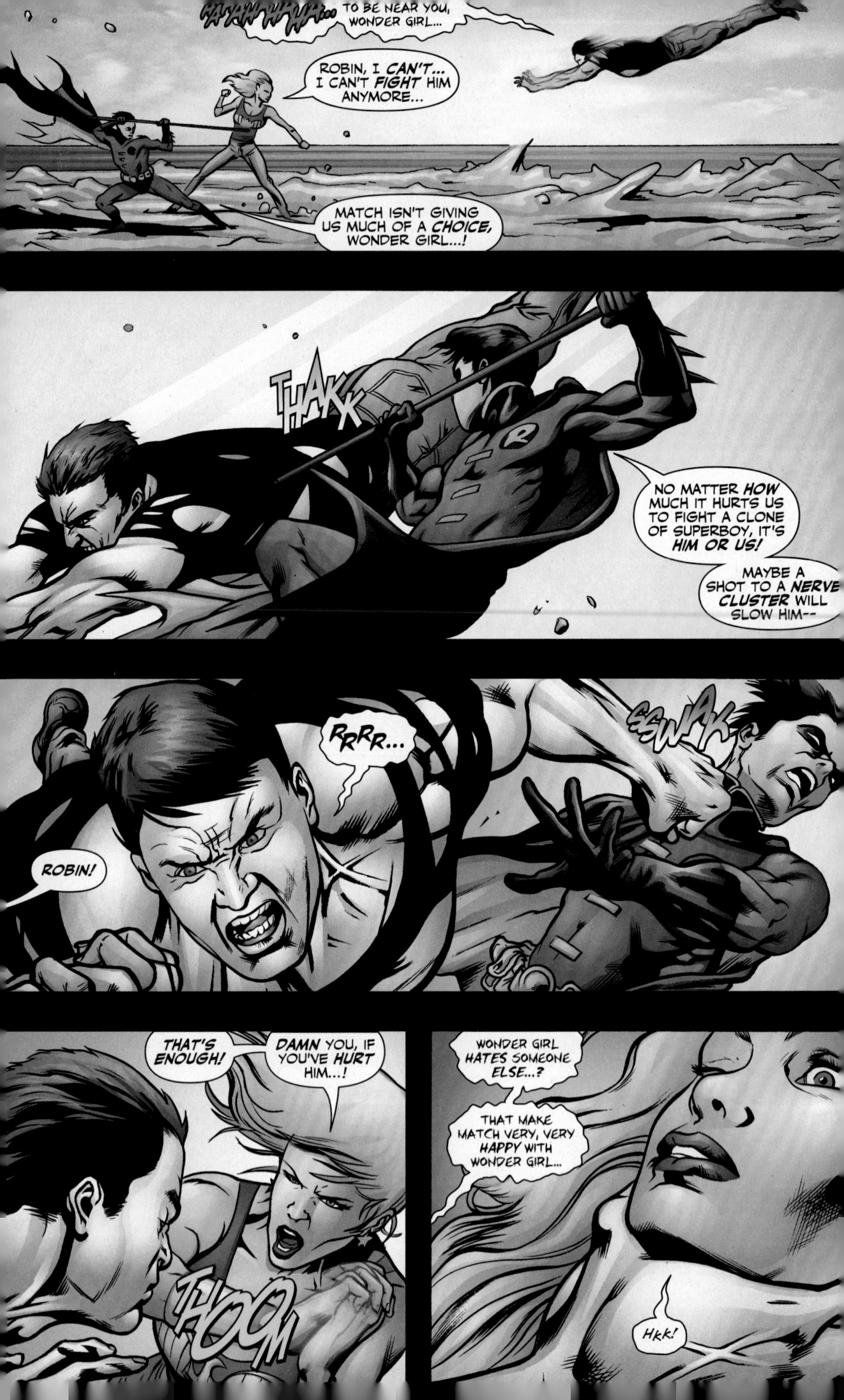
HA HA HA HA... TO BE NEAR YOU, WONDER GIRL...
ROBIN, I CAN'T... I CAN'T FIGHT HIM ANYMORE...
MATCH ISN'T GIVING US MUCH OF A CHOICE, WONDER GIRL...!
THAKK
NO MATTER HOW MUCH IT HURTS US TO FIGHT A CLONE OF SUPERBOY, IT'S HIM OR US!
MAYBE A SHOT TO A NERVE CLUSTER WILL SLOW HIM--
RRRR...
SSWAK
ROBIN!
THAT'S ENOUGH!
DAMN YOU, IF YOU'VE HURT HIM...!
THOOM
WONDER GIRL HATES SOMEONE ELSE...?
THAT MAKE MATCH VERY, VERY HAPPY WITH WONDER GIRL...
Hkk!

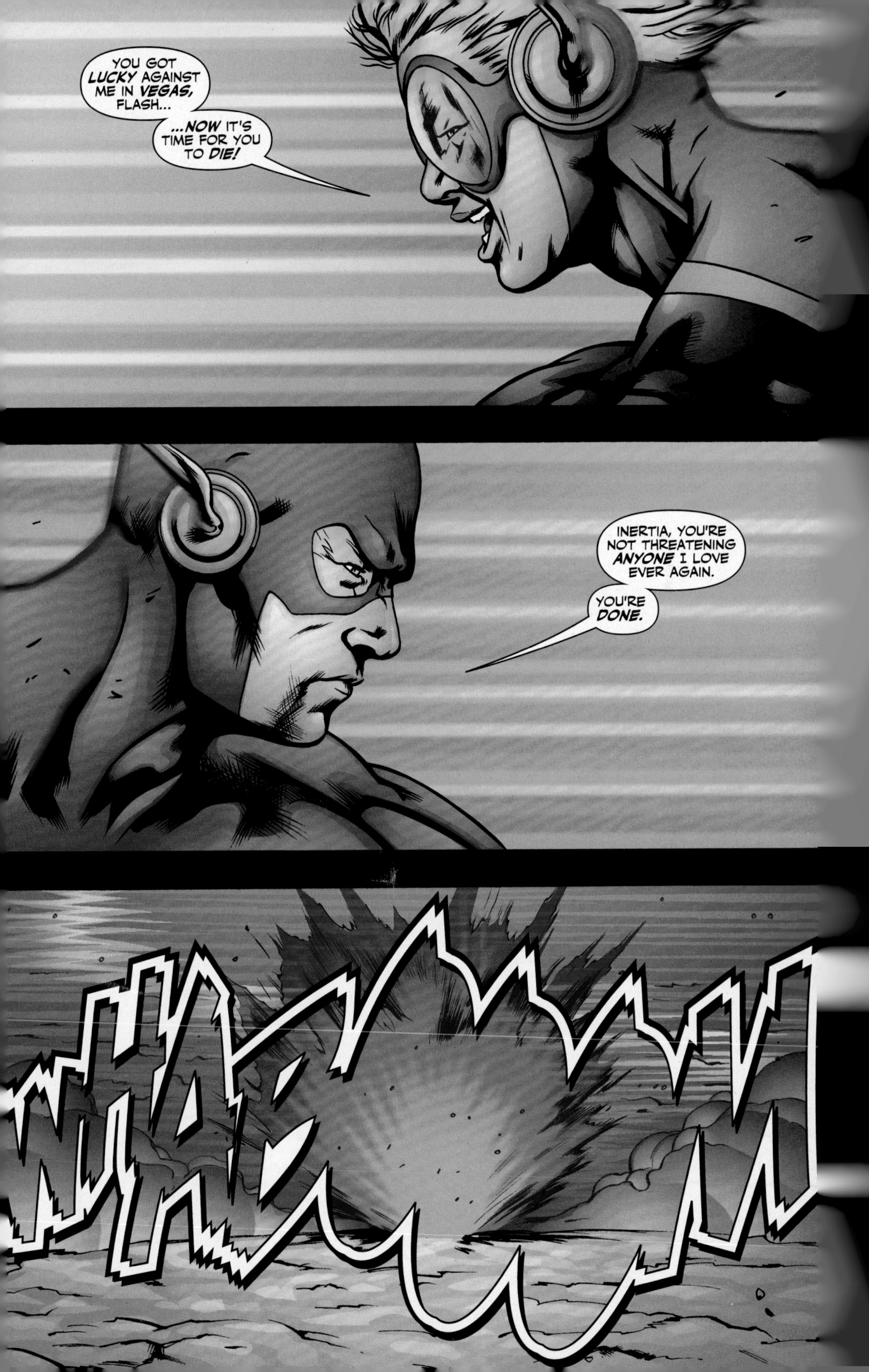
YOU GOT LUCKY AGAINST ME IN VEGAS, FLASH...
...NOW IT'S TIME FOR YOU TO DIE!
INERTIA, YOU'RE NOT THREATENING ANYONE I LOVE EVER AGAIN.
YOU'RE DONE.
WHAM

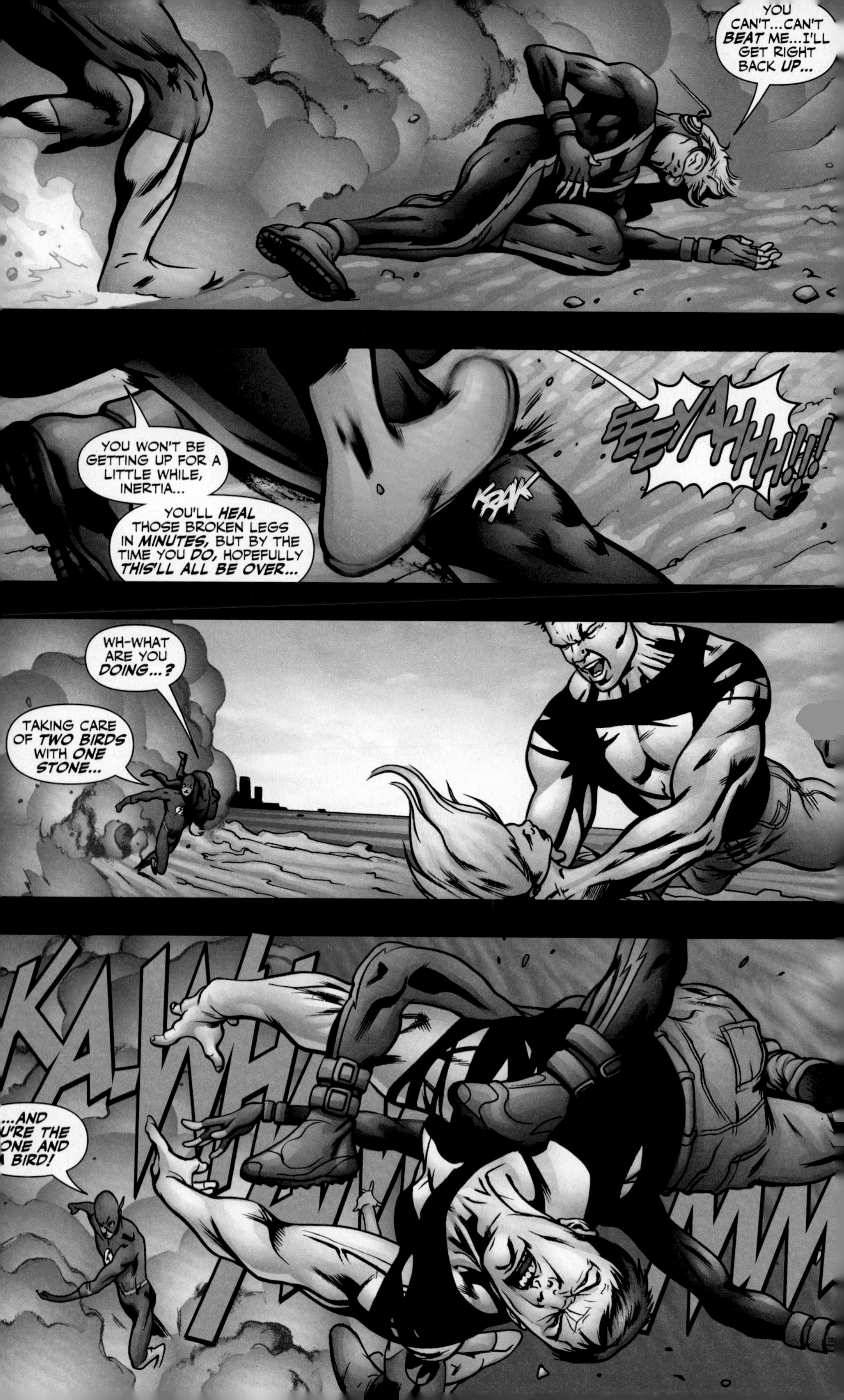

YOU CAN'T...CAN'T BEAT ME...I'LL GET RIGHT BACK UP...
YOU WON'T BE GETTING UP FOR A LITTLE WHILE, INERTIA...
YOU'LL HEAL THOSE BROKEN LEGS IN MINUTES, BUT BY THE TIME YOU DO, HOPEFULLY THIS'LL ALL BE OVER...
KRAK
EEEEYAHHH!!!!
WH-WHAT ARE YOU DOING...?
TAKING CARE OF TWO BIRDS WITH ONE STONE...
...AND U'RE THE ONE AND A BIRD!

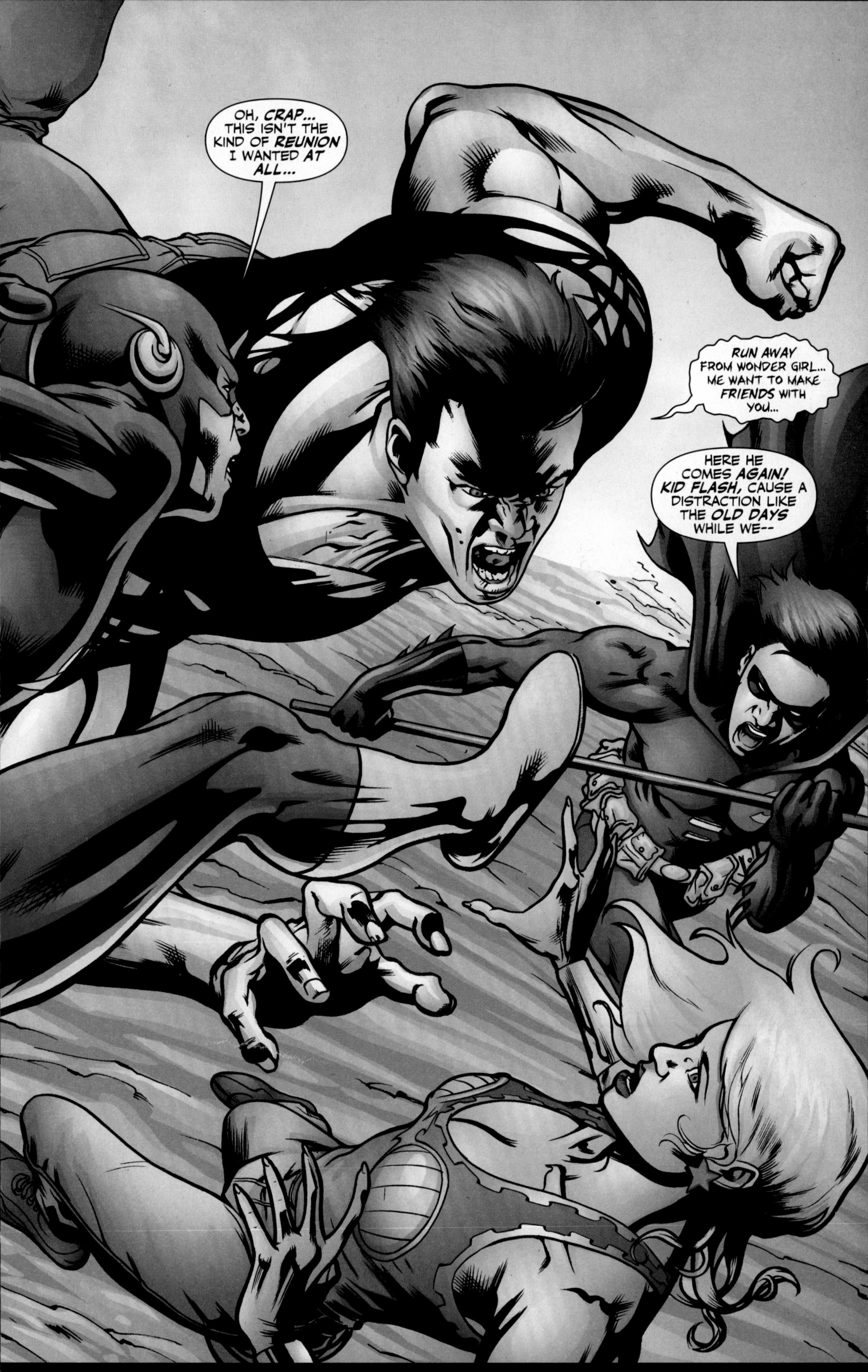
OH, CRAP... THIS ISN'T THE KIND OF REUNION I WANTED AT ALL...
RUN AWAY FROM WONDER GIRL... ME WANT TO MAKE FRIENDS WITH YOU...
HERE HE COMES AGAIN! KID FLASH, CAUSE A DISTRACTION LIKE THE OLD DAYS WHILE WE--

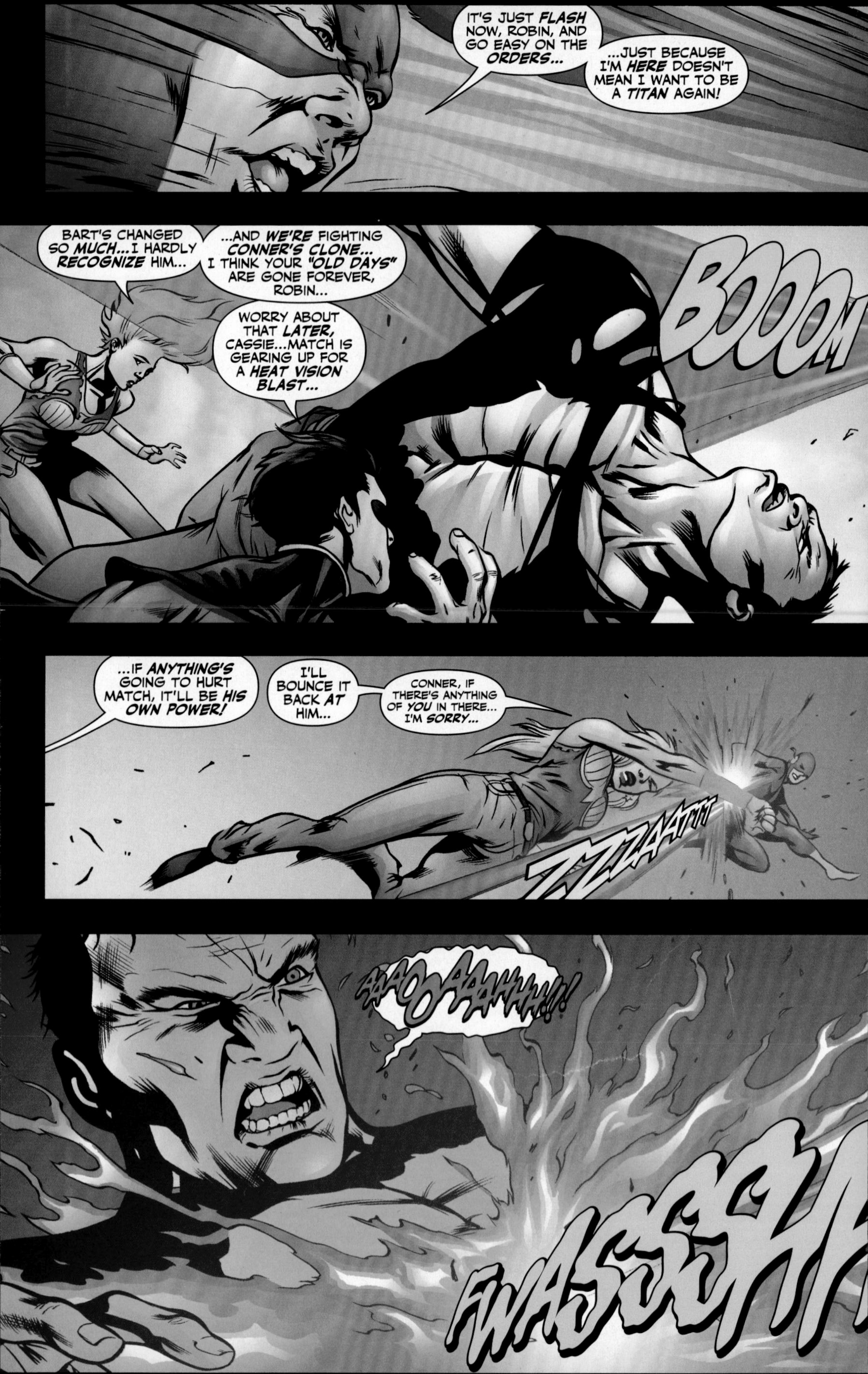
IT'S JUST FLASH NOW, ROBIN, AND GO EASY ON THE ORDERS...
...JUST BECAUSE I'M HERE DOESN'T MEAN I WANT TO BE A TITAN AGAIN!
BART'S CHANGED SO MUCH...I HARDLY RECOGNIZE HIM...
...AND WE'RE FIGHTING CONNER'S CLONE... I THINK YOUR "OLD DAYS" ARE GONE FOREVER, ROBIN...
WORRY ABOUT THAT LATER, CASSIE...MATCH IS GEARING UP FOR A HEAT VISION BLAST...
BOOOM
...IF ANYTHING'S GOING TO HURT MATCH, IT'LL BE HIS OWN POWER!
I'LL BOUNCE IT BACK AT HIM...
CONNER, IF THERE'S ANYTHING OF YOU IN THERE... I'M SORRY...
ZZZAATTT
AAAOOAAAHHH!!!
FWASSSH

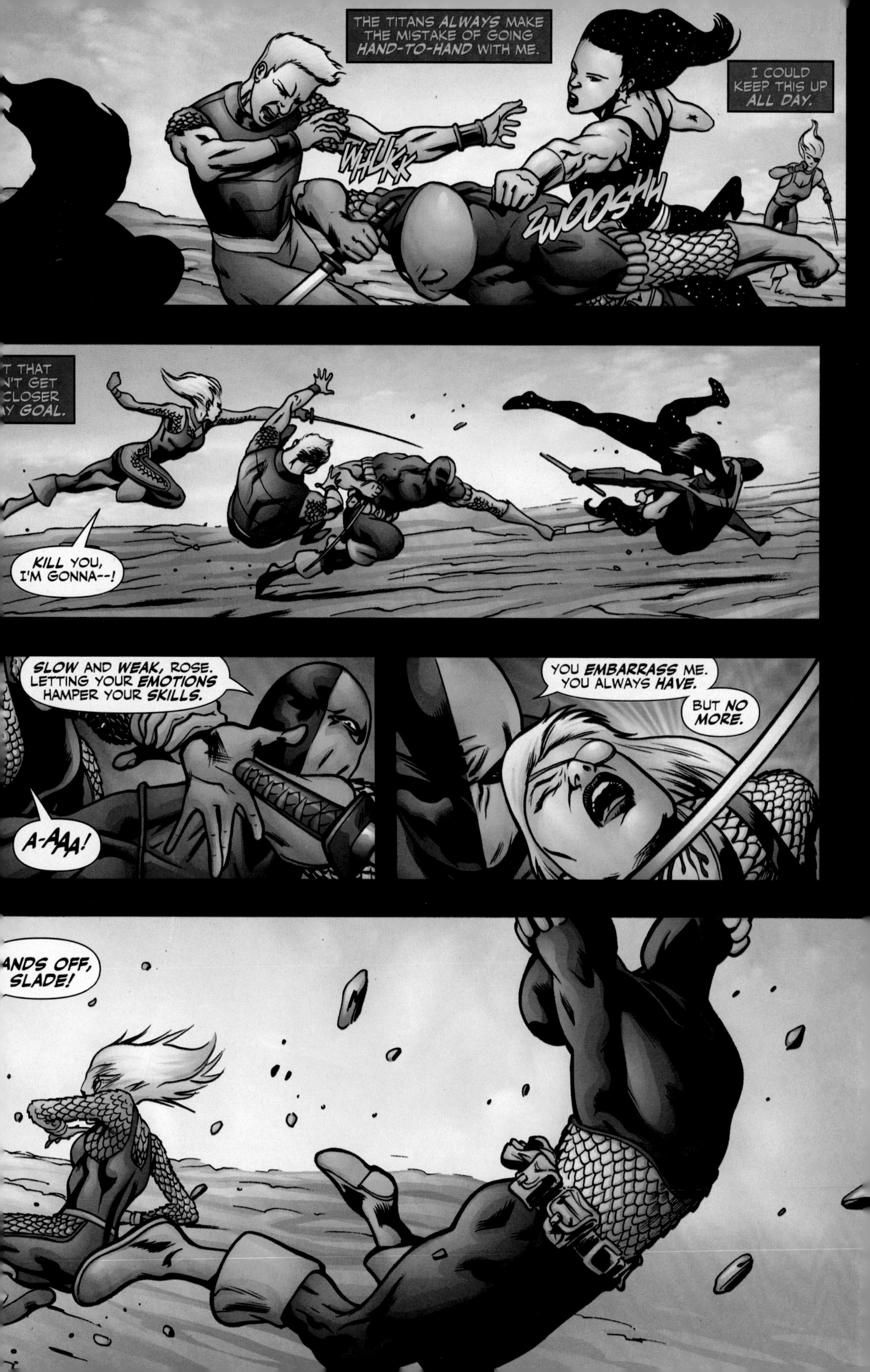
THE TITANS ALWAYS MAKE THE MISTAKE OF GOING HAND-TO-HAND WITH ME.
I COULD KEEP THIS UP ALL DAY.
WHUKK
ZWOOSHH
T THAT
N'T GET
CLOSER
Y GOAL.
KILL YOU, I'M GONNA--!
SLOW AND WEAK, ROSE. LETTING YOUR EMOTIONS HAMPER YOUR SKILLS.
A-AAA!
YOU EMBARRASS ME. YOU ALWAYS HAVE.
BUT NO MORE.
ANDS OFF, SLADE!

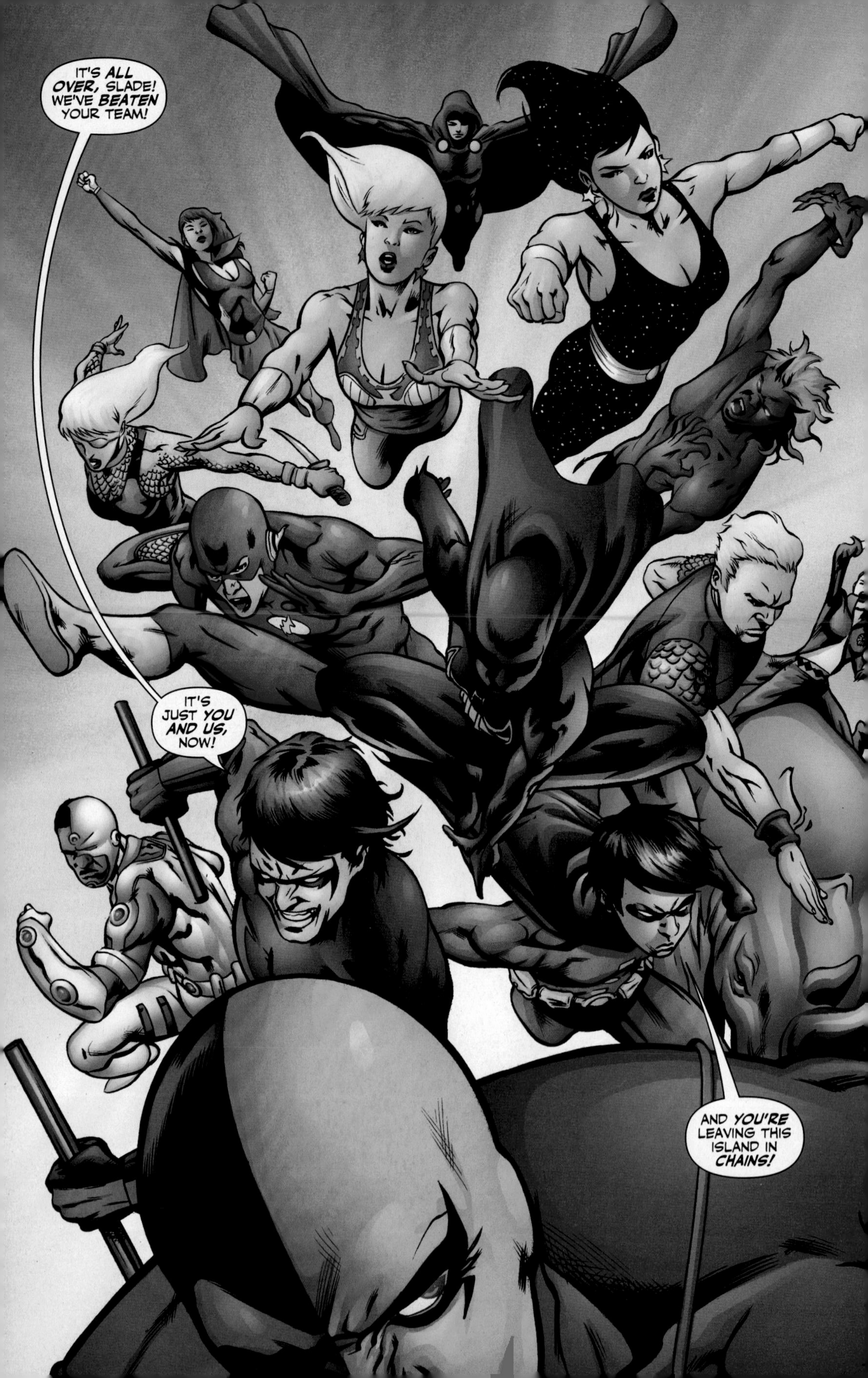
IT'S ALL OVER, SLADE! WE'VE BEATEN YOUR TEAM!
IT'S JUST YOU AND US, NOW!
AND YOU'RE LEAVING THIS ISLAND IN CHAINS!

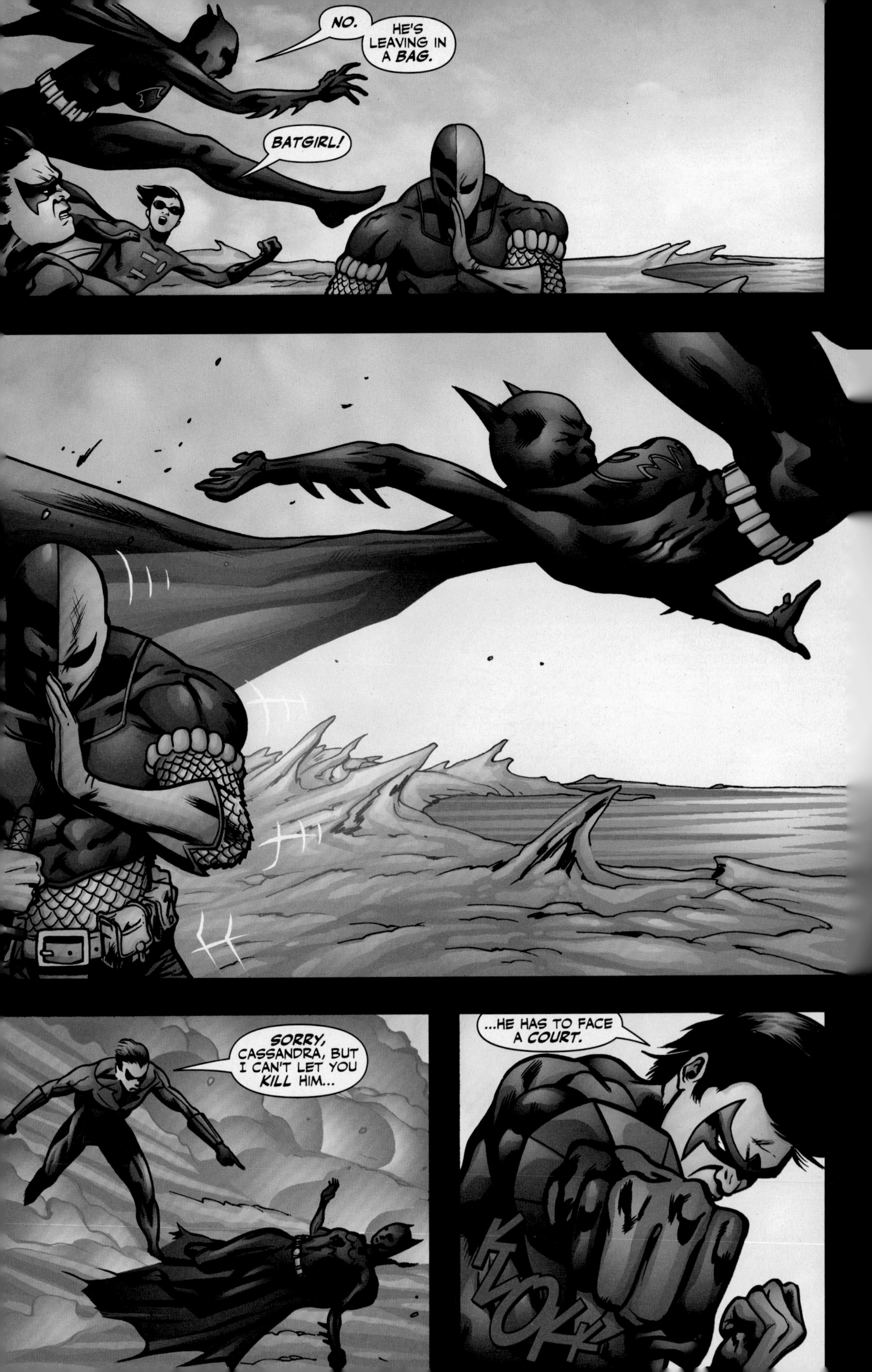
NO.
HE'S LEAVING IN A BAG.
BATGIRL!
SORRY, CASSANDRA, BUT I CAN'T LET YOU KILL HIM...
...HE HAS TO FACE A COURT.
KNOK!

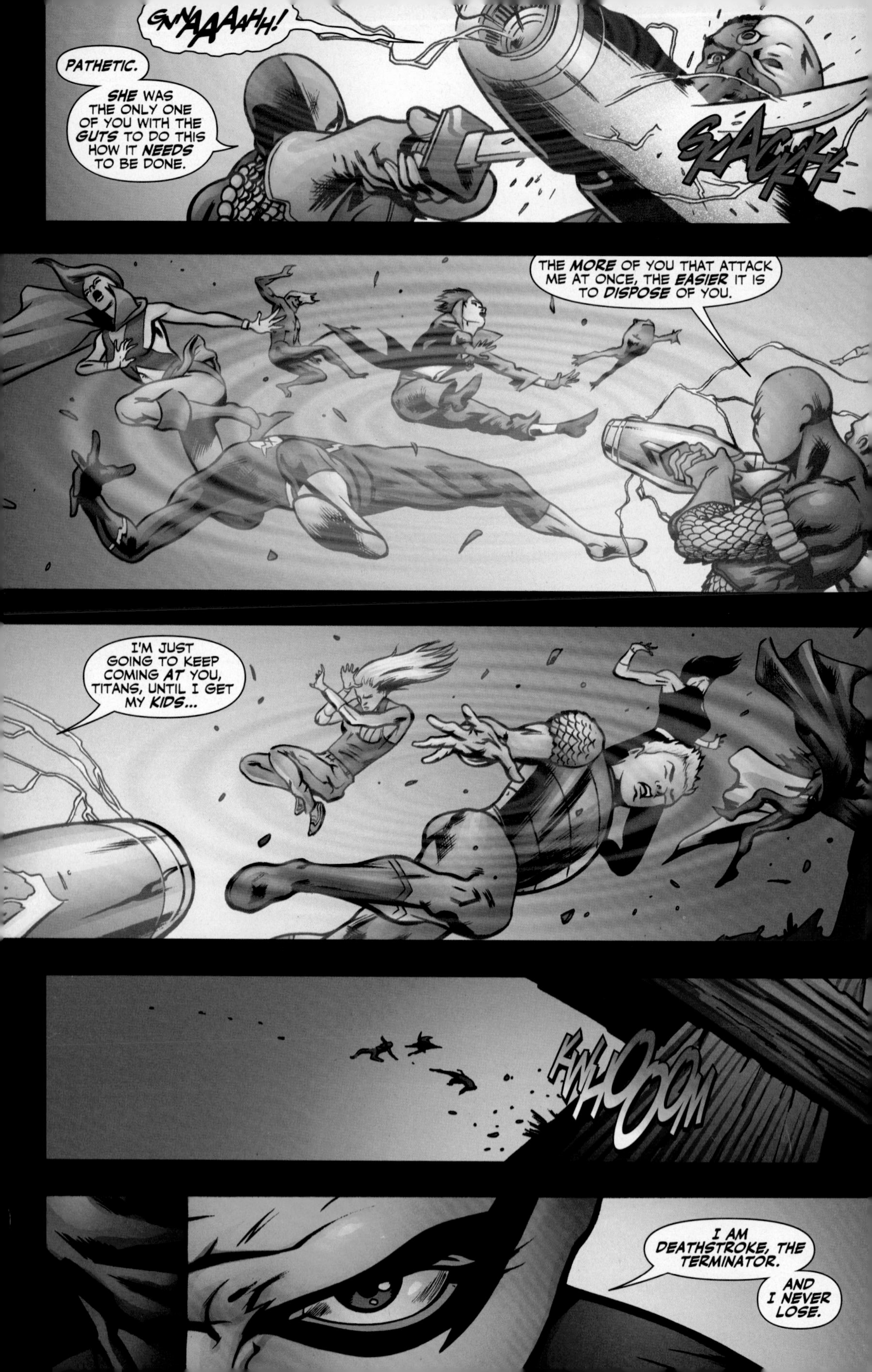
GNYAAAAHH!
PATHETIC.
SHE WAS THE ONLY ONE OF YOU WITH THE GUTS TO DO THIS HOW IT NEEDS TO BE DONE.
SKLACKKK
THE MORE OF YOU THAT ATTACK ME AT ONCE, THE EASIER IT IS TO DISPOSE OF YOU.
I'M JUST GOING TO KEEP COMING AT YOU, TITANS, UNTIL I GET MY KIDS...
KWHOOOM
I AM DEATHSTROKE, THE TERMINATOR.
AND I NEVER LOSE.

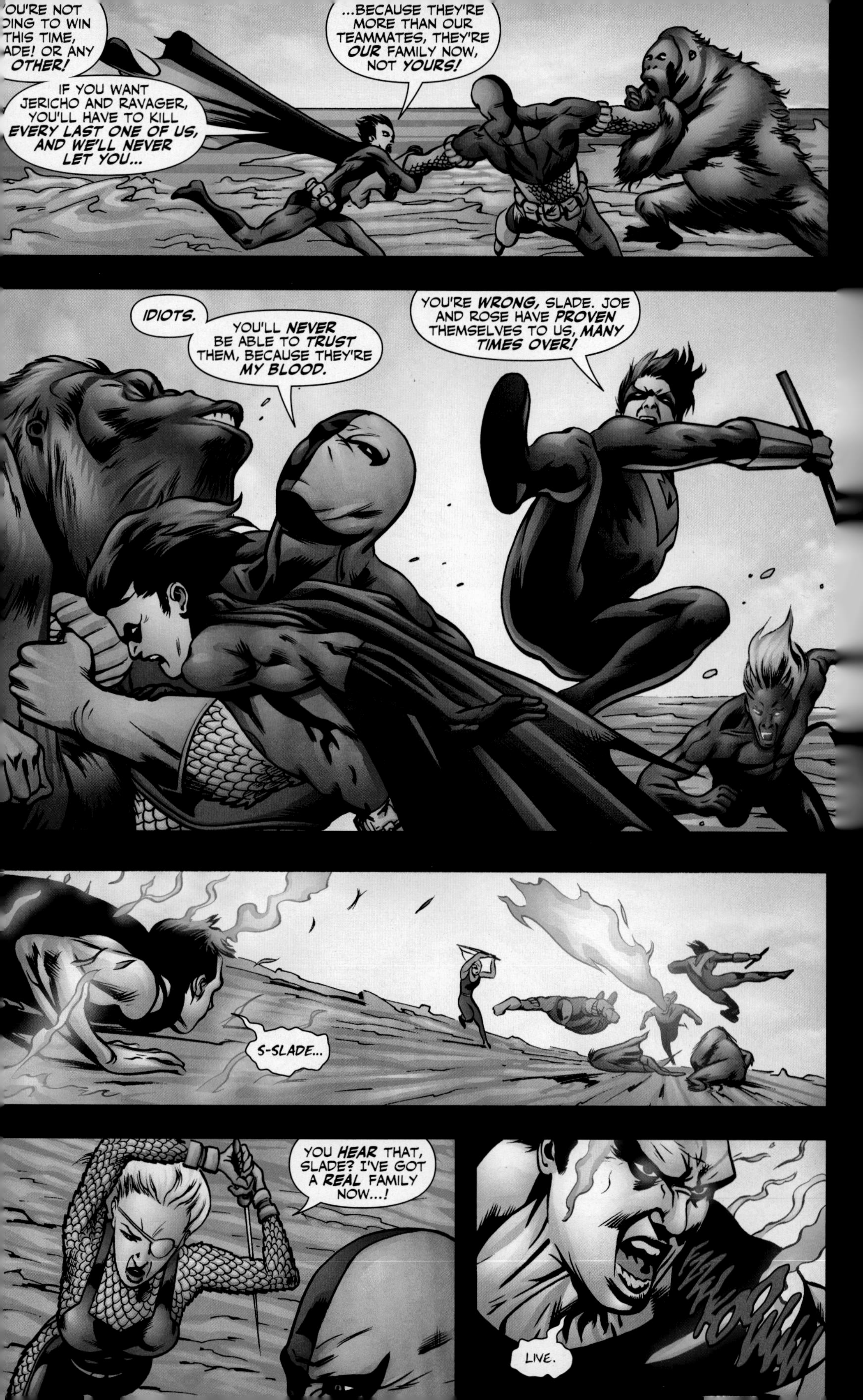

OU'RE NOT
OING TO WIN
THIS TIME,
ADE! OR ANY
OTHER!
IF YOU WANT JERICHO AND RAVAGER, YOU'LL HAVE TO KILL EVERY LAST ONE OF US, AND WE'LL NEVER LET YOU...
...BECAUSE THEY'RE MORE THAN OUR TEAMMATES, THEY'RE OUR FAMILY NOW, NOT YOURS!
IDIOTS.
YOU'LL NEVER BE ABLE TO TRUST THEM, BECAUSE THEY'RE MY BLOOD.
YOU'RE WRONG, SLADE. JOE AND ROSE HAVE PROVEN THEMSELVES TO US, MANY TIMES OVER!
S-SLADE...
YOU HEAR THAT, SLADE? I'VE GOT A REAL FAMILY NOW...!
LIVE.

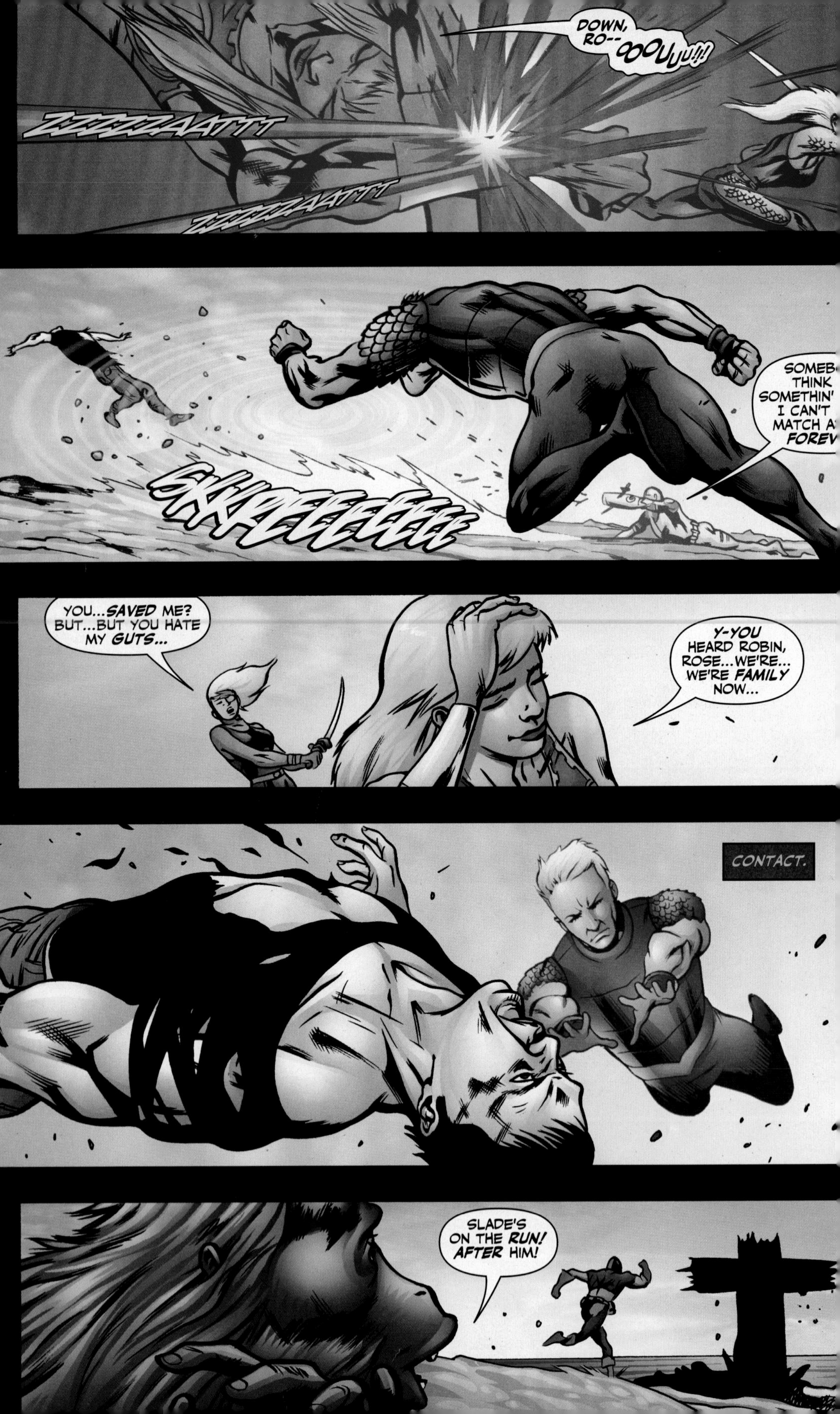
DOWN, RO-- OOOUUU!!!
ZZZZZAATTT
ZZZZZAATTT
SOMEB THINK SOMETHIN' I CAN'T MATCH A FOREV
YOU...SAVED ME? BUT...BUT YOU HATE MY GUTS...
Y-YOU HEARD ROBIN, ROSE...WE'RE... WE'RE FAMILY NOW...
CONTACT.
SLADE'S ON THE RUN! AFTER HIM!

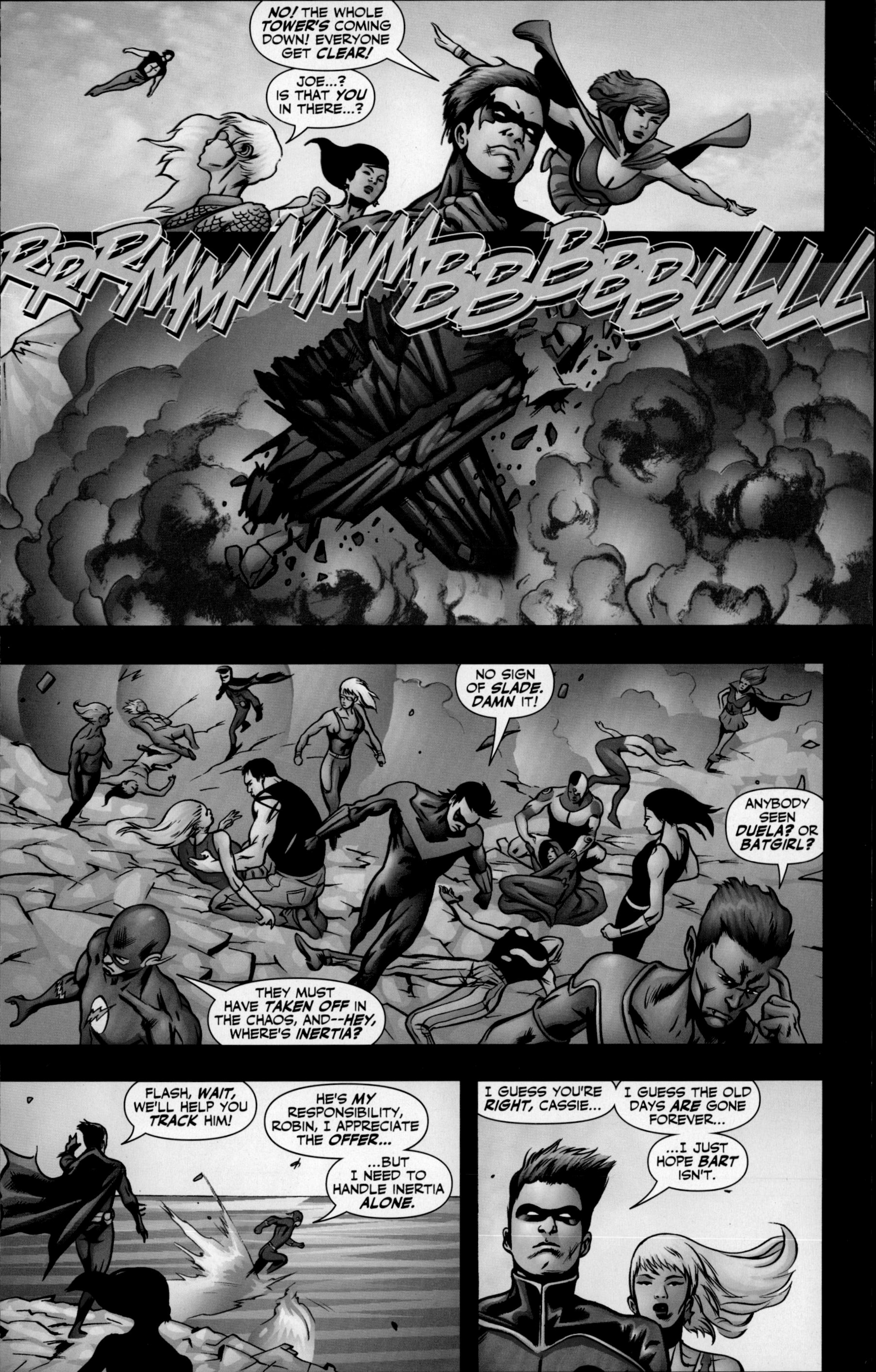
NO! THE WHOLE TOWER'S COMING DOWN! EVERYONE GET CLEAR!
JOE...? IS THAT YOU IN THERE...?
RRRMMMMMMBBBBBBLLL
NO SIGN OF SLADE. DAMN IT!
ANYBODY SEEN DUELA? OR BATGIRL?
THEY MUST HAVE TAKEN OFF IN THE CHAOS, AND--HEY, WHERE'S INERTIA?
FLASH, WAIT, WE'LL HELP YOU TRACK HIM!
HE'S MY RESPONSIBILITY, ROBIN, I APPRECIATE THE OFFER...
...BUT I NEED TO HANDLE INERTIA ALONE.
I GUESS YOU'RE RIGHT, CASSIE...
I GUESS THE OLD DAYS ARE GONE FOREVER...
...I JUST HOPE BART ISN'T.

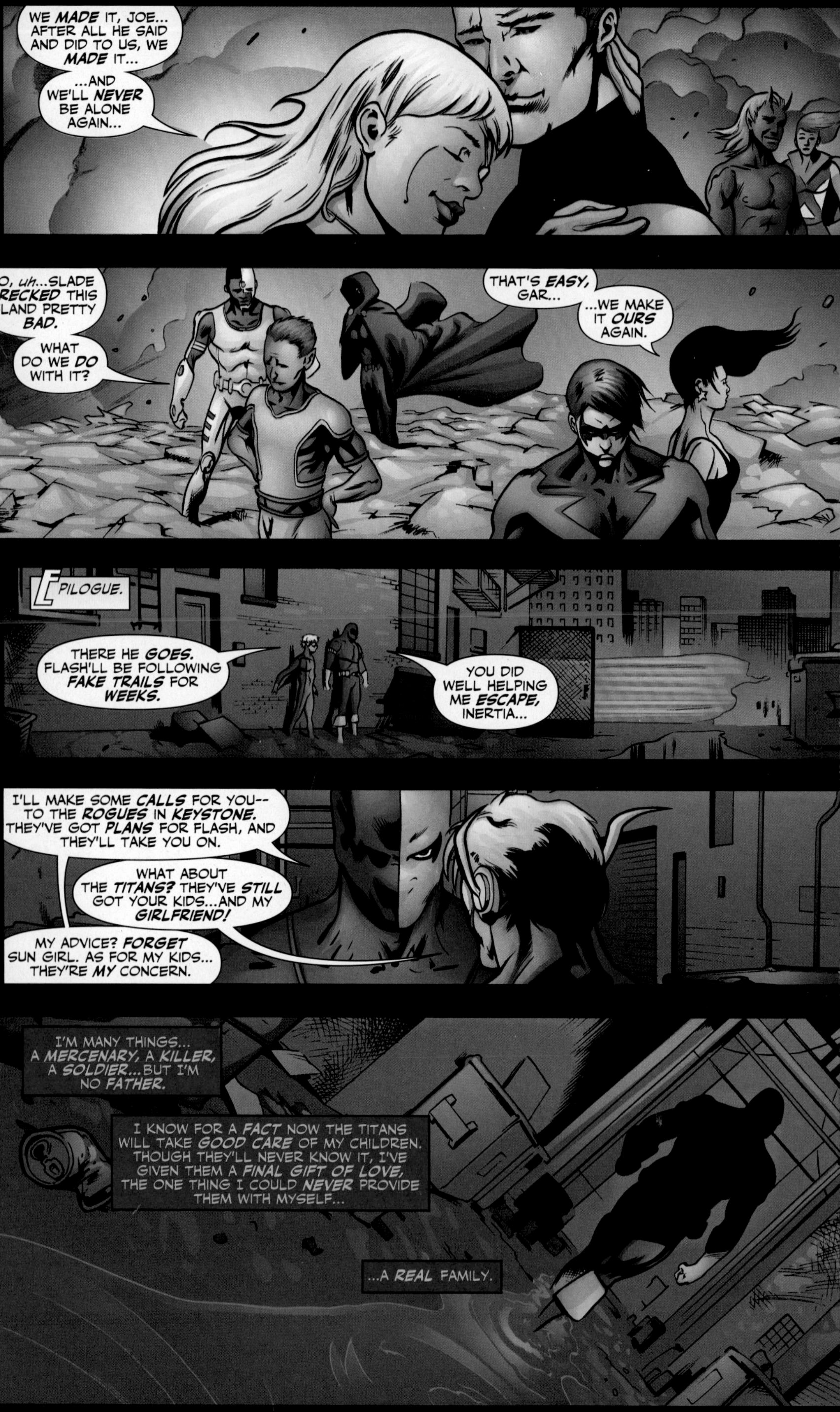

WE MADE IT, JOE... AFTER ALL HE SAID AND DID TO US, WE MADE IT...
...AND WE'LL NEVER BE ALONE AGAIN...
SO, uh...SLADE WRECKED THIS ISLAND PRETTY BAD.
WHAT DO WE DO WITH IT?
THAT'S EASY, GAR...
...WE MAKE IT OURS AGAIN.
EPILOGUE.
THERE HE GOES. FLASH'LL BE FOLLOWING FAKE TRAILS FOR WEEKS.
YOU DID WELL HELPING ME ESCAPE, INERTIA...
I'LL MAKE SOME CALLS FOR YOU-- TO THE ROGUES IN KEYSTONE. THEY'VE GOT PLANS FOR FLASH, AND THEY'LL TAKE YOU ON.
WHAT ABOUT THE TITANS? THEY'VE STILL GOT YOUR KIDS...AND MY GIRLFRIEND!
MY ADVICE? FORGET SUN GIRL. AS FOR MY KIDS... THEY'RE MY CONCERN.
I'M MANY THINGS... A MERCENARY, A KILLER, A SOLDIER...BUT I'M NO FATHER.
I KNOW FOR A FACT NOW THE TITANS WILL TAKE GOOD CARE OF MY CHILDREN. THOUGH THEY'LL NEVER KNOW IT, I'VE GIVEN THEM A FINAL GIFT OF LOVE, THE ONE THING I COULD NEVER PROVIDE THEM WITH MYSELF...
...A REAL FAMILY.

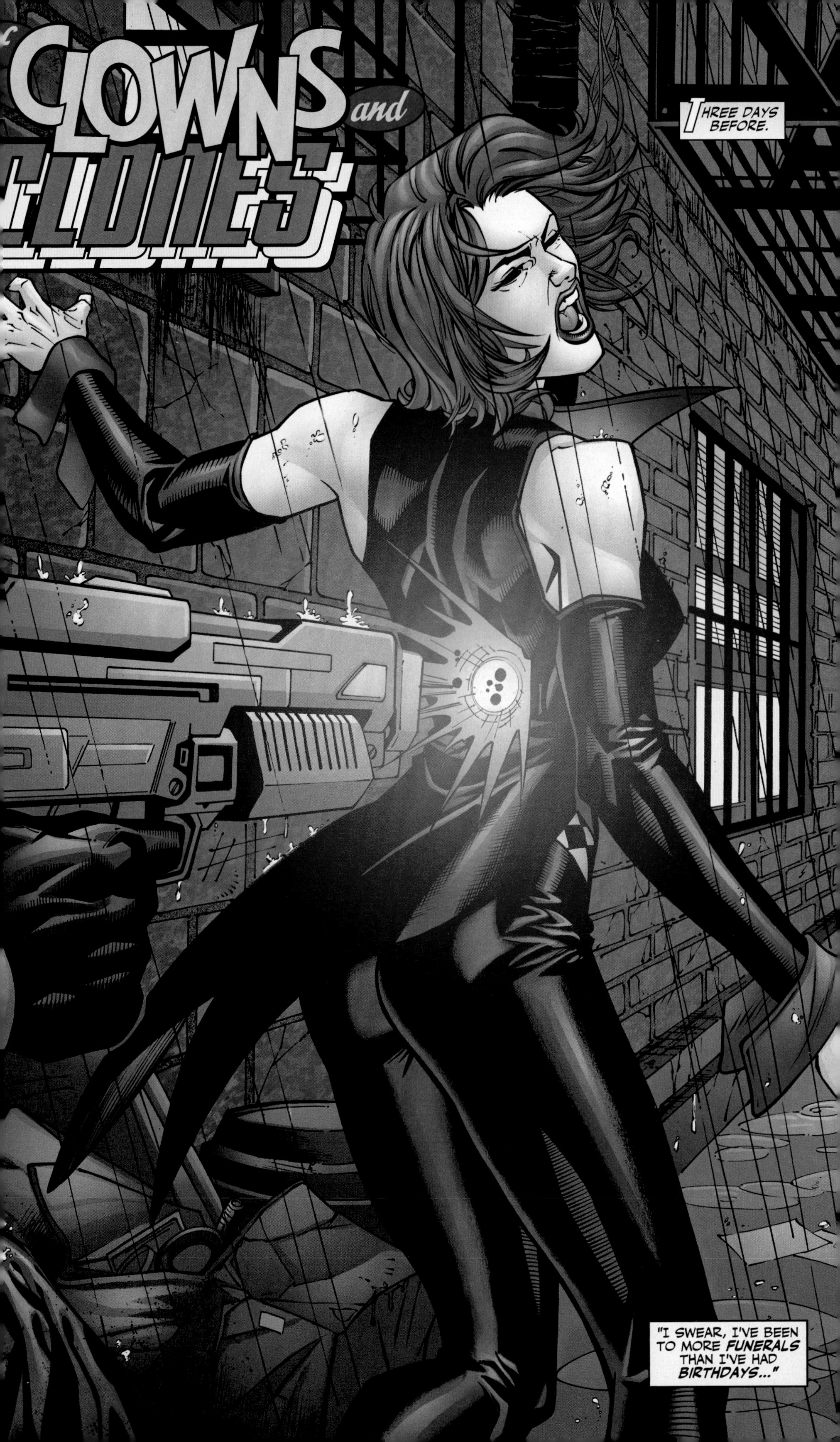
CLOWNS and
THREE DAYS BEFORE.
"I SWEAR, I'VE BEEN TO MORE FUNERALS THAN I'VE HAD BIRTHDAYS..."

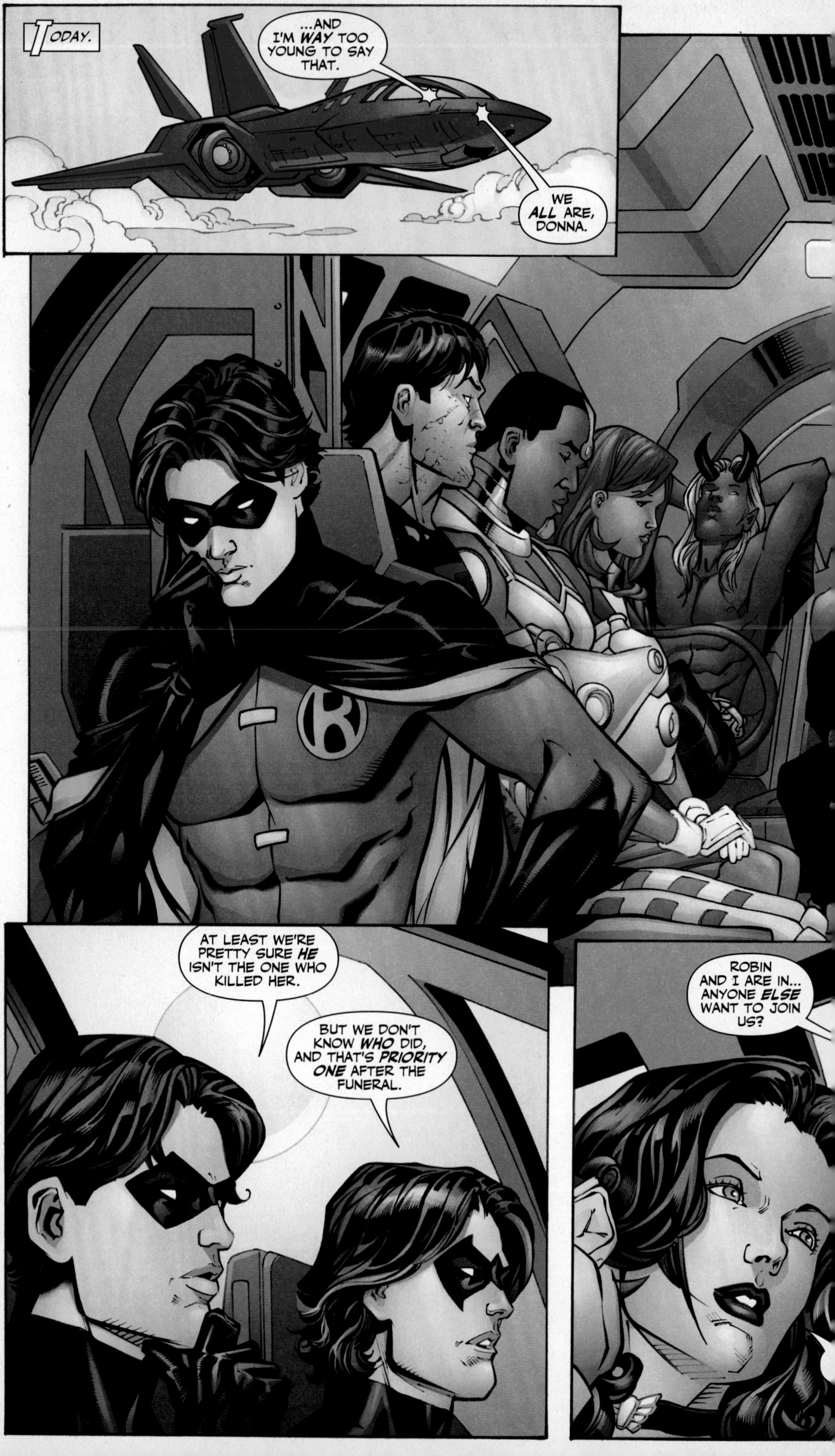
TODAY.
...AND I'M WAY TOO YOUNG TO SAY THAT.
WE ALL ARE, DONNA.
AT LEAST WE'RE PRETTY SURE HE ISN'T THE ONE WHO KILLED HER.
BUT WE DON'T KNOW WHO DID, AND THAT'S PRIORITY ONE AFTER THE FUNERAL.
ROBIN AND I ARE IN... ANYONE ELSE WANT TO JOIN US?

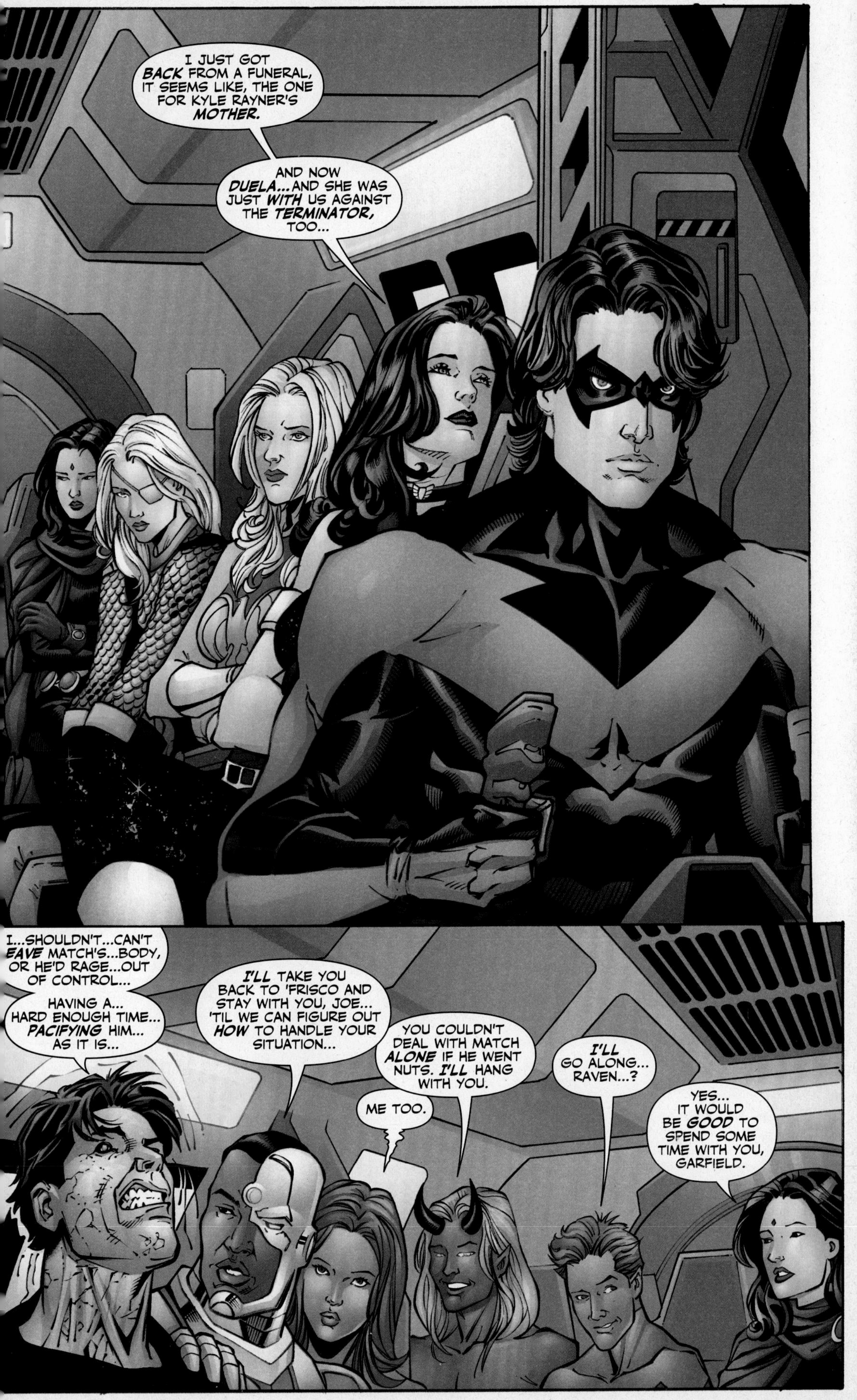
I JUST GOT BACK FROM A FUNERAL, IT SEEMS LIKE, THE ONE FOR KYLE RAYNER'S MOTHER.
AND NOW DUELA...AND SHE WAS JUST WITH US AGAINST THE TERMINATOR, TOO...
I...SHOULDN'T...CAN'T EAVE MATCH'S...BODY, OR HE'D RAGE...OUT OF CONTROL...
HAVING A... HARD ENOUGH TIME... PACIFYING HIM... AS IT IS...
I'LL TAKE YOU BACK TO 'FRISCO AND STAY WITH YOU, JOE... 'TIL WE CAN FIGURE OUT HOW TO HANDLE YOUR SITUATION...
ME TOO.
YOU COULDN'T DEAL WITH MATCH ALONE IF HE WENT NUTS. I'LL HANG WITH YOU.
I'LL GO ALONG... RAVEN...?
YES... IT WOULD BE GOOD TO SPEND SOME TIME WITH YOU, GARFIELD.

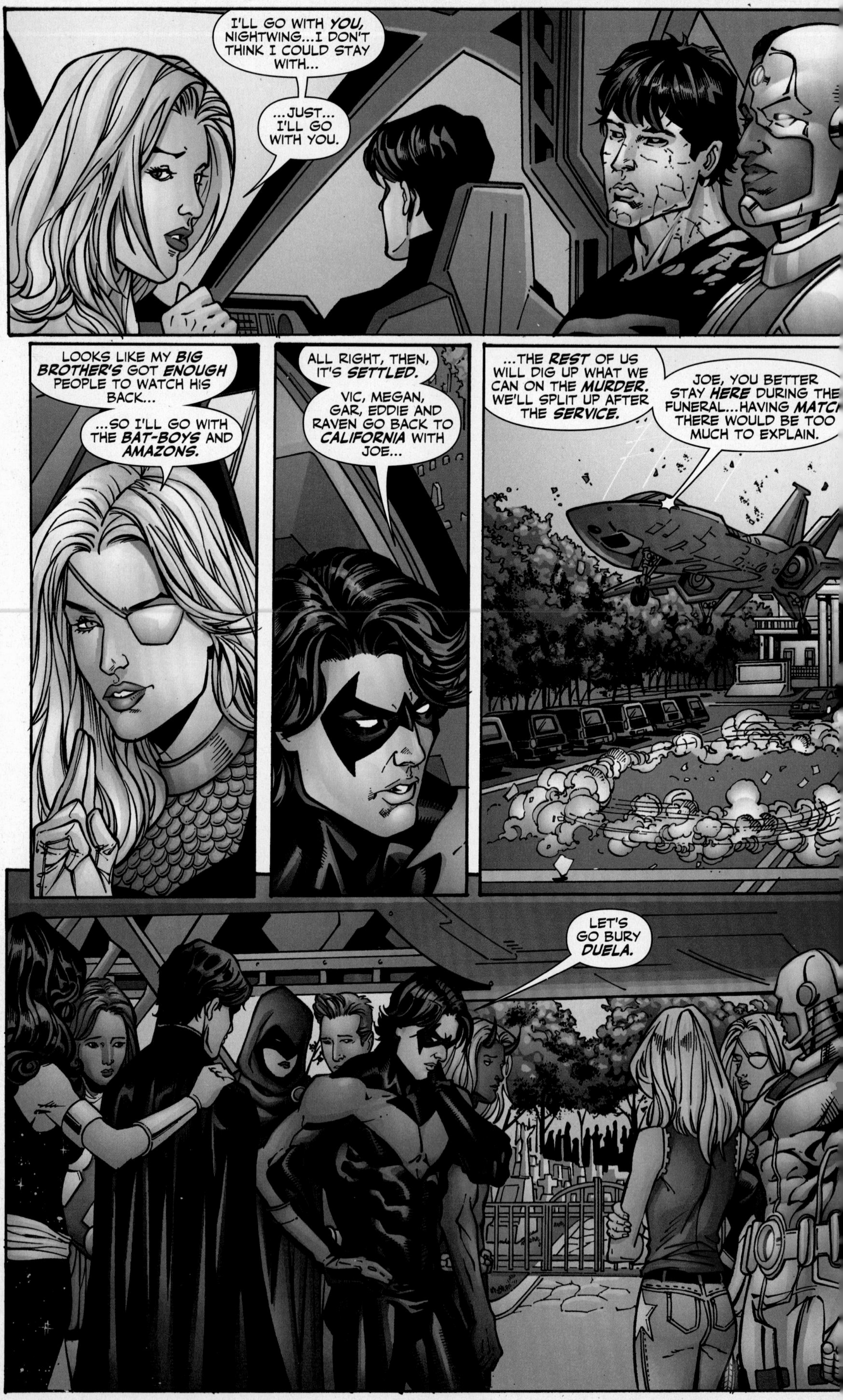
I'LL GO WITH YOU, NIGHTWING...I DON'T THINK I COULD STAY WITH...
...JUST... I'LL GO WITH YOU.
LOOKS LIKE MY BIG BROTHER'S GOT ENOUGH PEOPLE TO WATCH HIS BACK...
...SO I'LL GO WITH THE BAT-BOYS AND AMAZONS.
ALL RIGHT, THEN, IT'S SETTLED.
VIC, MEGAN, GAR, EDDIE AND RAVEN GO BACK TO CALIFORNIA WITH JOE...
...THE REST OF US WILL DIG UP WHAT WE CAN ON THE MURDER. WE'LL SPLIT UP AFTER THE SERVICE.
JOE, YOU BETTER STAY HERE DURING THE FUNERAL...HAVING MATCH THERE WOULD BE TOO MUCH TO EXPLAIN.
LET'S GO BURY DUELA.

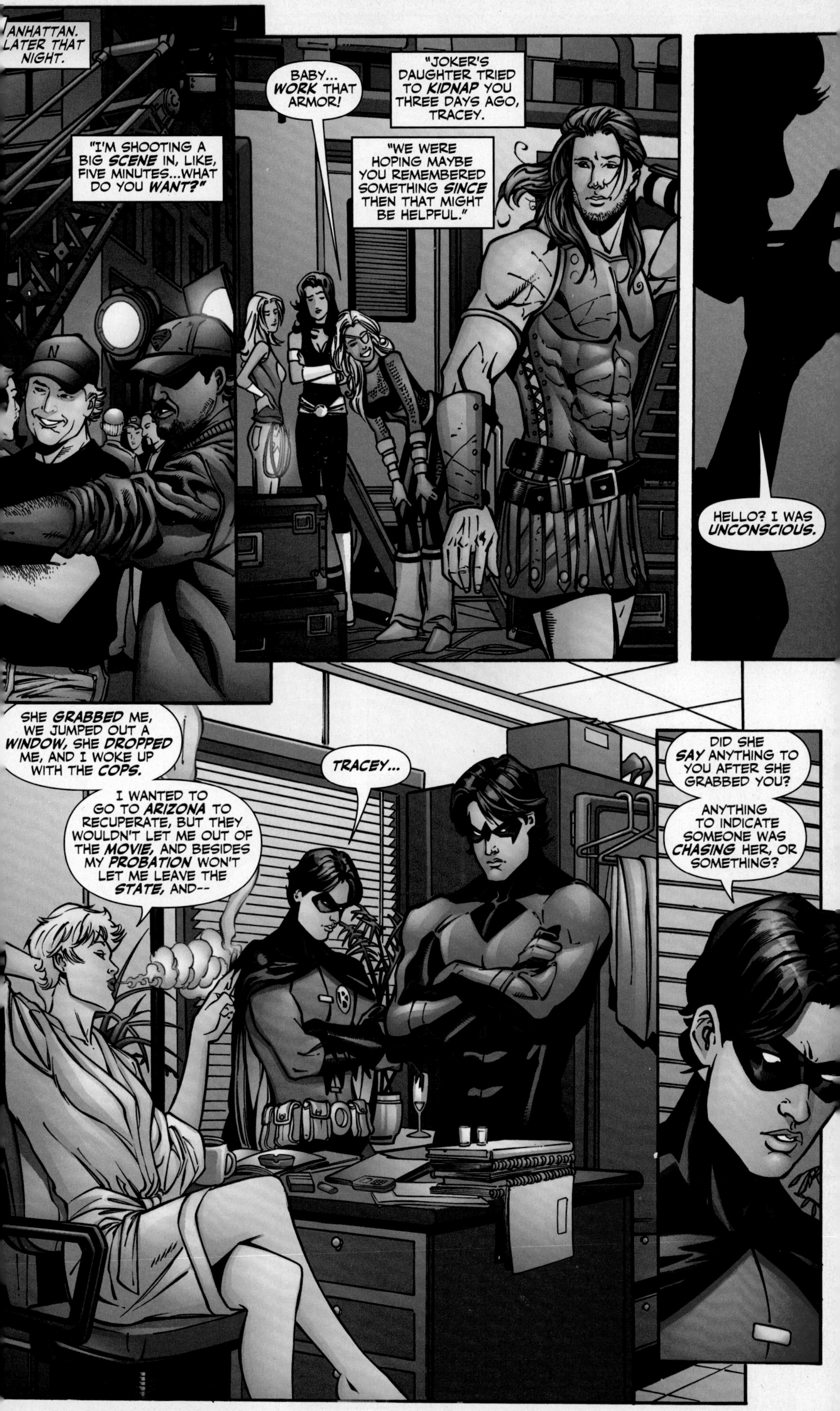
ANHATTAN. LATER THAT NIGHT.
"I'M SHOOTING A BIG SCENE IN, LIKE, FIVE MINUTES...WHAT DO YOU WANT?"
BABY... WORK THAT ARMOR!
"JOKER'S DAUGHTER TRIED TO KIDNAP YOU THREE DAYS AGO, TRACEY.
"WE WERE HOPING MAYBE YOU REMEMBERED SOMETHING SINCE THEN THAT MIGHT BE HELPFUL."
HELLO? I WAS UNCONSCIOUS.
SHE GRABBED ME, WE JUMPED OUT A WINDOW, SHE DROPPED ME, AND I WOKE UP WITH THE COPS.
I WANTED TO GO TO ARIZONA TO RECUPERATE, BUT THEY WOULDN'T LET ME OUT OF THE MOVIE, AND BESIDES MY PROBATION WON'T LET ME LEAVE THE STATE, AND--
TRACEY...
DID SHE SAY ANYTHING TO YOU AFTER SHE GRABBED YOU?
ANYTHING TO INDICATE SOMEONE WAS CHASING HER, OR SOMETHING?

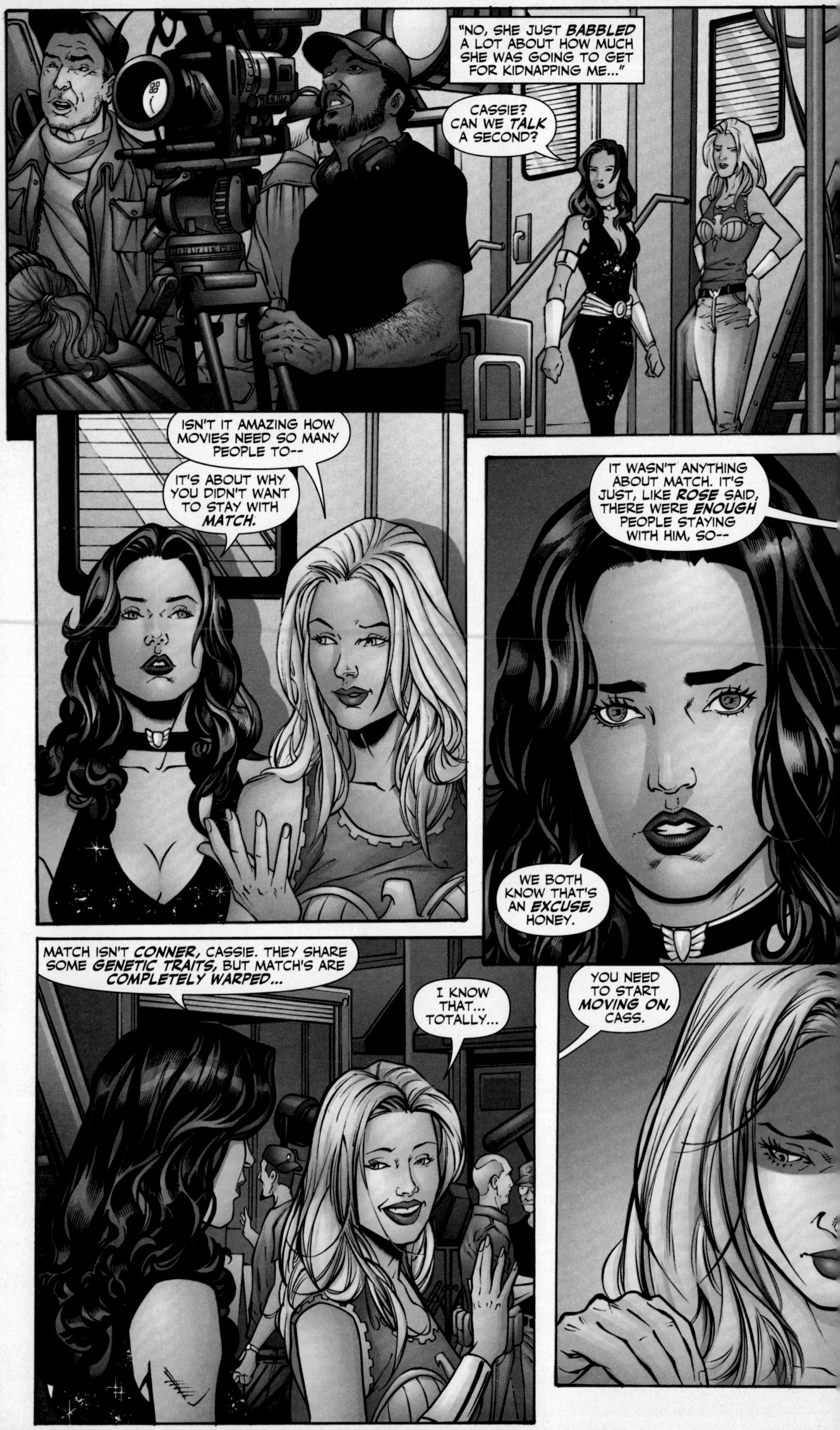
"NO, SHE JUST BABBLED A LOT ABOUT HOW MUCH SHE WAS GOING TO GET FOR KIDNAPPING ME..."
CASSIE? CAN WE TALK A SECOND?
ISN'T IT AMAZING HOW MOVIES NEED SO MANY PEOPLE TO--
IT'S ABOUT WHY YOU DIDN'T WANT TO STAY WITH MATCH.
IT WASN'T ANYTHING ABOUT MATCH. IT'S JUST, LIKE ROSE SAID, THERE WERE ENOUGH PEOPLE STAYING WITH HIM, SO--
WE BOTH KNOW THAT'S AN EXCUSE, HONEY.
MATCH ISN'T CONNER, CASSIE. THEY SHARE SOME GENETIC TRAITS, BUT MATCH'S ARE COMPLETELY WARPED...
I KNOW THAT... TOTALLY...
YOU NEED TO START MOVING ON, CASS.

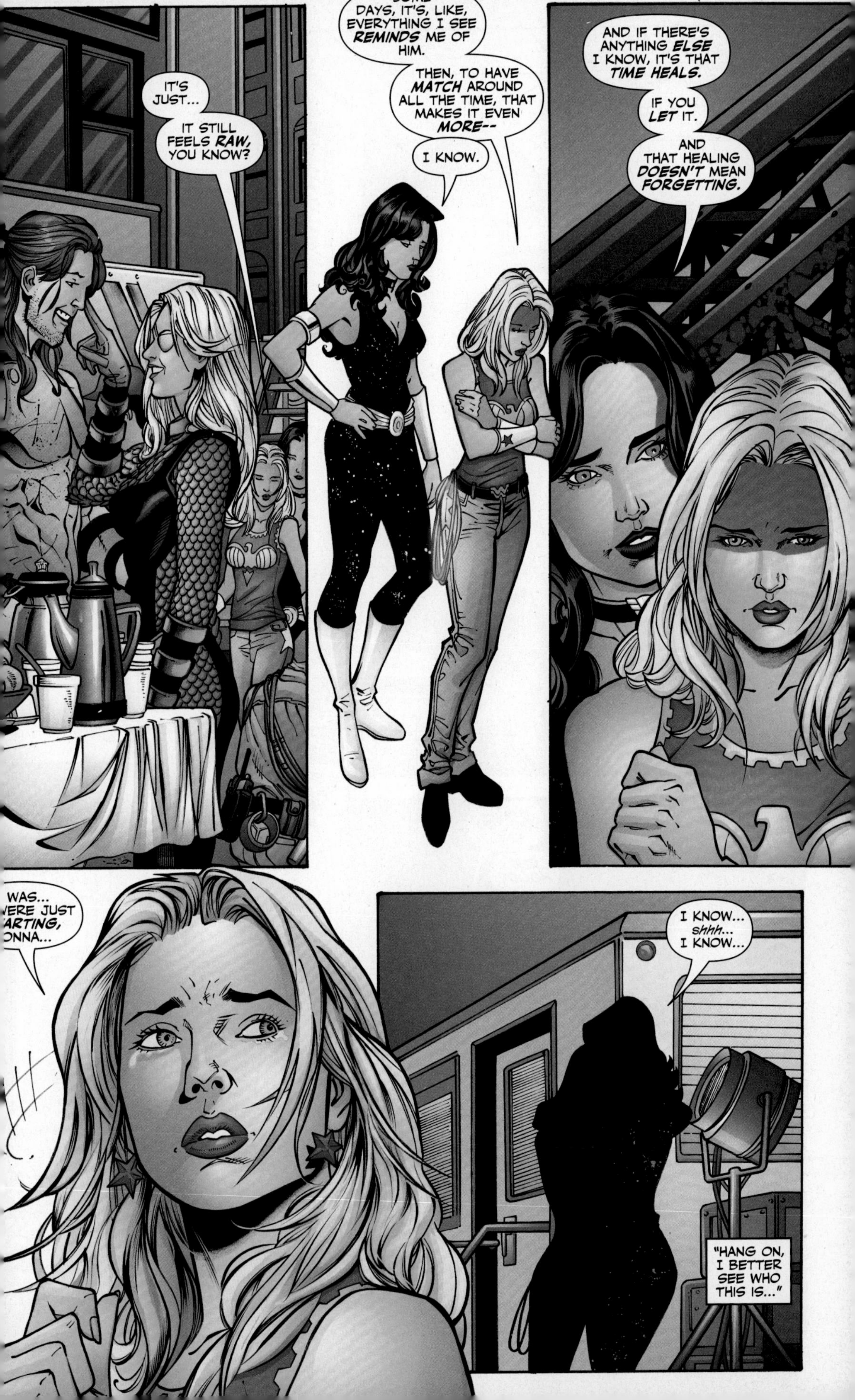
IT'S JUST...
IT STILL FEELS RAW, YOU KNOW?
SOME DAYS, IT'S, LIKE, EVERYTHING I SEE REMINDS ME OF HIM.
THEN, TO HAVE MATCH AROUND ALL THE TIME, THAT MAKES IT EVEN MORE--
I KNOW.
AND IF THERE'S ANYTHING ELSE I KNOW, IT'S THAT TIME HEALS.
IF YOU LET IT.
AND THAT HEALING DOESN'T MEAN FORGETTING.
WAS... WERE JUST ARTING, ONNA...
I KNOW... shhh... I KNOW...
"HANG ON, I BETTER SEE WHO THIS IS..."

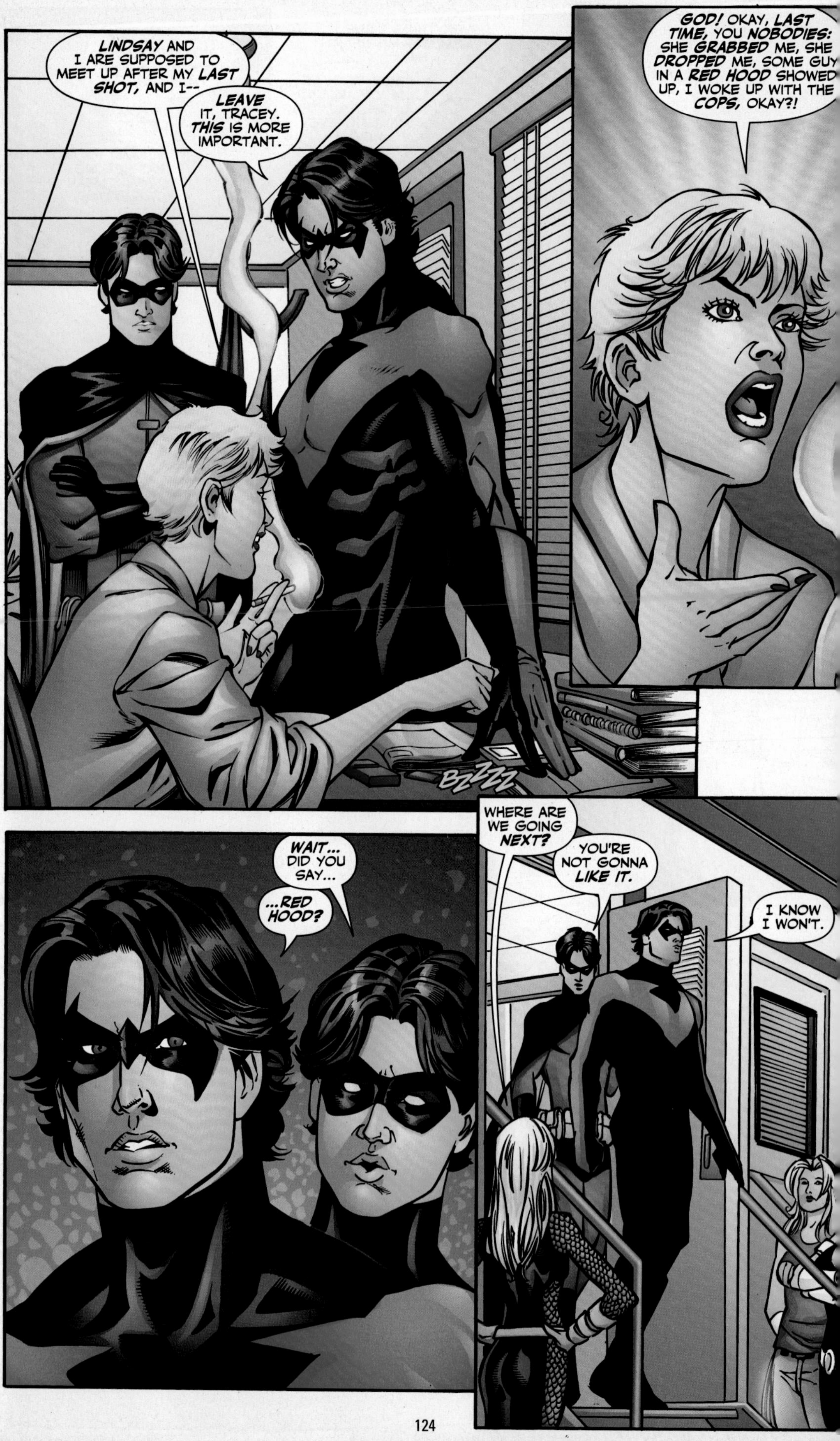

LINDSAY AND I ARE SUPPOSED TO MEET UP AFTER MY LAST SHOT, AND I--
LEAVE IT, TRACEY. THIS IS MORE IMPORTANT.
BZZZZ
GOD! OKAY, LAST TIME, YOU NOBODIES: SHE GRABBED ME, SHE DROPPED ME, SOME GUY IN A RED HOOD SHOWED UP, I WOKE UP WITH THE COPS, OKAY?!
WAIT... DID YOU SAY...
...RED HOOD?
WHERE ARE WE GOING NEXT?
YOU'RE NOT GONNA LIKE IT.
I KNOW I WON'T.

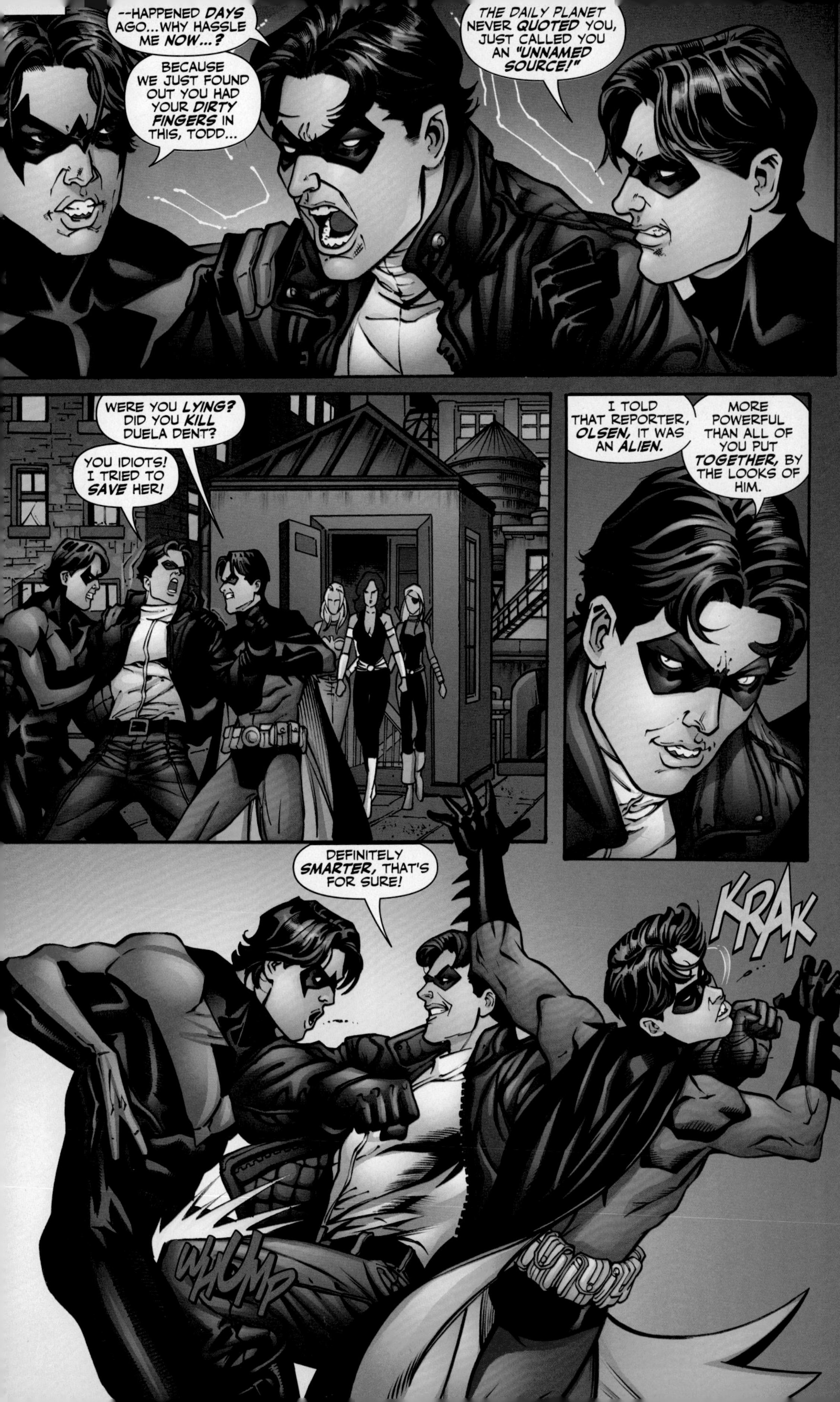
--HAPPENED DAYS AGO...WHY HASSLE ME NOW...?
BECAUSE WE JUST FOUND OUT YOU HAD YOUR DIRTY FINGERS IN THIS, TODD...
THE DAILY PLANET NEVER QUOTED YOU, JUST CALLED YOU AN "UNNAMED SOURCE!"
WERE YOU LYING? DID YOU KILL DUELA DENT?
YOU IDIOTS! I TRIED TO SAVE HER!
I TOLD THAT REPORTER, OLSEN, IT WAS AN ALIEN.
MORE POWERFUL THAN ALL OF YOU PUT TOGETHER, BY THE LOOKS OF HIM.
DEFINITELY SMARTER, THAT'S FOR SURE!
KRAK
WHUMP

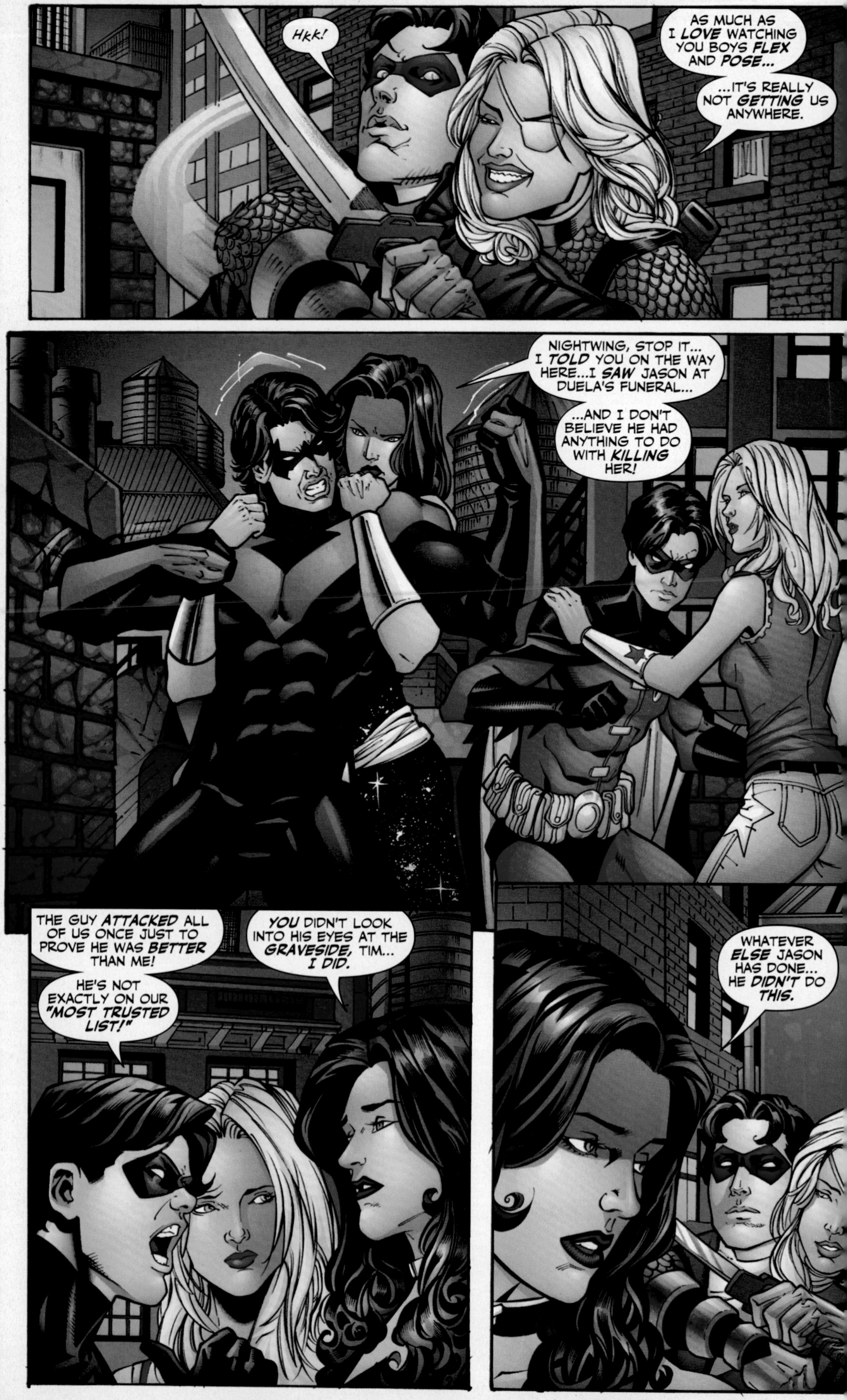
Hkk!
AS MUCH AS I LOVE WATCHING YOU BOYS FLEX AND POSE...
...IT'S REALLY NOT GETTING US ANYWHERE.
NIGHTWING, STOP IT... I TOLD YOU ON THE WAY HERE...I SAW JASON AT DUELA'S FUNERAL...
...AND I DON'T BELIEVE HE HAD ANYTHING TO DO WITH KILLING HER!
THE GUY ATTACKED ALL OF US ONCE JUST TO PROVE HE WAS BETTER THAN ME!
HE'S NOT EXACTLY ON OUR "MOST TRUSTED LIST!"
YOU DIDN'T LOOK INTO HIS EYES AT THE GRAVESIDE, TIM... I DID.
WHATEVER ELSE JASON HAS DONE... HE DIDN'T DO THIS.

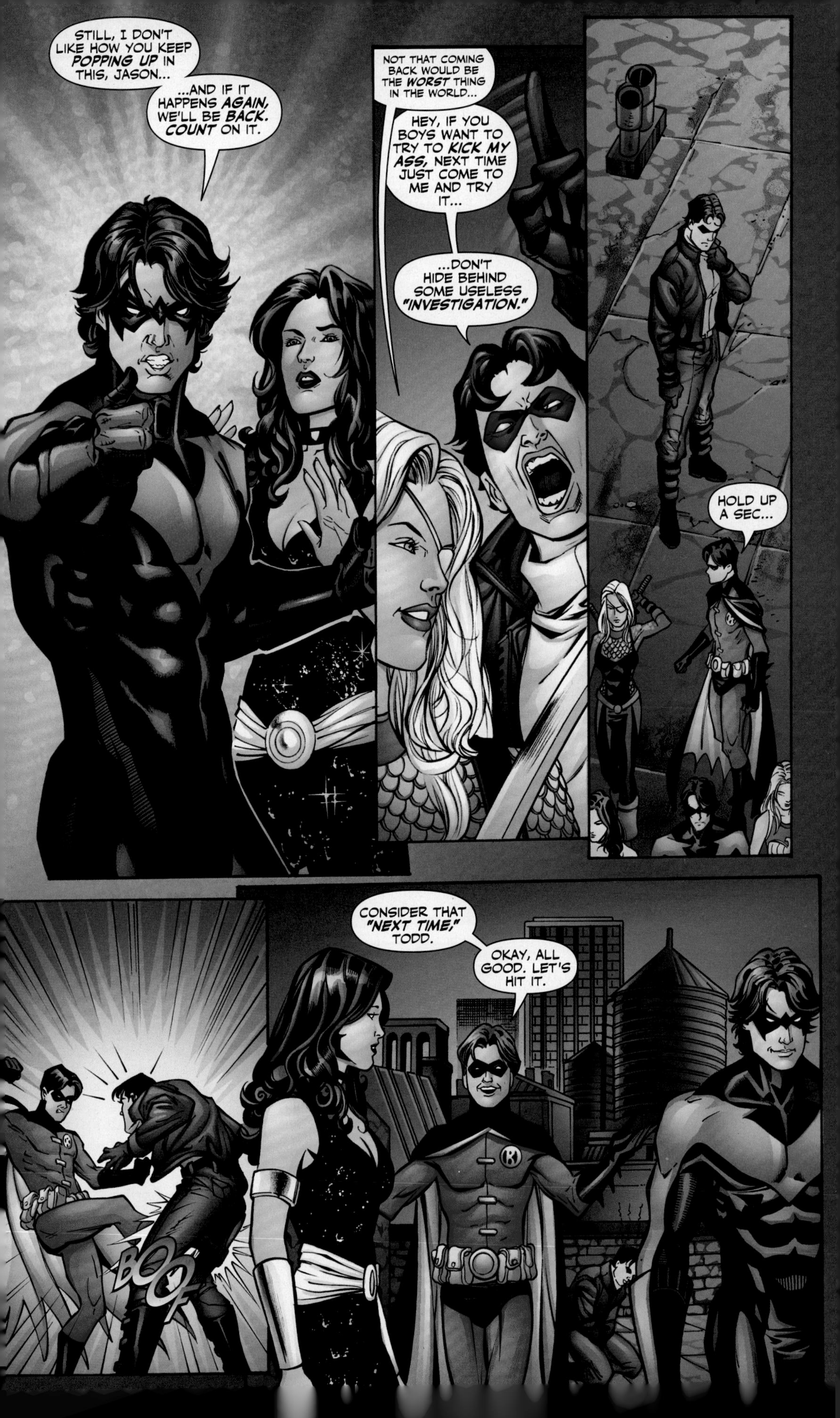
STILL, I DON'T LIKE HOW YOU KEEP POPPING UP IN THIS, JASON...
...AND IF IT HAPPENS AGAIN, WE'LL BE BACK. COUNT ON IT.
NOT THAT COMING BACK WOULD BE THE WORST THING IN THE WORLD...
HEY, IF YOU BOYS WANT TO TRY TO KICK MY ASS, NEXT TIME JUST COME TO ME AND TRY IT...
...DON'T HIDE BEHIND SOME USELESS "INVESTIGATION."
HOLD UP A SEC...
CONSIDER THAT "NEXT TIME," TODD.
OKAY, ALL GOOD. LET'S HIT IT.
BOOF

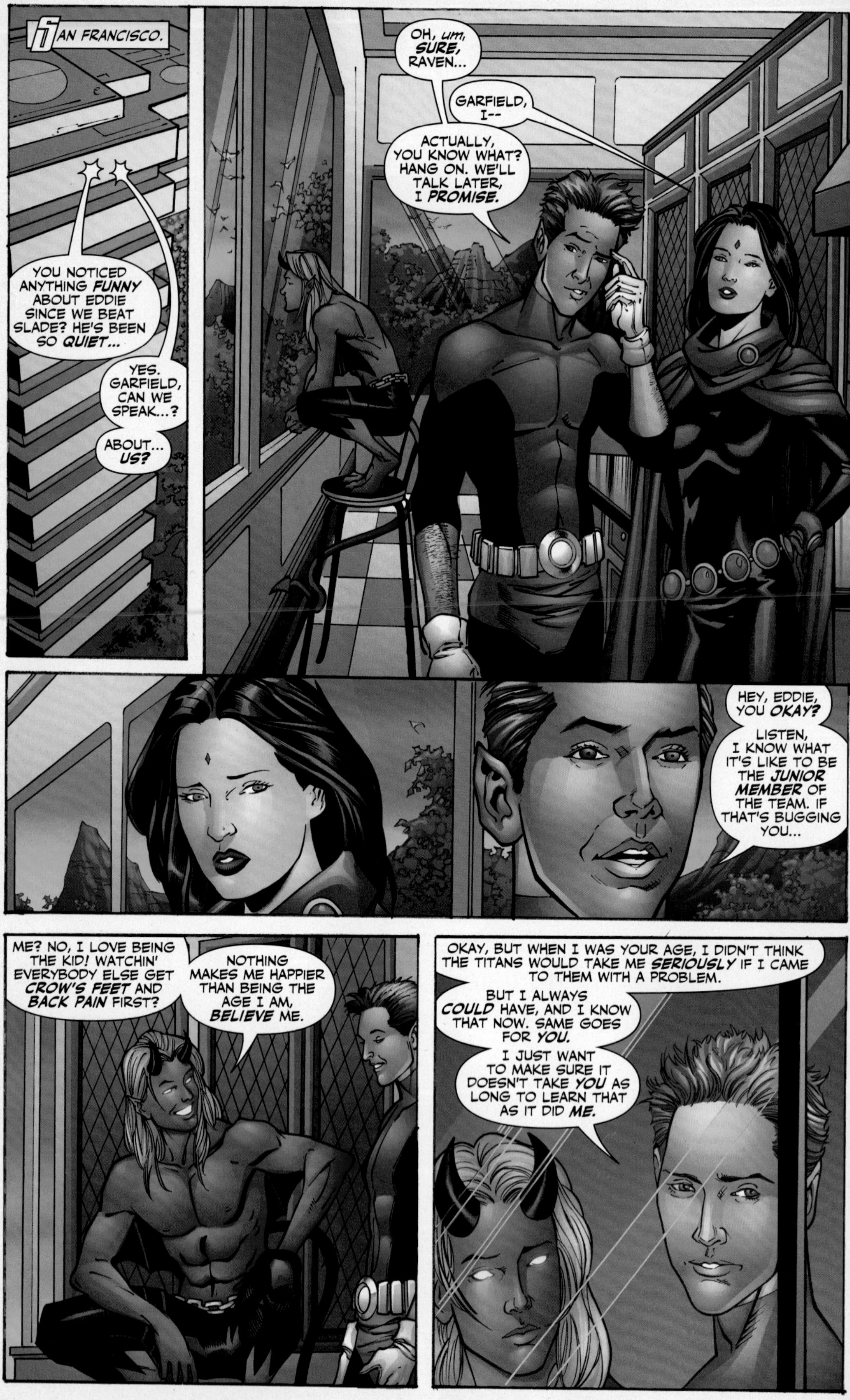
SAN FRANCISCO.
YOU NOTICED ANYTHING FUNNY ABOUT EDDIE SINCE WE BEAT SLADE? HE'S BEEN SO QUIET...
YES. GARFIELD, CAN WE SPEAK...?
ABOUT... US?
OH, um, SURE, RAVEN...
GARFIELD, I--
ACTUALLY, YOU KNOW WHAT? HANG ON. WE'LL TALK LATER, I PROMISE.
HEY, EDDIE, YOU OKAY?
LISTEN, I KNOW WHAT IT'S LIKE TO BE THE JUNIOR MEMBER OF THE TEAM. IF THAT'S BUGGING YOU...
ME? NO, I LOVE BEING THE KID! WATCHIN' EVERYBODY ELSE GET CROW'S FEET AND BACK PAIN FIRST?
NOTHING MAKES ME HAPPIER THAN BEING THE AGE I AM, BELIEVE ME.
OKAY, BUT WHEN I WAS YOUR AGE, I DIDN'T THINK THE TITANS WOULD TAKE ME SERIOUSLY IF I CAME TO THEM WITH A PROBLEM.
BUT I ALWAYS COULD HAVE, AND I KNOW THAT NOW. SAME GOES FOR YOU.
I JUST WANT TO MAKE SURE IT DOESN'T TAKE YOU AS LONG TO LEARN THAT AS IT DID ME.

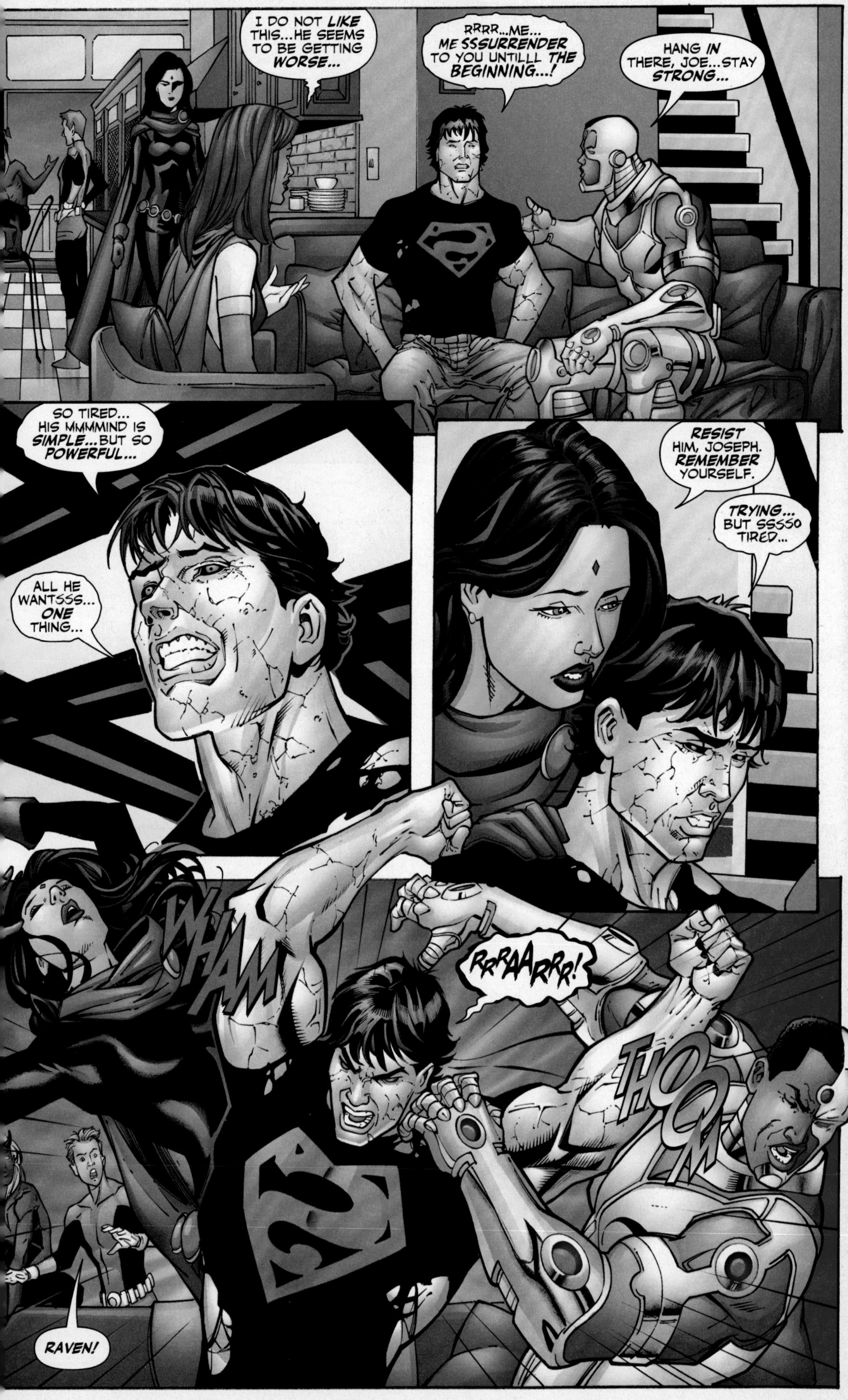

I DO NOT LIKE THIS...HE SEEMS TO BE GETTING WORSE...
RRRR...ME... ME SSSURRENDER TO YOU UNTILLL THE BEGINNING...!
HANG IN THERE, JOE...STAY STRONG...
SO TIRED... HIS MMMMIND IS SIMPLE...BUT SO POWERFUL...
ALL HE WANTSSS... ONE THING...
RESIST HIM, JOSEPH. REMEMBER YOURSELF.
TRYING... BUT SSSSO TIRED...
WHAM
RRRAARRR!
THOOM
RAVEN!

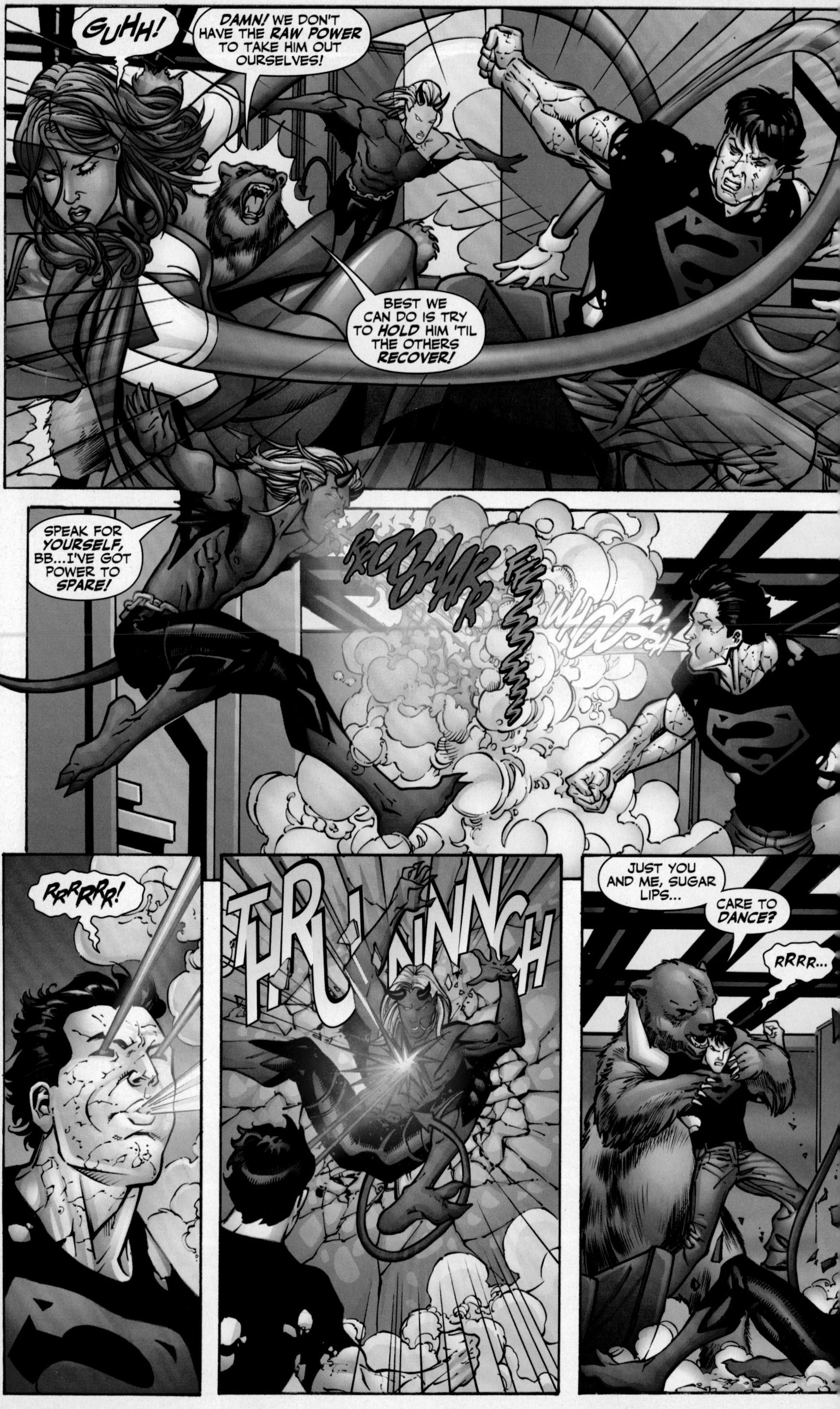
GUHH!
DAMN! WE DON'T HAVE THE RAW POWER TO TAKE HIM OUT OURSELVES!
BEST WE CAN DO IS TRY TO HOLD HIM 'TIL THE OTHERS RECOVER!
SPEAK FOR YOURSELF, BB...I'VE GOT POWER TO SPARE!
WHOOSH
RRRRR!
THRUNNNCH
JUST YOU AND ME, SUGAR LIPS...
CARE TO DANCE?
RRRR...

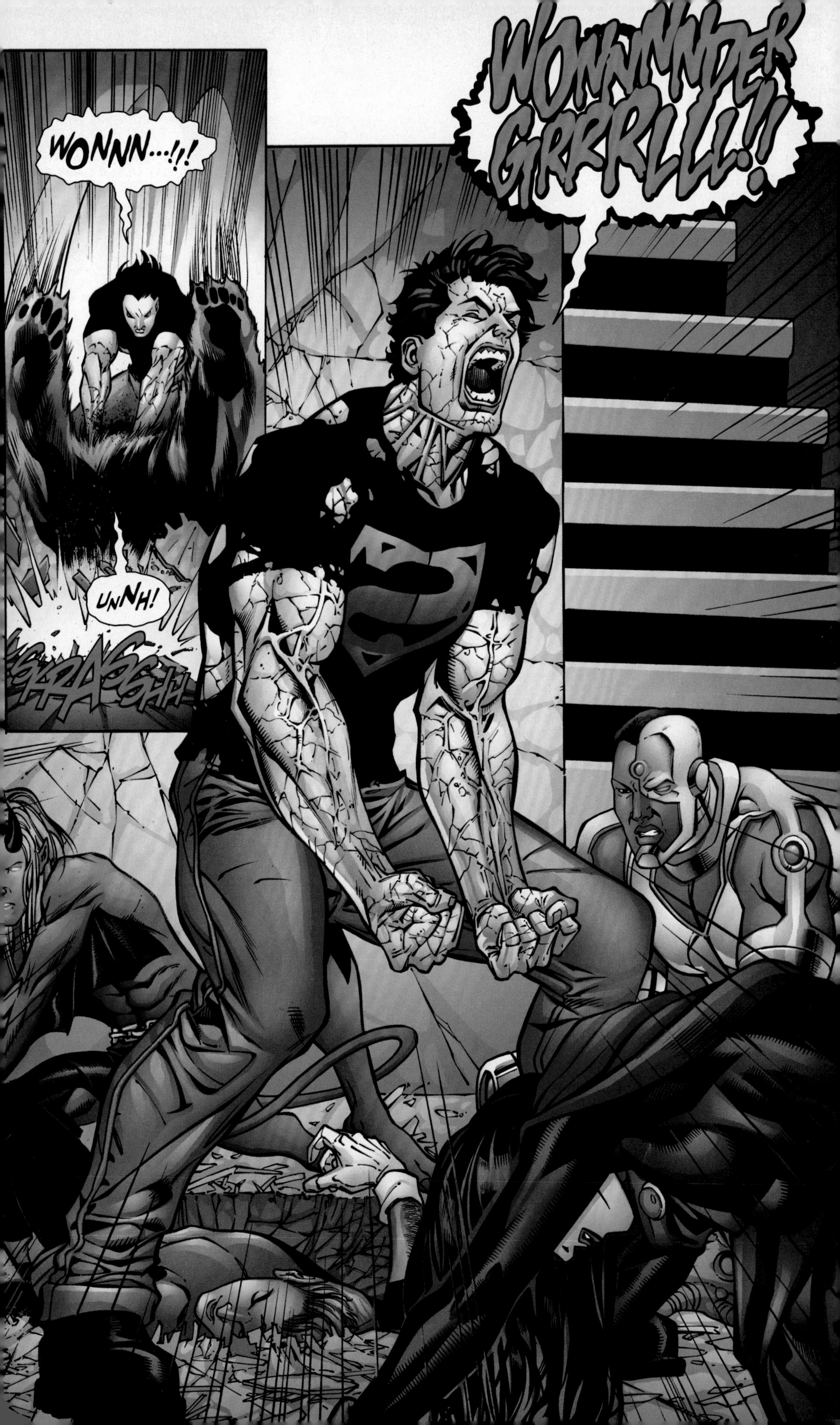
WONNN...!!!
UNNH!
SKRASSH
WONNNNDER GRRRLLL!!

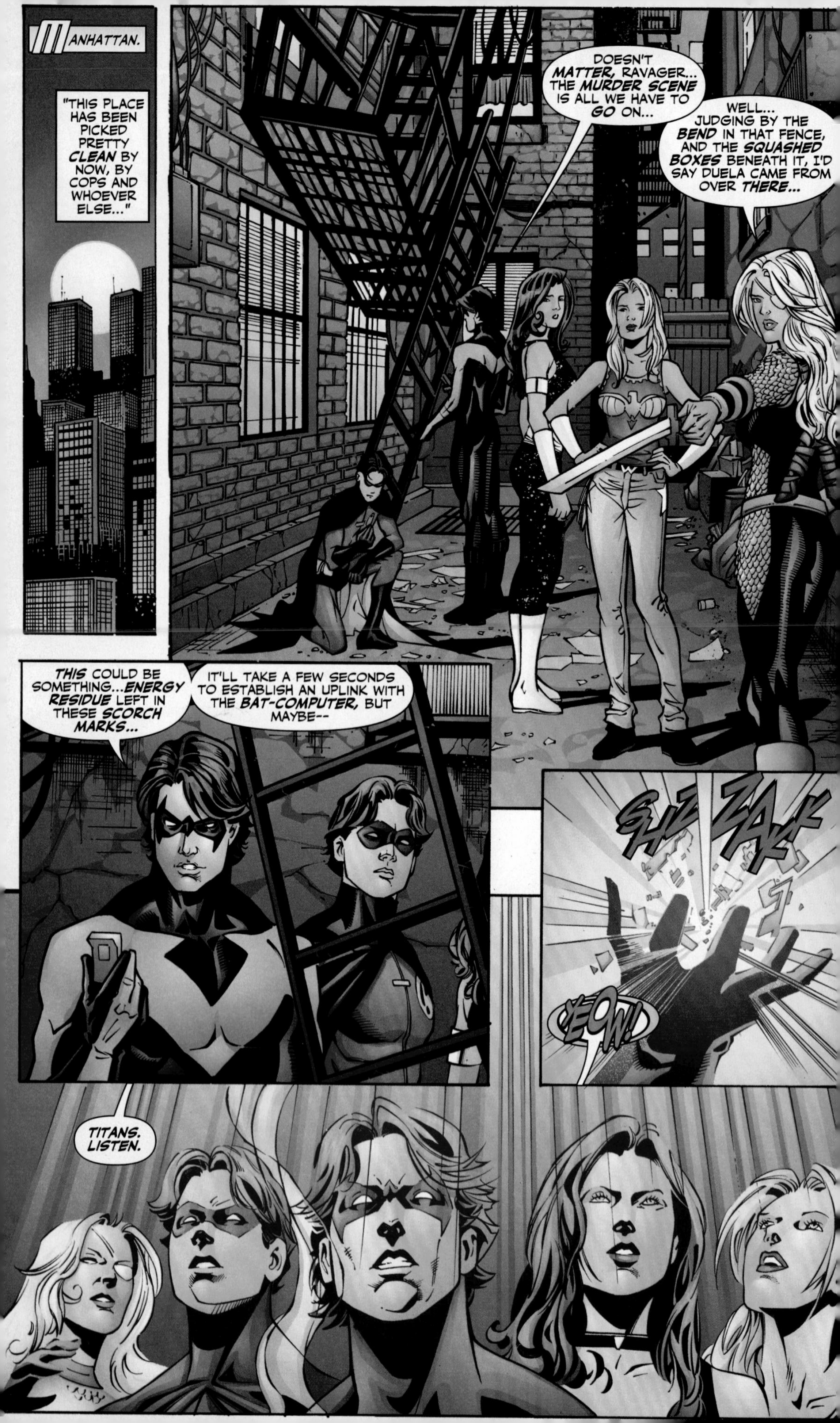
MANHATTAN.
"THIS PLACE HAS BEEN PICKED PRETTY CLEAN BY NOW, BY COPS AND WHOEVER ELSE..."
DOESN'T MATTER, RAVAGER... THE MURDER SCENE IS ALL WE HAVE TO GO ON...
WELL... JUDGING BY THE BEND IN THAT FENCE, AND THE SQUASHED BOXES BENEATH IT, I'D SAY DUELA CAME FROM OVER THERE...
THIS COULD BE SOMETHING...ENERGY RESIDUE LEFT IN THESE SCORCH MARKS...
IT'LL TAKE A FEW SECONDS TO ESTABLISH AN UPLINK WITH THE BAT-COMPUTER, BUT MAYBE--
SHZZZAK
YEOW!
TITANS. LISTEN.

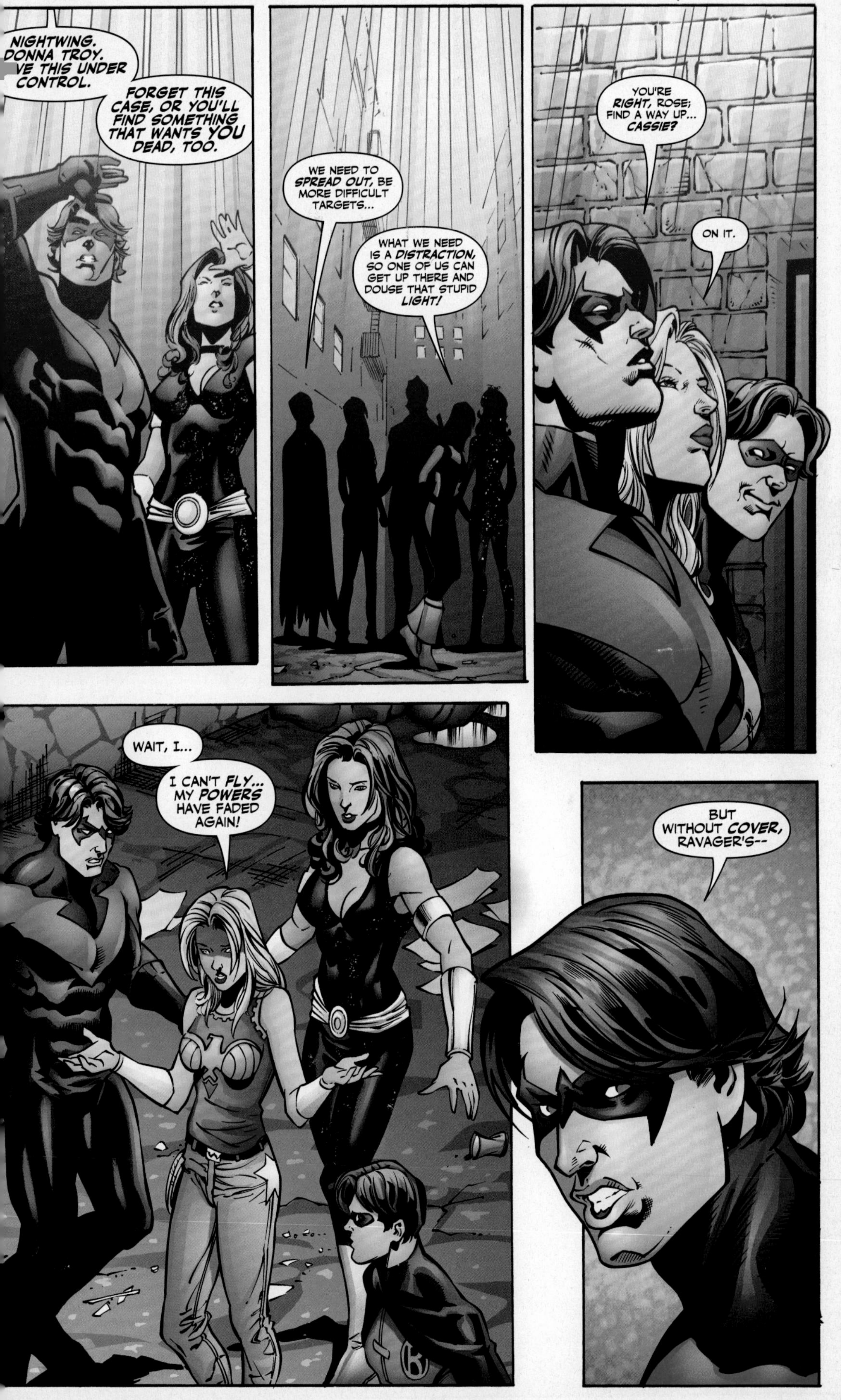
NIGHTWING. DONNA TROY. VE THIS UNDER CONTROL.
FORGET THIS CASE, OR YOU'LL FIND SOMETHING THAT WANTS YOU DEAD, TOO.
WE NEED TO SPREAD OUT, BE MORE DIFFICULT TARGETS...
WHAT WE NEED IS A DISTRACTION, SO ONE OF US CAN GET UP THERE AND DOUSE THAT STUPID LIGHT!
YOU'RE RIGHT, ROSE; FIND A WAY UP... CASSIE?
ON IT.
WAIT, I...
I CAN'T FLY... MY POWERS HAVE FADED AGAIN!
BUT WITHOUT COVER, RAVAGER'S--

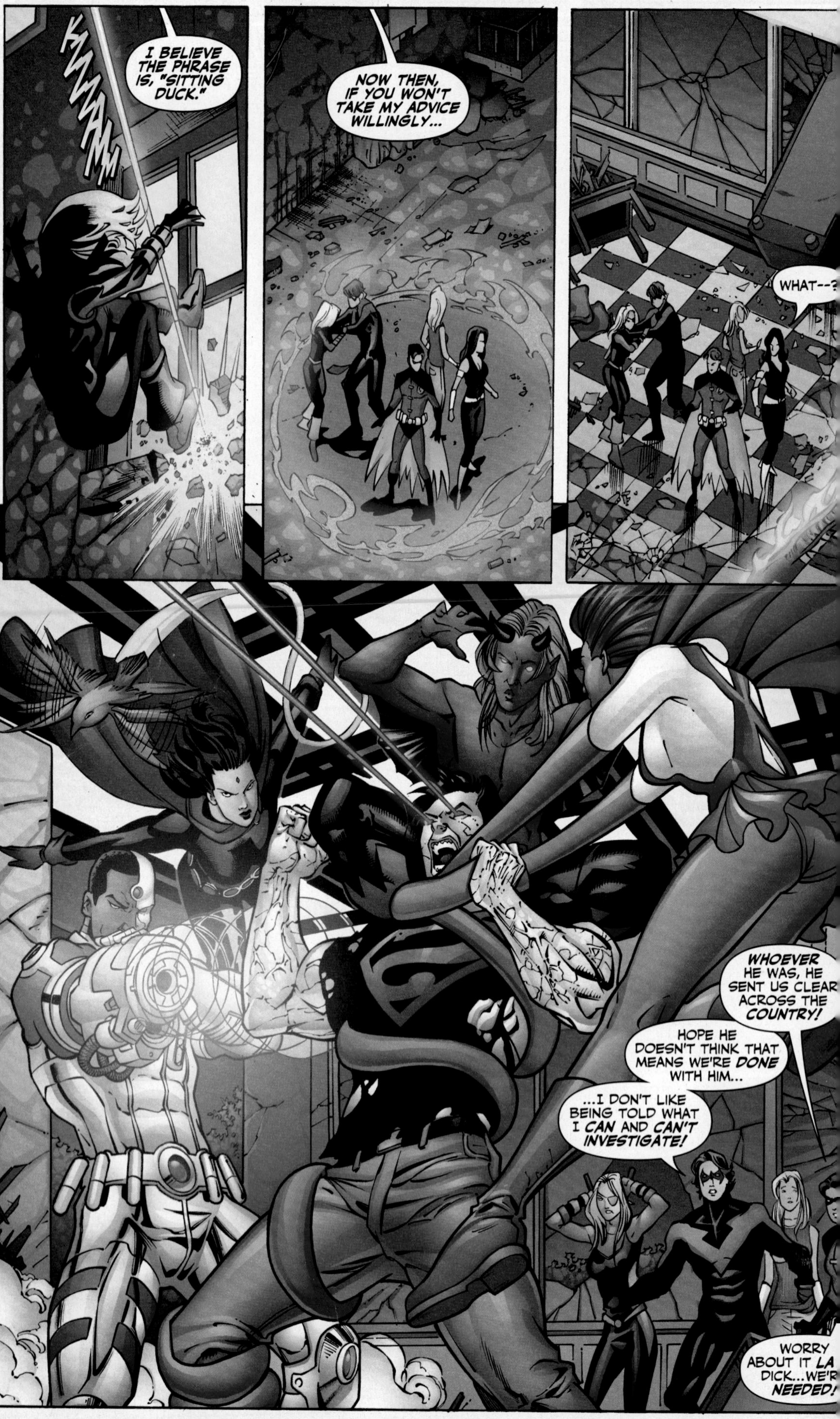
KWAAMM
I BELIEVE THE PHRASE IS, "SITTING DUCK."
NOW THEN, IF YOU WON'T TAKE MY ADVICE WILLINGLY...
WHAT--?
WHOEVER HE WAS, HE SENT US CLEAR ACROSS THE COUNTRY!
HOPE HE DOESN'T THINK THAT MEANS WE'RE DONE WITH HIM...
...I DON'T LIKE BEING TOLD WHAT I CAN AND CAN'T INVESTIGATE!
WORRY ABOUT IT LA
DICK...WE'R
NEEDED!

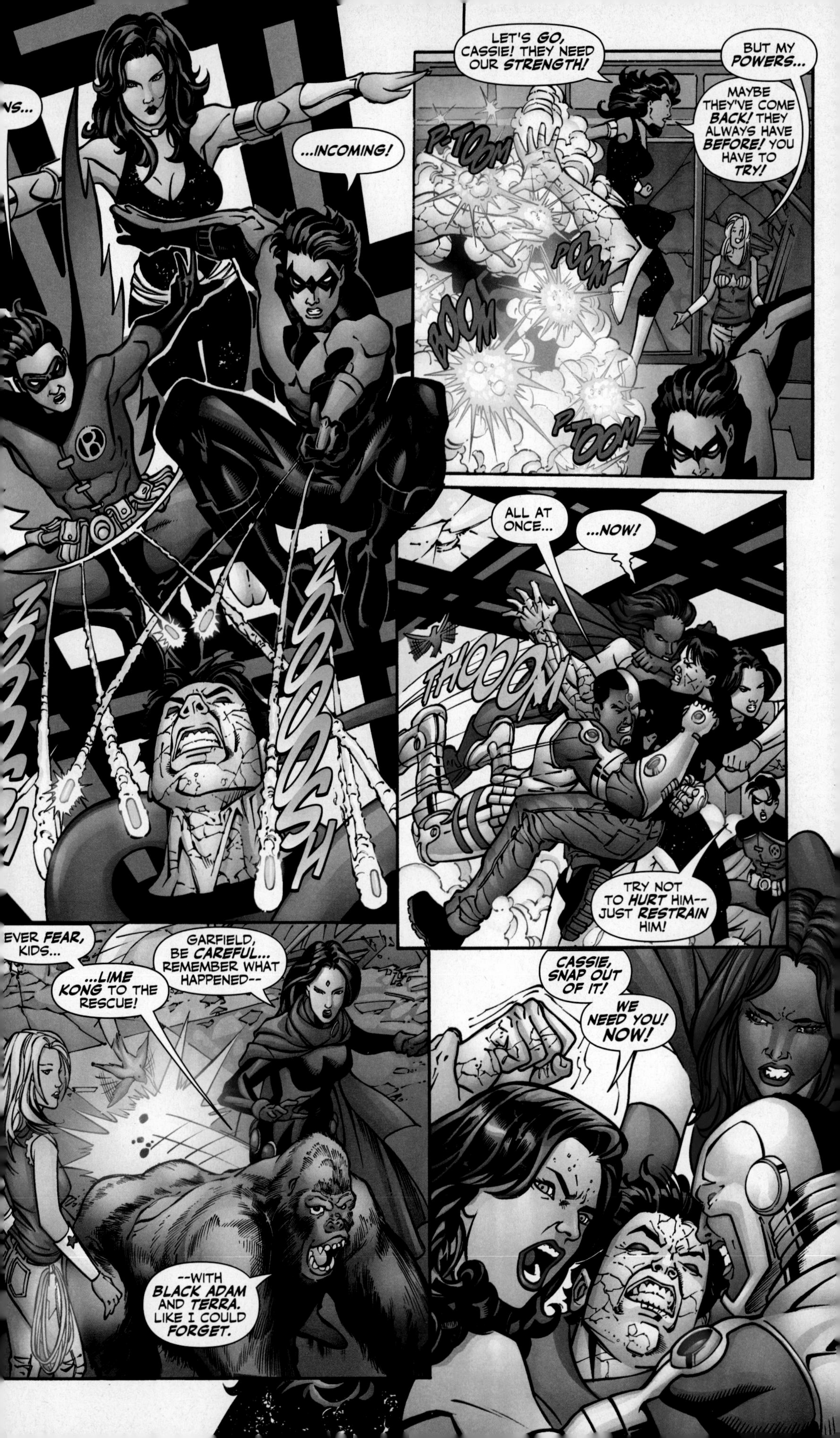

...NS...
...INCOMING!
ZZOOOOOSH
ZZOOOOOSH
LET'S GO, CASSIE! THEY NEED OUR STRENGTH!
BUT MY POWERS...
MAYBE THEY'VE COME BACK! THEY ALWAYS HAVE BEFORE! YOU HAVE TO TRY!
P-TOOM
POOM
BOOM
P-TOOM
ALL AT ONCE...
...NOW!
THOOOM
TRY NOT TO HURT HIM--JUST RESTRAIN HIM!
...EVER FEAR, KIDS...
...LIME KONG TO THE RESCUE!
GARFIELD, BE CAREFUL... REMEMBER WHAT HAPPENED--
--WITH BLACK ADAM AND TERRA. LIKE I COULD FORGET.
CASSIE, SNAP OUT OF IT!
WE NEED YOU! NOW!

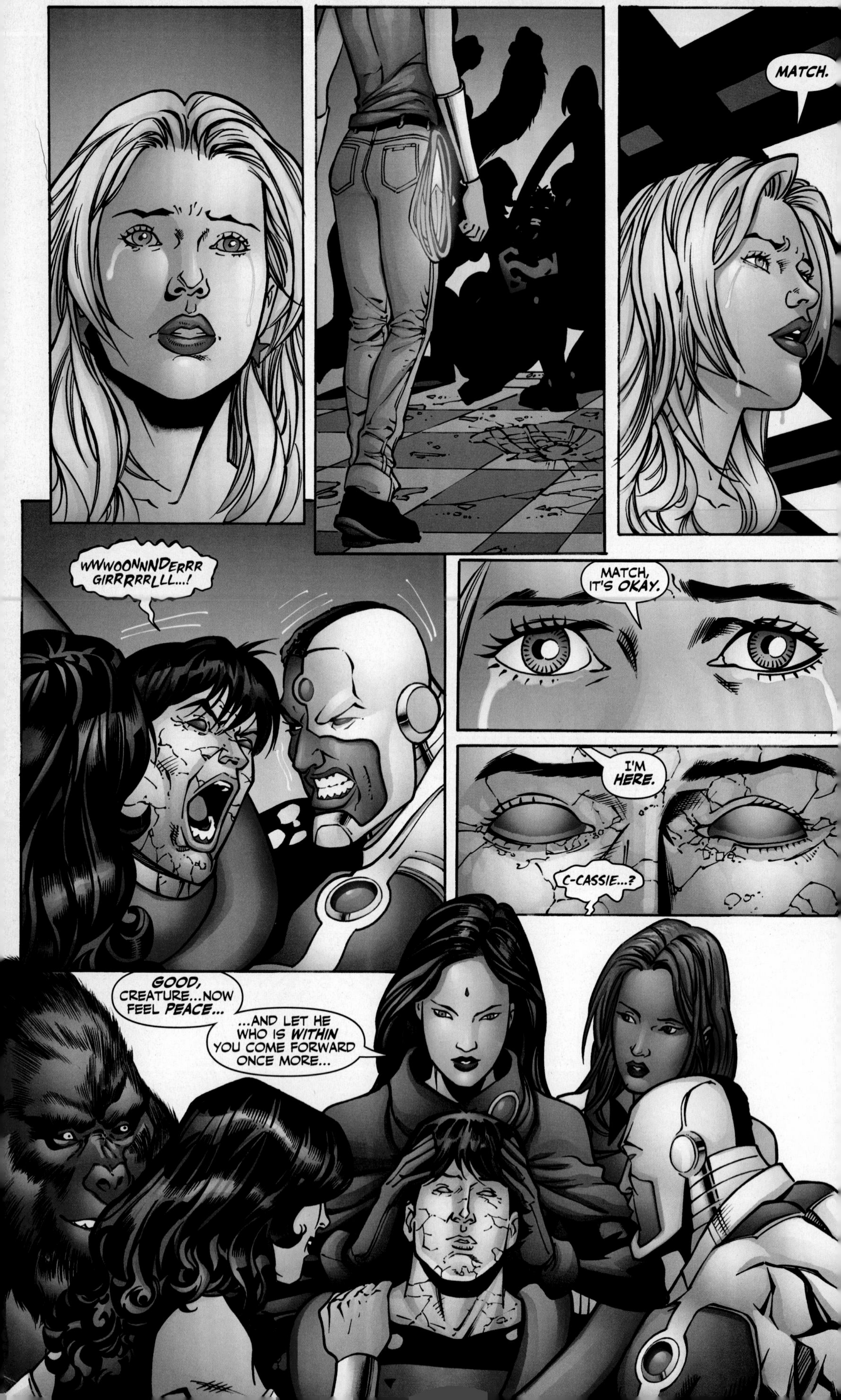
MATCH.
WWWOONNNDERRR GIRRRRRLLL...!
MATCH, IT'S OKAY.
I'M HERE.
C-CASSIE...?
GOOD, CREATURE...NOW FEEL PEACE...
...AND LET HE WHO IS WITHIN YOU COME FORWARD ONCE MORE...

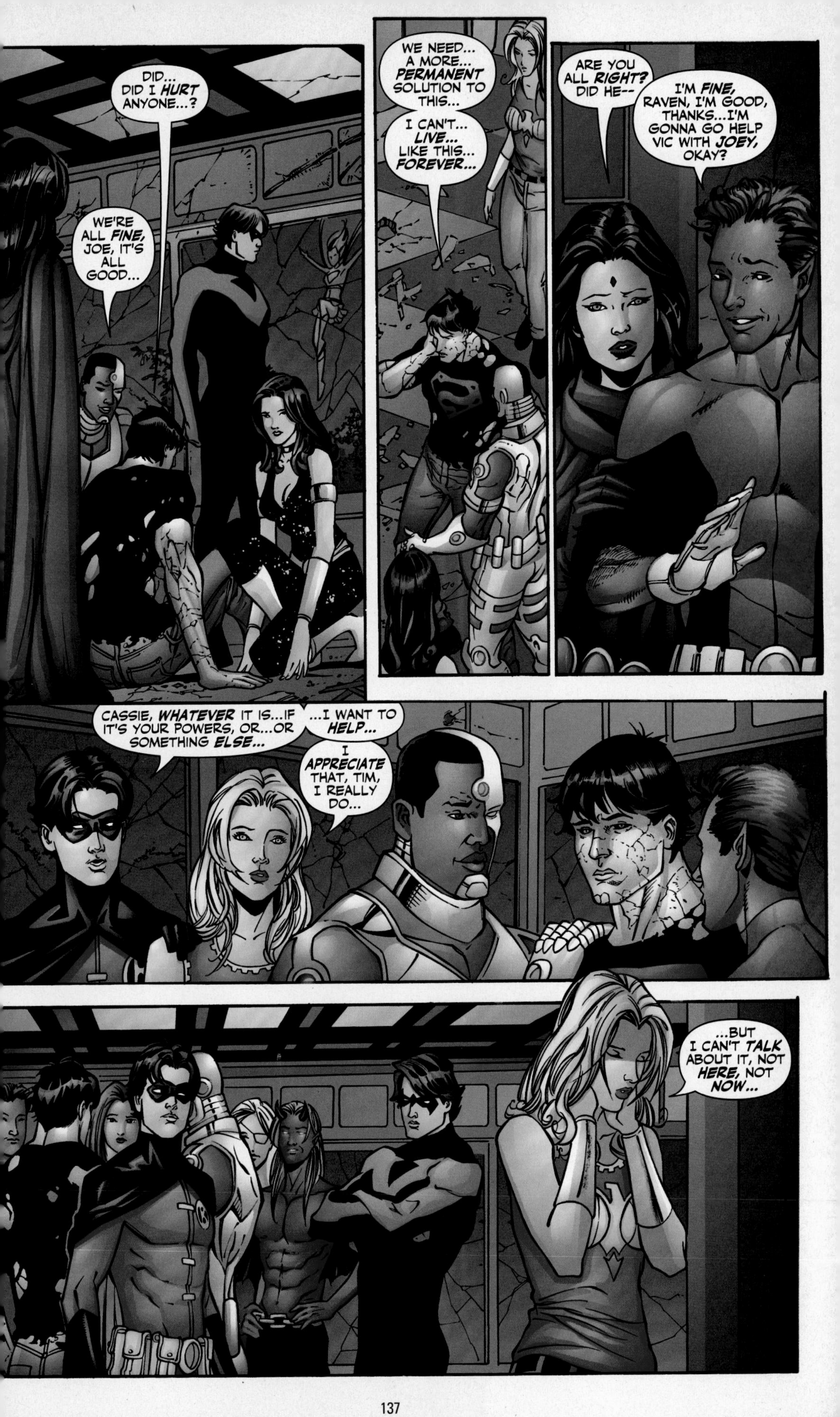
DID... DID I HURT ANYONE...?
WE'RE ALL FINE, JOE, IT'S ALL GOOD...
WE NEED... A MORE... PERMANENT SOLUTION TO THIS...
I CAN'T... LIVE... LIKE THIS... FOREVER...
ARE YOU ALL RIGHT? DID HE--
I'M FINE, RAVEN, I'M GOOD, THANKS...I'M GONNA GO HELP VIC WITH JOEY, OKAY?
CASSIE, WHATEVER IT IS...IF IT'S YOUR POWERS, OR...OR SOMETHING ELSE...
...I WANT TO HELP...
I APPRECIATE THAT, TIM, I REALLY DO...
...BUT I CAN'T TALK ABOUT IT, NOT HERE, NOT NOW...

Issue #42
Colored by
the Hories

Issue #43
Colored by
the Hories

Issue #44
Inked by
Jonathan Glapion
Colored by
the Hories

Issue #45
Inked by
Jonathan Glapion
Colored by
Moose Baumann

Issue #46
Colored by
Moose Baumann

Issue #47
Art by
Randy Green,
Sandra Hope,
Rod Reis

Covers by
Tony Daniel

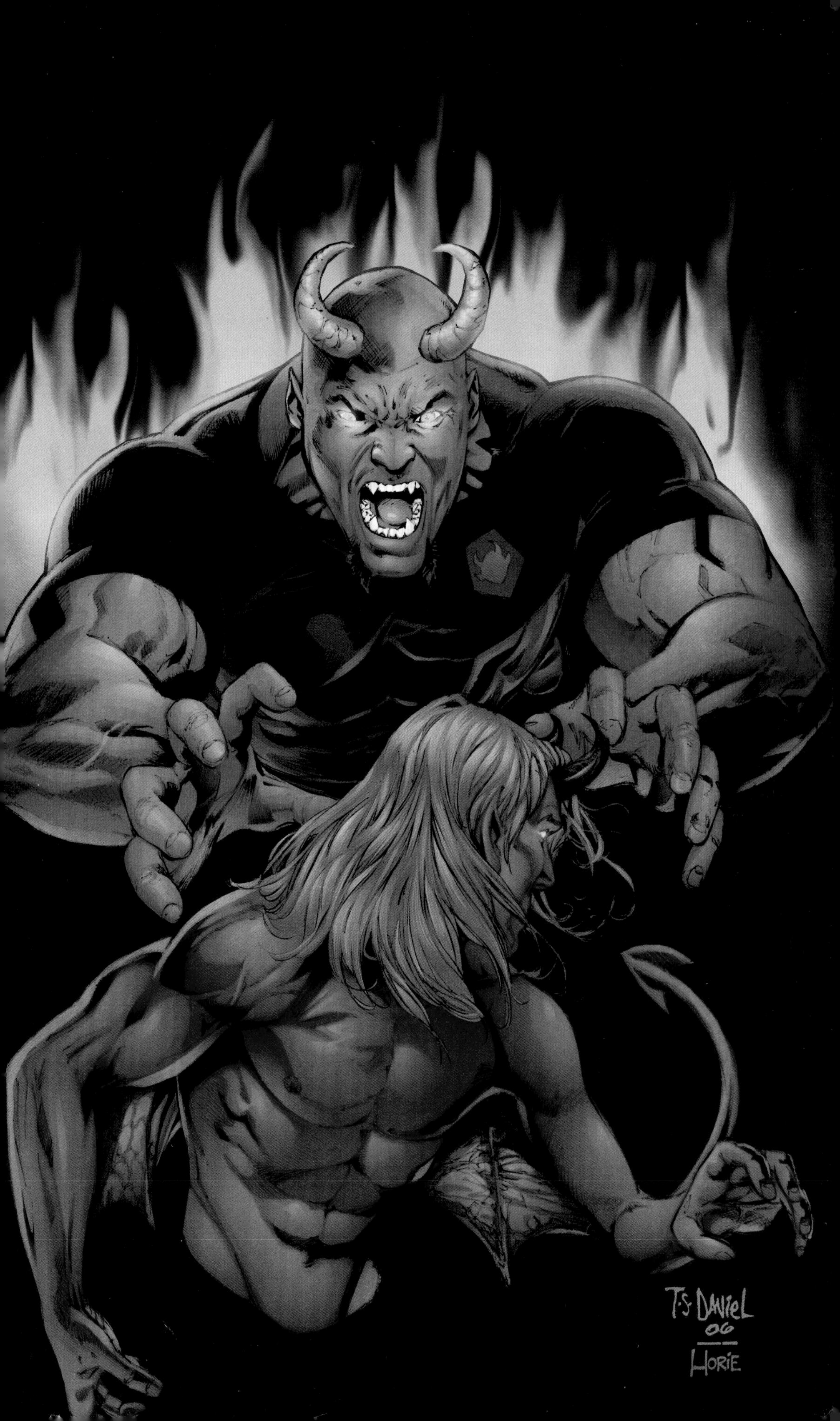
T.S. DANIEL
06
HORIE

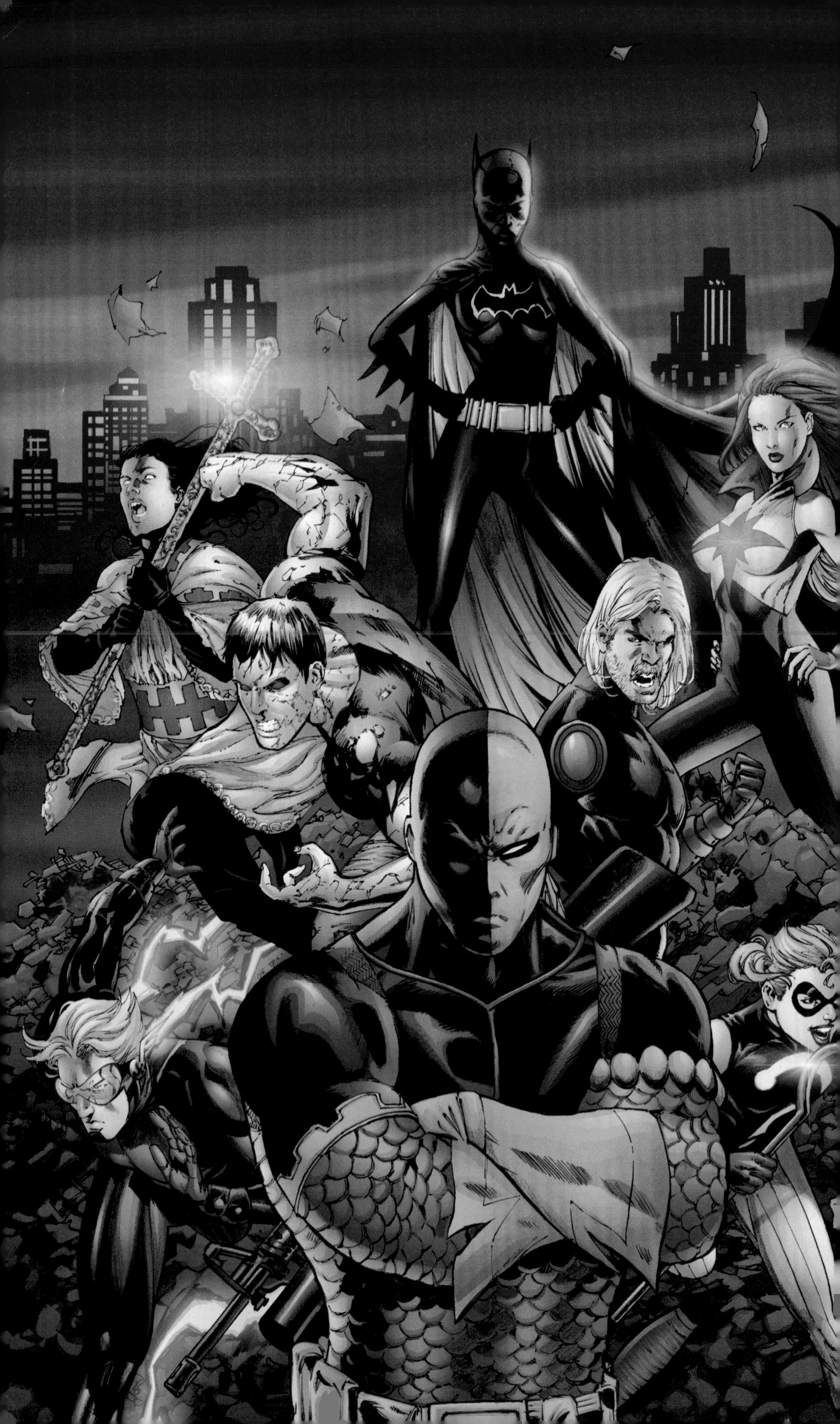

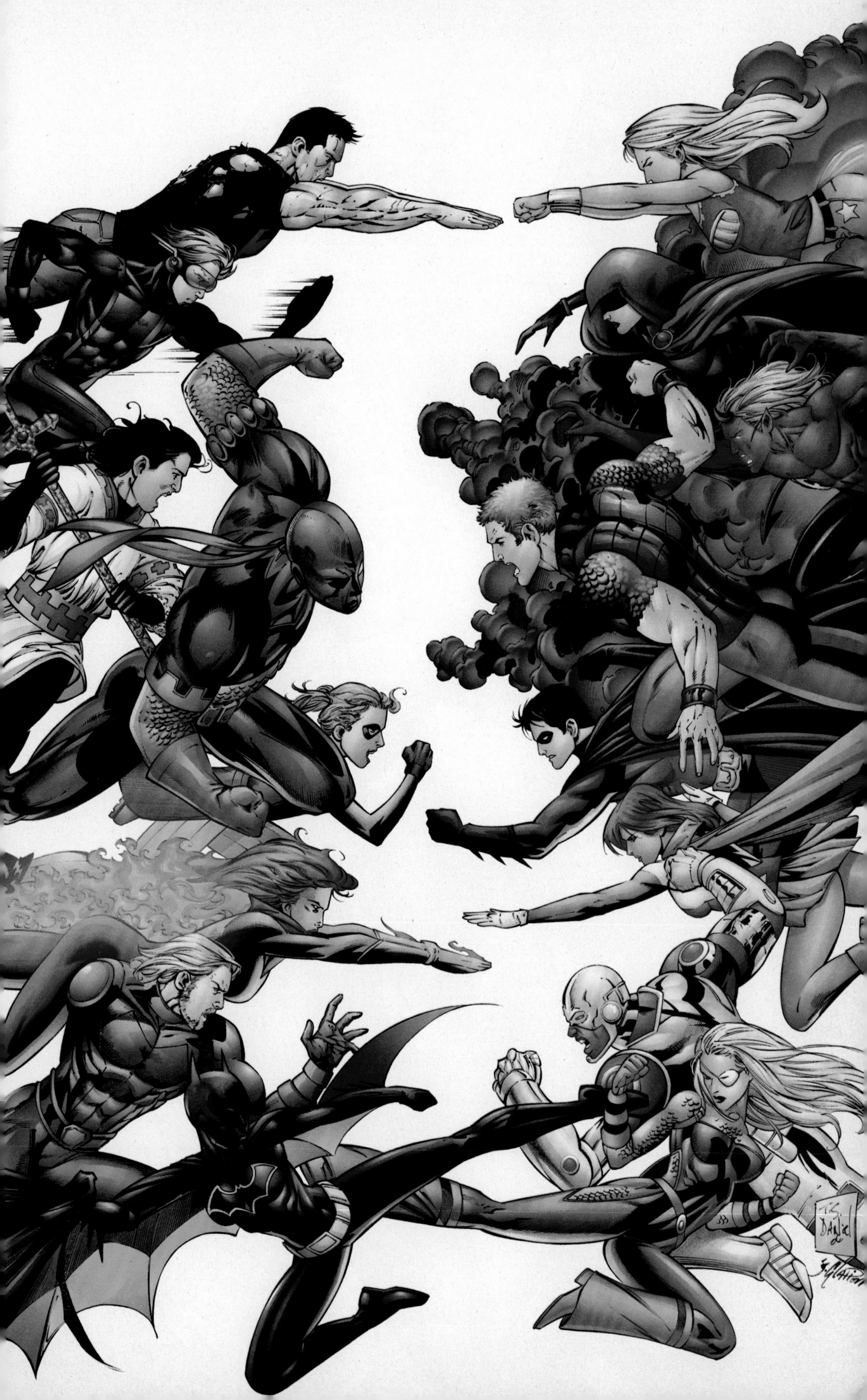

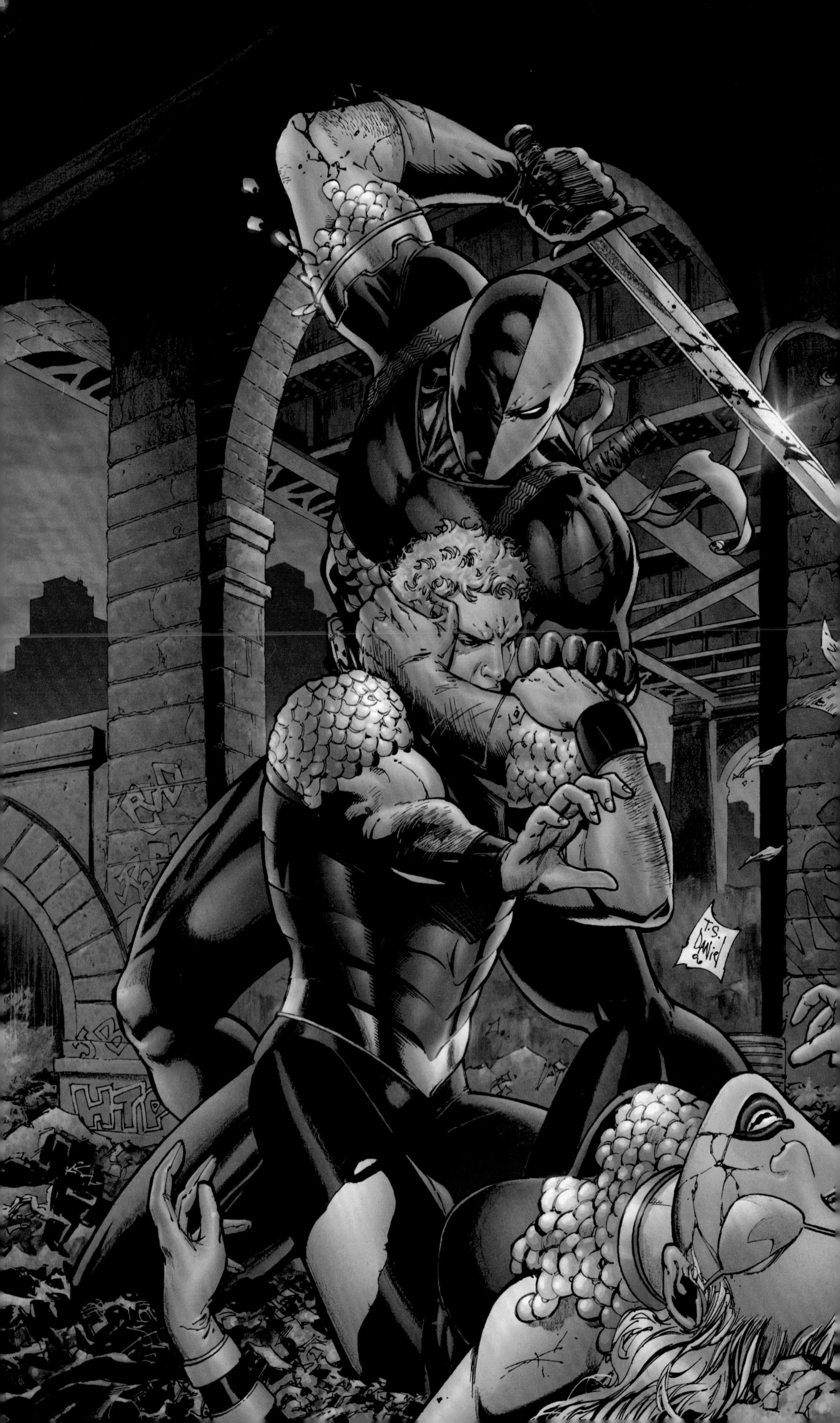

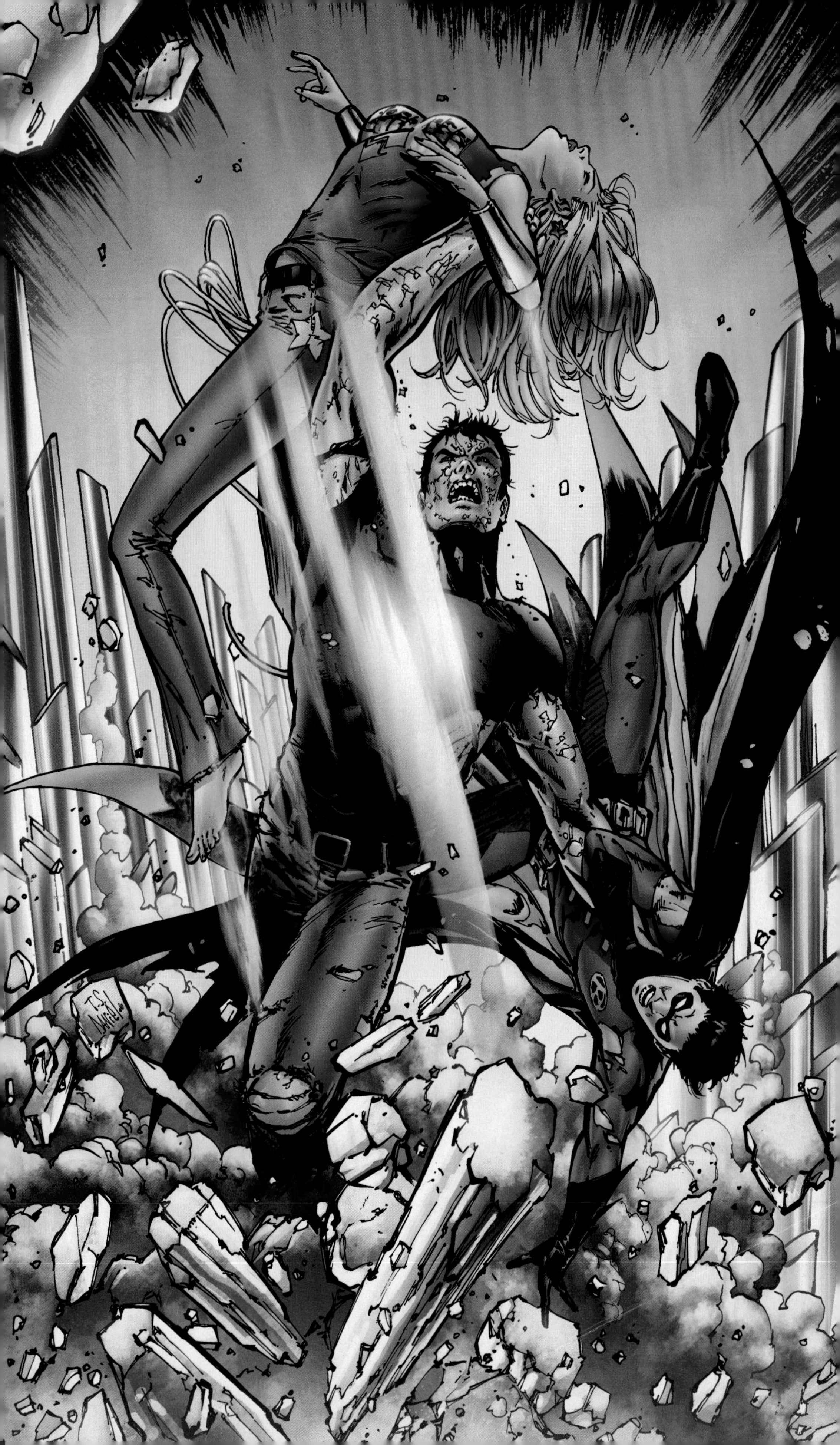

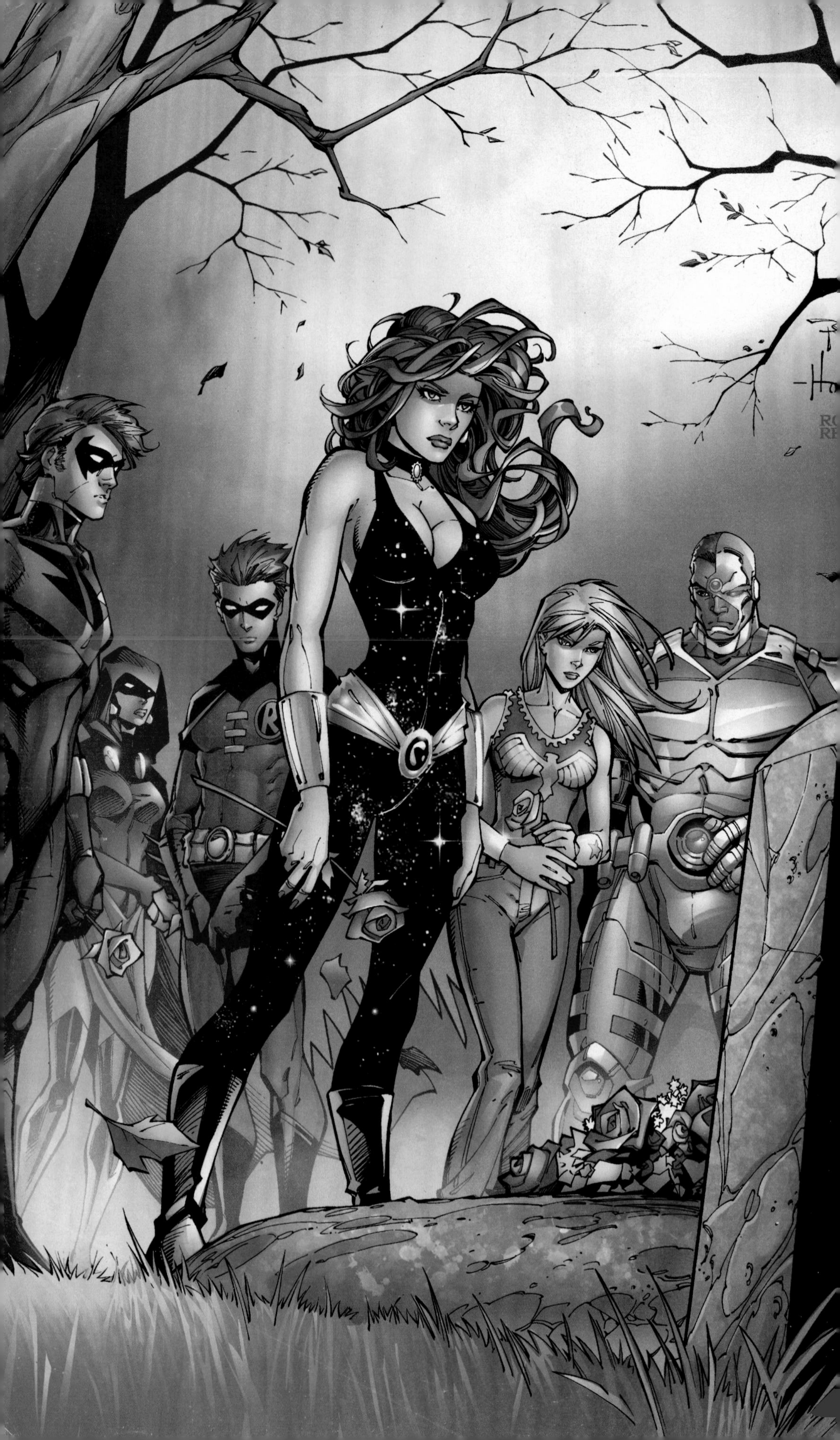

EAST COAST / WEST COAST RIVALRY!

Deathstroke, the Titans' deadliest and most tenacious foe, is back!

Seeking vengeance for the family he believes the Teen Titans have taken from him, the assassin puts together his own villainous squad consisting of some of the Titans' most menacing adversaries — and even a few of their allies!

With his new "Titans East," Deathstroke has more than enough raw power to defeat his enemies. How will the Teen Titans defend themselves from the inevitable assault led by a rival who knows them the best and hates them the most?

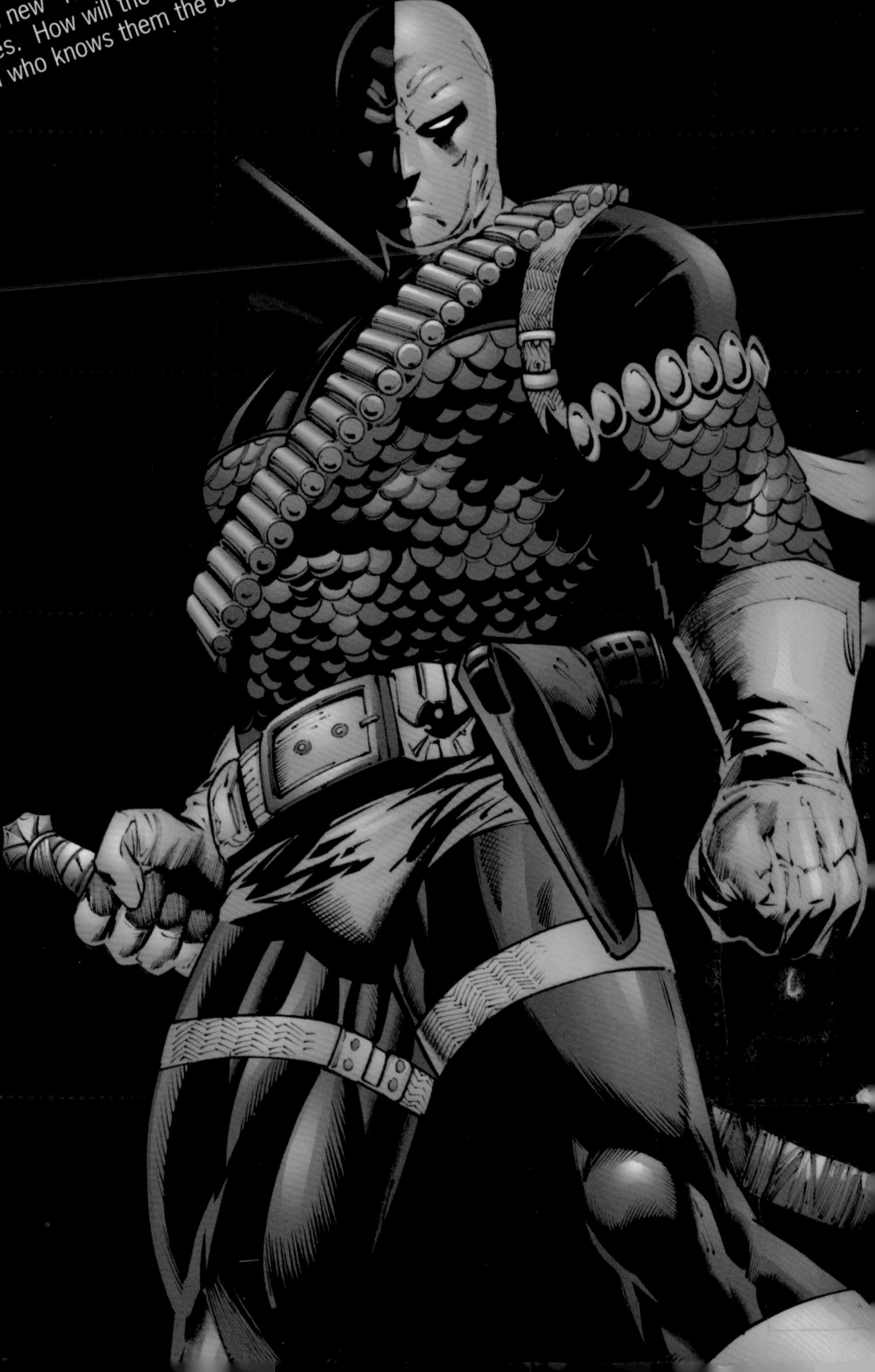

dccomics.com

$14.99 USA $17.99 CAN ISBN: 978-1-4012-1447-0

51499